WIRED

A ROMANCE

WIRED

A ROMANCE

GARY WOLF

RANDOM HOUSE

NEW YORK

Library of Congress Cataloging-in-Publication Data
Wolf, Gary.
Wired—a romance / Gary Wolf.
p.   cm.
Includes index.
ISBN 0-375-50290-4
1. Rossetto, Louis. 2. Wired (San Francisco, Calif.) 3. Publishers and publishing—
United States—Biography. 4. Businesspeople—United States—Biography.
5. Mass media—United States. 6. Internet industry—United States.
7. Online information services industry—United States. I. Title.
Z473.R75W65   2003   070.5'092—dc21
[B]   2002036992

Random House website address: www.atrandom.com
Printed in the United States of America on acid-free paper
24689753
First Edition

Book design by J. K. Lambert

If you have difficulty envisioning something as trivial as the imminent end of elections, you'll be totally unprepared to cope with the prospect of the forthcoming demise of spoken language and its replacement by a global consciousness.

—Marshall McLuhan, 1969

CONTENTS

Introduction xi

PART I

Chapter 1. From Nowhere 3

Chapter 2. The Blessing .... .15

Chapter 3. Pilgrims .... .25

Chapter 4. Feedback .... .39

Chapter 5. Fascinated, Revolted, Mesmerized .... .57

Chapter 6. Victories .... .75

PART II

Chapter 7. The Grotto .... .93

Chapter 8. Carl .... .115

Chapter 9. A Shower of Money .... .145

Chapter 10. The Roll-Up .... .161

Chapter 11. Sincerity .... .189

Chapter 12. The Road Show .... .201

Chapter 13. Sacrifice .... .217

Chapter 14. The End .... .239

Acknowledgments .... .263

Index .... .265

INTRODUCTION

A proper romance ought to pit youth against age, innocence against worldliness, and show the triumph of love over all temptation. We begin, then, with some disadvantages. Our hero is in his forties. He scorns idealism as naïveté. And his domestic life has a distinctly argumentative cast. Nonetheless, this book is called a romance, and I think it is accurately named.

A romance should at least have a hint of the supernatural. Here we are more lucky. Fauns and angels are not permissible in journalism, but there are other forces in the world that hauntingly express themselves through individuals. Original ideas often appear unexpectedly in several places at once; like ghosts, they are in the air. Once such ideas begin to spread, they can have an uncanny, almost demonic effect, causing otherwise rational people to act strangely. The story that follows is a romance in exactly this sense: it traces the effect of a fantastic idea—the idea that computers will make every existing authority obsolete—as it worked through and upon the man who conjured it up.

Thirty years ago a young man was featured on the cover of *The New York Times Magazine*. He was a pioneer of a new political movement called libertarianism. The goal of the libertarians was to abolish the government, but they did not succeed, and the young man left the United States and resettled in Europe for two decades. When he returned he upended the media business, captured the attention of millions, and seduced some of the country's most powerful financiers. He even spoke, again, of the end of government.

He was no longer a libertarian, because libertarianism was a political label, and he had become an enemy of politics. The transformation he advocated was more profound than that. He spoke of a new social life unimpeded by national borders; of communities transcending time and geography. His message was, in part, about technology, and the financial mania it precipitated resembled other incidents of hysteria that came in the wake of important inventions—railroads, automobiles, electricity, radio. But he was not an inventor, nor even a very great businessman. He was simply a talented storyteller who offered a glimpse of a future in which all outmoded constraints would be swept aside.

His success coincided with a great stock-market bubble. How much was he to blame for it? When economic historians sort out the confusion of the last ten years, they will doubtless give some of the responsibility to administrators of the central bank who lowered interest rates at a key moment, flooding the market with cheap money that quickly found its way into stocks. But the supply of money is only one side of the story. The other side is demand. In the optimism of the bubble years, enthusiasm for the story of the digital revolution made huge speculative investments seem reasonable; this in itself caused credit to loosen.

An interesting illustration of the duel engines that fuel financial bubbles—loose credit and enthusiasm for a good story—can be found in the temporary success of John Law, an economist and gambler who launched the first modern bubble in the early eighteenth century. Under sponsorship of the French court, Law formed a bank that issued paper money backed by significant specie reserves. He increased confidence and credit began to flow. But that was not all he did. Law also took control of a company with monopoly rights to settlement and trade in the Louisiana territories, and sold several waves of shares to the public. After some manipulation of currency supplies by the court and Law's bank, shares in the Mississippi Company took off. With an initial value of five hundred, Mississippi shares eventually doubled, and then ran up to ten thousand in a frenzy of speculation. In the dénouement, all were ruined.

Why did investors clamor to buy shares in the Mississippi Company at so many times their offering price? The wealth of the Americas was the perfect speculator's tale. It was rumored to be infinite, and it was impossible to investigate firsthand. Before the fever broke, every segment of society was infected, and after it broke, every participant suffered.

At the end it no longer mattered that America contained every natural advantage for farmers, traders, and well-capitalized chartered monopolies. A bubble, while dependent upon its story, renders the story's truth irrelevant. This is because, paradoxically, a bubble feeds upon skepticism. Today's skeptics are tomorrow's buyers. People who decline to purchase shares at five hundred, who laugh at them at a thousand, and revile them at fifteen hundred eagerly snatch them up at two thousand when the spectacle of friends and neighbors celebrating their profits becomes too much to bear. As the bubble grows, the story becomes more and more popular, for it is the buyer's indispensable justification and

excuse. Only when the story's truth is more or less universally acknowledged do prices plateau and then plummet. Skepticism, a
key ingredient, has run out.

The romance that follows is not a full account of the mania that
enlivened the late nineties and brought so many unlikely characters to the fore. It is merely the story of its story. Instant communication and ubiquitous computers were on the verge of creating
unprecedented wealth and freedom; humanity was at the dawn of
a new era. This story had, if no sole author, at least a preeminent
champion. His name was Louis Rossetto, and his platform was
Wired.

PART I

CHAPTER 1

FROM NOWHERE

Louis Rossetto had a strange effect on people. He was like a magnet whose grip increased dramatically at close range. Listeners might be dismissive at a distance, and dubious as he opened his mouth, but then he pulled them in and held them close. He always seemed to be better informed than anybody else in the room. He had sources from Afghanistan and contacts in Sri Lanka. He knew Dutch, Italian, and Portuguese. Because he was so coherent, and because when he had made his point he fell silent and waited calmly for a response, Louis had a peculiar way of compelling his acquaintances to express agreement with things that they were not really sure of. This could be embarrassing later and sometimes even made people swing the other way and say they hated him.

John Plunkett was unnerved the first time he got a glimpse of Louis through the window of an elegant office building on the Quai d'Anjou, in Paris. John was a big man with a deceptively placid expression. Normally he worked as a graphic designer in New York City making annual reports for big corporations. "Selling shit on a stick," he called it. But at the moment John was short on money and looking for a job. He had seen an ad for a designer in the *International Herald Tribune,* and after scheduling an interview he decided to walk by the office and have a look. Truck traffic paused in front of the building, obscuring his view, so he crossed the street and peered between the drapes. He saw a tiny computer sitting on a desk, with an orange screen and black letters too small for him to make out. In front of the screen a tall man sat completely still, his face expressionless. He looked like some kind of hippie or derelict, out of place behind these old stone walls and six-paned windows. The man suddenly turned toward the street and stared. Something about his unblinking expression, its lack of acknowledgment or human recognition, startled the designer, and he fled. Later John would interpret this encounter as a premonition, but light fades early in Paris in the fall and perhaps Louis Rossetto's gaze registered nothing because he only saw his own face in the window, reflecting back.

Designers are never implicated, John told himself, after he took the job with Real Invest. Real Invest was a discreet financial operation that offered individual banking services and untraceable European investments for Americans who preferred to keep their capital gains out of the hands of the Internal Revenue Service. Bill Sigal, the owner, would eventually flee Paris one step ahead of the police. John found Sigal to be a slightly threatening person, self-assured and ruthless in his extraction of cash investments from midwestern rubes (whom he called, as a sort of shorthand, "dentists"), but Plunkett's job was only to redesign the company's newsletter, called *Globescan,* and he took no more responsibility for the malodorous quality of the Sigal enterprise than he did for the assertions made to stockholders of his corporate clients.

Later John would describe Real Invest as a "lure for expatriate bums looking for an angle." On the other hand, were they really bums? The man who had startled him at the window may have been a drifter and an odd duck, a character from another time and a kind of political exile, but he was only a bum if the word conjured meanings beyond mere vagrancy: boisterous anarchism, say, and hatred of authority, and a love of mayhem as a source of both entertainment and sustenance. Add these antiquated associations into the mix, and you still wouldn't have it right, because the old type of bum—the Wobbly, the hobo, the one-big-union man—was an enemy of capitalism, while Louis Rossetto had a master's degree in business administration from Columbia University, where he specialized in marketing and finance. He was an amateur scholar of the Haymarket riots and a deep reader of libertarian economics. Many years after their first meeting, when their partnership had brought John both international acclaim and a deep sense of personal grievance, he would remember his conversations with Louis as the most interesting he had ever had in his life.

Louis was the editor of *Globescan,* which he typeset himself using the primitive tools of the new microcomputer industry. In this he was heir to a tradition of profound innovation. His own father had been an employee of the Mergenthaler Linotype Company, whose founder, Ottmar Mergenthaler, invented the world's first commercially successful automatic typesetting machine. The Linotype revolutionized the newspaper business. In the fifties Louis's father had helped develop one of the first electronic phototypesetting machines, the Linotron, and by the time Louis was a teenager, typesetting had migrated from the noisy floor of publishing plants to production departments or even directly into the editorial offices of small publications.

Louis was well placed to make something of this legacy. By nature inquisitive and stubborn, he had an outsider's toughness that made him difficult to intimidate. In Great Neck, the Long Island suburb where he grew up, his neighbors had been affluent, Jewish, and politically liberal; Louis was Italian and his family was conservative. Arriving at Columbia in 1967, when the Students for a Democratic Society were attempting to close down the university, he declared himself for Nixon. That year campus revolutionaries battled the police, who beat them along with bystanders. Louis Rossetto watched the Columbia crisis unfold and devoted himself to political study, moving steadily out through the ramifying veins of conservatism until he got to the finest capillaries where the isolatos of the right—the libertarians—mingled with the isolatos of the left—the anarchists. For a short time he was the unlikely president of the Columbia Young Republicans, but he was a shaggy-haired, antiwar troublemaker, out of sync with the party's mainstream. Eventually, he went to work as a volunteer staff member at an anarchist journal, *The Abolitionist*. The thing to be abolished was government. Louis stood at the waist-high table, running warm paste over the backs of the galleys. He knew that advances in typesetting meant more than added convenience for typesetters. For him, cheap printing was a tool of revolt, though not the sort of revolt his peers may have had in mind. *The New York Times Magazine* put Louis on the cover as a representative of a new type of radical. Inside, Louis repeated the libertarian slogan: "Ask not what your country can do for you, ask what your country is doing *to* you."

Disillusion on the left has long been a cliché, but as the decade turned, Louis was influenced by a less publicized trend: disillusion on the right. The right, after all, was the side that really seemed to be losing the revolution. As corporations made peace with the counterculture, and the last of the anti–New Deal, Roosevelt-hating, small-town businessmen entered their dotage, you had to wonder what was going to happen to the untimely personalities who wanted to carry on in the older Republican image: the rugged, storybook individualists; the enterprising moguls-to-be whose rights of accumulation were abrogated by the income tax; the bright young men and women of '68—of Nixon for President in '68—whose field of activity was swamped by inflation, stagnation, and Republican price controls. Nobody knew yet what a comeback the entrepreneurial ideal would make. President Reagan was still ten years away.

Louis's opinion that the government should be abolished did not prevail. As soon as he graduated, he started business school at Columbia, but by the time he emerged he was certain he did not want to work for a boring American corporation. Then came Watergate. This was an exciting development. Social conflict always opens avenues for unusual talents. As the televised hearings unfolded, Louis saw a chance to escape from what he thought of as the corporate draft. His subject was in front of him and in two months he had written a novel. It was a potboiler called *Takeover.* The premise was a coup by Richard Nixon. It had one sex scene, one chase scene, and extensive political exposition.

In December 1973 the young novelist was out at his parents'

house on Long Island, waiting for a call from his agent. So far there had been no buyers. The temperature was 31 degrees, and it was raining. By midnight, all the trees and branches were covered with an inch of ice, and he lay in his bed listening to the weaker limbs break off. It seemed that he would not escape the corporate draft after all. The next morning, with everything in sight frozen and dead branches a foot deep on the ground, he got his call and found out that a small publisher named Lyle Stuart had agreed to bring out the book. The money was negligible, and Nixon resigned before it came out, ruining the joke, but this was beside the point. Louis would get, after all, his spy's disguise, his public costume, his word to put on the blank line of the entrance documents when he came and left the country. He was a writer.

For ten years he survived on odds and ends: a few magazine stories, some carpentry. He never wrote another novel, but he always made just enough money and he had extraordinary luck at showing up in zones of conflict that were just breaking down into chaos, circumstances in which a person of courage never has trouble getting a square meal. In the mid-seventies he found himself in Rome, where he befriended Piernico Solinas and ghostwrote the young assistant director's book about the making of *Caligula,* a "sex colossal" written by Gore Vidal, funded by Bob Guccione, and directed by Tinto Brass. *Caligula* was filmed during the peak of the sexual revolution, when it seemed more or less reasonable for a well-known director to demonstrate the exact manner in which he wanted cunnilingus performed on an actress. The moral of Salinas's account, *Ultimate Porno,* is that authority is an illusion, and that established hierarchies are easily hijacked by individuals of conviction and stamina. This was a valuable lesson.

Louis seemed to have a second sense for incipient revolution, and he made it to Peru in time for the start of the Shining Path uprising, to Sri Lanka for the outbreak of the Tamil rebellion, to Italy for the bombings and kidnappings by the Red Brigades. He was not consciously chasing trouble, but he was rarely afraid and his curiosity was intense. In Afghanistan as a freelance, he would write one of the first newspaper reports describing how the anti-Soviet mujahedeen were using American-supplied antiaircraft missiles to turn the tide of the war. The world's second-most powerful empire was being held at bay by a ragtag insurgency with the help of the right high-tech tools; it was incredible to witness and inspiring to think back upon. Louis got to the front by hiking in from Pakistan with a gang of part-time fighters.

Eventually, he settled in Amsterdam. Amsterdam was cheap, with easy transportation and other amenities, and though he was opposed on principle to Holland's quasi-socialist welfare system, Louis loved the famously tolerant lifestyle of the Dutch metropolis, where marijuana was sold openly in the cafés. Because his father had been born an Italian citizen, Louis successfully asserted his right to live and work in Europe.

Like John Plunkett, Louis had read Real Invest's advertisement in the *International Herald Tribune*. At the office overlooking the Seine, Plunkett designed the newsletter's logo, while Louis flew down from Amsterdam every two weeks to cull news stories from the international press and write editorials that attempted to dislodge Real Invest customers from their narrow prejudices. Bill

Sigal liked to emphasize the value of international investing. There was no reason for Americans to leave their money languishing in domestic securities when the world economy was undergoing such exciting changes.

One day Louis passed a handsome woman who was walking out of the company's office on the Quai d'Anjou. He barely had time to notice her before she bounced by him onto the street. But of course he did notice. "There is something about me that gets attention," Jane Metcalfe said later. "I have never been able to just slip in someplace."

She met him again soon afterward, at a party where they sat on the floor together smoking pot out of a pipe made from a cardboard tube. She liked Louis immediately. He was soft-spoken but very forceful. He had traveled the world and his opinions were his own; there was nothing he said that resembled a newspaper editorial. But, perhaps most important, he seemed immune to social pressure. He was charting his own course, just as she had vowed to do.

Among the stylish Americans who spent time on the Ile Saint-Louis, Jane Metcalfe was sometimes mistaken for a wealthy heiress. "Her grandfather owned a railroad," one of her admirers recalled, long after she moved away. "Her father was a Princeton man who owned a bank." But this description was misleading, for by the time Jane was born the Metcalfe family was not rich. When Jane was growing up her mother lived in a state mental hospital. Her father was a bon vivant, and she was raised by a devoted nanny whose room and board comprised a large percentage of her pay. Still, with her natural confidence and vivacity, Jane had managed to hold her own as a scholarship student at Louisville Colle-

giate, Kentucky's elite secondary school. At school she wore a uni-
form, after school she wore tennis whites. This took care of the
problem of clothes. She became president of her class and captain
of her field-hockey team. Jane's friends back in Louisville may
have expected her to spend some time out of town acquiring social
polish before returning to be safely married to a rich man, but instead she graduated from the University of Colorado with a degree
in political science, moved to Paris, and refused to return. She was
absolutely determined to alter her destiny. On the other hand, the
values of Louisville society were in some ways not so different
from the values of Paris, and, on the Île Saint-Louis, people wondered what Jane, who was beautiful, game for anything, and rumored to be rich, was doing with this eccentric man who had a
motley career and no money. Louis, as one of Jane's older and
more worldly friends told her directly, had all the signs of being a
lifelong loser. "You could do so much better!" he said. But these
conventional ideas were not her own. Jane's crush on Louis had no
calculation in it, except for the deepest calculation that identifies
happiness with passion.

Like the others, Jane had found her job in the building at 37
Quai d'Anjou by answering a newspaper advertisement. Soon she
was traveling back and forth to Geneva, carrying funds, and she
was responsible for a certain amount of reassuring correspondence. At first she admired Sigal and found him glamorous. "He
was very global in his thinking," she later said. But Jane's signature was on letters to Bill Sigal's clients that contained statements
like "We received your funds" and "The funds are in your account." She knew that the second statement was sometimes un-
true. The more she was entangled in the business, the more

worried she became. She guessed it would end badly. Finally Jane quit and found a sales position with a vendor of hotel supplies. She was twenty-four.

Meanwhile, in a *Globescan* editorial, Louis Rossetto took aim at President Ronald Reagan's huge, deficit-financed military buildup, which, as an enemy of statism, he naturally opposed. But the boobs to whom Real Invest's services were pitched were good conservative people, and Ronald Reagan was their hero. With an aggravating sincerity that would later confound more important enemies than Bill Sigal, Louis was treating *Globescan* as an independent pamphlet on liberal economics rather than a printed infomercial. A fierce argument ensued. Bill and Louis yelled at each other for a few minutes, then Louis was fired. John Plunkett quit Real Invest at about the same time and returned to the United States.

The year was 1985. Louis, at thirty-five, was approaching the age when a peripatetic lifestyle threatens to become permanent and youthful wandering turns into habitual homelessness. After leaving Real Invest he made two moves that appeared to contradict each other. Characteristically, he bought a ticket to South Africa, where he had always wanted to travel. Uncharacteristically, he applied for what had once been known as a straight job, editing technical documents for Ink Taalservice, a small translation and technical publishing house in Amsterdam. Ink made him an offer. Louis asked for a few weeks to decide, then flew to Cape Town.

There was a state of emergency in South Africa, with violence in the homelands, but Louis drove from Cape Town to Durban along the coast and picked up every hitchhiker he saw, running his little rental car like a bus, sometimes with every seat full. He ferried African National Congress organizers who explained to him why it was inevitable that Russia would defeat America, and black soldiers just back from Angola in T-shirts that said I KILL TERRORISTS. Whether his foreignness trumped his race, or his natural immunity to social pressure and insinuation protected him from threats that would have frightened a more sensitive person, or whether, merely by chance, the flows of political hostility swirled around him without coming close—whatever the reason, Louis thought South Africa during the crisis was delightful. The people were friendly and warm, and free with their opinions. The countryside was beautiful and the cities were outwardly tranquil. The bohemian life on the margins, which he also explored, lolled on undisturbed. He stayed for three weeks and wondered if he would ever go back to Europe.

The gap between what he had seen in the press about South Africa and what he experienced firsthand made a deep impression. In the township of Ceskei Louis visited the little town of Port Saint John, on the Indian Ocean. It was due south from Johannesburg and had been a vacation resort, but now that it was part of a nominally independent black republic it had fallen into disfavor and most of the whites had fled. As he drove down the road—by himself, for once—he saw little kids coming toward the shoulder, each one rubbing a closed fist into an open hand. He wondered if it was a political sign or a form of begging. The town was falling apart but extremely comfortable. The Indian Ocean was warm. The beer was inexpensive. And it turned out that the sign the kids were making was for South African smoke, incredible grass, for which they were asking mere pennies. It started to sink in, then, what it could be like to live there, to just hang on, hang around. There would always be a way to scrape together a living sending dispatches on the revolution.

He took his car out of town a few miles to where one of the few white residents lived in a little farmhouse full of modern appliances and hi-tech stereo equipment. When he arrived the man was getting stoned using a brick he had hollowed out into a pipe. Louis told his host, who was a drug dealer, that a real estate agent in Port Elizabeth had advised him to always carry a gun. He had ignored the advice and had driven all the way to Port Saint John with a shifting crowd of hitchhiking passengers and never been the victim of a crime. The drug dealer snorted. He said he never locked his door when he was away, never mind carrying a gun. "You make your own decision about how much of the common story to believe," he said, smoking his brick.

Louis did not admire the man personally, but he recognized how much liberty you could acquire in one of these border zones that were half catastrophe and half paradise, especially if you were invulnerable to the received opinions most people mistook for reality. The drug dealer was living a life of ease in a state of emergency, and it represented both the ultimate achievement and the end of the road. Louis woke up the next morning and decided to go back to Amsterdam. Many years later, when he noticed a look of shock on the face of one of his colleagues or partners when he violated some small bit of business etiquette—and he noticed this only rarely—he would marvel at the narrow boundaries of their world, and at what they were capable of taking seriously.

CHAPTER 2

THE BLESSING

Folktale protagonists are disinherited or orphaned at the start; businessmen are fired. Louis Rossetto's new job at Ink was to produce materials for the Fokker 100, a new, intercity, twin-engine jet. But almost as soon as he showed up the Fokker project was canceled. This was fantastic luck. The myriad public services of the Dutch capital had given Louis a cushion as he pursued his self-education, and now its strict labor laws came into play. Full-time employees could not be given the boot with impunity. Rather than pay for his termination, Ink gave Louis a job babying the company's computer printers into producing decent output, a scandalously difficult task before the invention of desktop-publishing software.

Peter Rutten, a brooding, dark-haired, Delft-born writer who was busy making instruction manuals for computers that controlled part of Holland's flood-control system, thought Louis's commitment to his job was bizarre. Who really cared if every font in every size could be reproduced correctly using these intermediate tools that would soon be obsolete? But Louis's head was always in one of the printers; he was irrationally, almost defiantly dedicated.

Originally, Peter guessed that this was an American trait, a sample of the work ethic he would find in the States if he ever realized one of his dreams and managed to emigrate. He soon realized his mistake. Louis was not lazy, but neither was he typically ambitious, nor particularly interested in the happiness of his employers. His aims were entirely different. He thought computer publishing would change the world.

The type of revolution Louis anticipated was unfamiliar. Peter was surprised to discover that his new friend was unstirred by any of the standard progressive rhetoric current among Dutch young people. For instance, though South Africa's apartheid system was the subject of widespread European protest, and the direst predictions about that country's future were commonplace, Louis just laughed at Peter's opinions, treating them as woefully secondhand. There was, Louis said, a reservoir of good feeling between the races in South Africa, and its future was not as bleak as it was being portrayed by the media. Louis hated the mainstream press. Its work product was *defective*. South Africa was not on the verge of apocalypse.

While dissenting on the topic of South Africa's future, Peter liked Louis's idea that the printing devices they were using at Ink, and the personal computers on which they were producing thousand-page instruction manuals, had the power to transform terms of debate that had heretofore seemed uncontestable. Desktop computers could transform media even more than the Mergenthaler linotype had. Also, there was something irresistible about the way Louis seemed to dwell outside the dominant currents of liberal or conservative thought. Peter stayed late with Louis as he practiced voodoo manipulation of the recalcitrant printers. They played trash-can basketball after everybody else had left the office and indulged in top-volume political arguments in the smoky bars alongside the canals, and Peter was gradually won over by the faith Louis had in a new journalistic dispensation. It was an appealing idea, especially if you were a Dutchman at the beginning of your career, for established newspapers and magazines in Holland were small and cliquish institutions, without the rate of growth that necessitated an influx of talent. Europe had been in a recession forever, telephone calls across national borders cost a small fortune, and kids wore buttons on their jackets that said NO FUTURE.

Louis worked all week at his new job in Amsterdam. But every Friday at about 7 P.M. he began the six-hundred-kilometer drive to Paris, arriving by midnight. If Jane was not back yet from a dinner engagement with one of her friends, he would sleep in his used Peugeot outside the courtyard of her apartment until she appeared and woke him up. They had still exchanged no promises, for he was as independent a human being as one was likely to encounter anywhere, while she never lacked for interesting company. But when they met each other they usually stayed up all night, finally going to sleep at daybreak and rising again in the late afternoon.

For Jane the French capital was losing its charm. In the spring of 1988 she decided to accept Louis's repeated invitations to try Amsterdam. She intended to work in the fashion industry, but the blocky cuts and drab colors of Dutch fashion baffled her, and just as she began to despair, Louis allowed that he needed a hand.

Louis was no longer the person in charge of the printers at Ink Taalservice. A few months earlier his boss, Jaap van der Meer, had asked him to edit a company magazine that would be titled *Computers and Translation*. Ink planned to use the magazine to help sell translation software and services. For less money, Ink could have hired two salespeople and had them pitch every major client in Europe, but when Louis pointed this out he was told to stop protesting and start editing.

On the first page of the first issue Jaap van der Meer announced to readers that "machine translators are about to begin penetrating the business market." On the fifth page of that very same issue Louis published a well-informed essay by a leading computer scientist demonstrating that machine translation was not only *not* about to penetrate the business market but was still technically unfeasible and would probably remain unfeasible for years. Louis was left to find his own editorial mission, and in keeping with his lifelong passion for a free, democratic, popular press he decided that the important developments were not in the area of automatic translation but in word processing, speech recognition, typesetting, page layout, and printing. He quickly won permission to change the name: *Computers and Translation* became *Language Technology*. The title lasted one year. It was nicely descriptive but lacked pizzazz. Soon Louis changed the name again, to *Electric Word*.

Louis was a pioneering user of the tools he wrote about and promoted. He produced his magazine on his desktop. The design was by Max Kisman, whose posters for Amsterdam dance clubs

Louis admired, and who alone among the designers Louis interviewed was willing to work in a production process that was entirely digital. Since all layout was done on the computer, Louis could change the text at the last minute and would often bicycle over to the apartment where his production manager was working late, to alter words or sentences on-screen.

The magazine was rife with printed errors. The problem was a result of thin resources and tight deadlines, but it was also a hint of another regime of publishing, both newer and older than the one still dominant during the magazine's three-year run. *Language Technology* and *Electric Word,* cranked out on a desktop with Louis staring over the designer's shoulder, anticipated the style of electronic publishing while looking back to a time when a printer might drag his press out to a public square in the heat of an election and churn out broadsides denouncing the authorities. With these new devices, magazines could be invented out of thin air.

Since it began as a promotional tool, advertising in *Language Technology* was an afterthought, but Louis always felt that his situation would be more secure if the magazine made money. Jane never got a paycheck from *Language Technology* or *Electric Word,* but she sold ads on commission, learning as she went.

As the editor of a magazine, Louis began to display all of his diverse talents and strengths. Jane loved to see his idiosyncrasy reveal itself as genius. Louis never treated the technical people he wrote about merely as a source of information or a collection of fascinating characters. Instead, they were his vanguard. Moreover, they were a secret vanguard, not because they conspired to remain unknown but because their ideas were embodied in machines most people were afraid of, and their activities, style of speech, mode of dress, and taste in entertainment were unappealing to journalists and popularizers. In *Language Technology* and *Electric Word* Louis sought to highlight the power of this new elite.

He had given himself a difficult assignment. The fulfillment of a world-historical destiny usually took a backseat, in the minds of engineers, to the pleasures of solving a technical challenge. They were, despite their intelligence and influence, a very unlikely vanguard. On the other hand, Louis did not concoct his philosophy out of nothing. Materials going back fifteen years were on hand, beginning with Ted Nelson's seminal manifesto, *Computer Lib,* published in 1974. Nelson, an inventor and polemicist, presented computer technology as a liberating social force. "Computer Power to the People" and "You Can and Must Understand Computers Now" were his slogans. The book sold fifty thousand copies in thirteen years, mostly to computer people, among whom it was widely known and loved.

Ted Nelson's understanding of his readers was intimate and accurate. In a short discussion of politics, he cited a poll that found 50 percent of the registered Libertarians in New York to be computer professionals. "The field is full of talented loners who have felt stifled by school and held back by undeserving fools," he wrote. "In a sense it is their natural political position."

Among the fans of *Computer Lib* were the founders of the microcomputer business. The invention of the Apple computer earned a hundred million dollars for Steve Wozniak, the most celebrated hacker, and produced billion-dollar subindustries. Apple itself had helped spread the idea that computers were a political force with a series of visionary advertising campaigns, beginning with its famous Super Bowl spot in 1984 that showed the Macintosh as a weapon against an oppressive state.

In *Language Technology* and *Electric Word* Louis was already reflecting the changes that had occurred since the milestone of the Macintosh. His magazine was meant to convey the challenge that goes along with startling good news. He described his readers as "thinking computer users involved in the global revolution of information technology."

Predictably, the sale of translation tools did not increase. After eight bimonthly issues, Jaap van der Meer called Louis in for a meeting and told him that his magazine was an ex-product and he was an ex-employee.

"Wow," Louis said. "That's harsh."

When Ink cut off support, Louis went in search of a buyer who would allow him to continue. He found Maurice Keizer, a Dutch businessman who had licensed the technology for rotating billboards made of thin plastic strips attached to an electric motor. Keizer had built a small company around this innovation and was expanding it by buying magazines. He owned a four-story building near the Vondelpark in Amsterdam, and in the summer of 1988 he gave Louis space in the basement. Next to Louis was Peter Rutten, who followed him from Ink, and next to Peter was Jane, who called every technology company who had somebody who could talk to her in English or French and tried to sell them an ad.

Keizer was slightly interested in the contents of *Electric Word,* but his guiding motive was money. He wanted to build a big magazine company quickly, transform investments into capital assets, and leverage himself from entrepreneurship to moguldom. He recognized *Electric Word* as an instruction manual for producing titles on the cheap, and he saw in Louis an easily exploitable resource whose somewhat extravagant ideas about the future were less important than his experience organizing all the pieces of a magazine—writing, design, layout, circulation, advertising—without expensive support.

A clash was inevitable. With each issue of *Electric Word* Louis grew more confident that he had discovered an engine of social change. Louis insisted that the people he wrote about were, as he put it, "the most powerful people on the planet." This hyperbole—if it was hyperbole—was interesting neither to Keizer nor to the very long series of publishers and financiers to whom Louis would later present it.

Keizer had many balls in the air, and his financial machinations were opaque. The mood in the basement office was tense as they sat at their desks made out of cheap doors on sawhorses and listened to Jane slam down the phone and swear in English after another brush-off, so there was plenty of fuel for argument, but even under the best of circumstances there was probably nothing Louis could have said to convince Keizer that *Electric Word* was not a toy or a hobby or a loss leader or a little trade magazine for people who carried calculators in leather cases on their belts but a portrait and a tool of a millennial transformation that was happening right in front of his eyes.

Electric Word never had more than fifteen thousand subscribers. When Maurice Keizer shut the magazine down in May 1990, Louis transferred his operation to a borrowed apartment and printed another issue using Keizer's credit with suppliers. On the cover was a headline reading INVEST IN THIS MAGAZINE! Louis, in his editor's note, announced that "thirty-six months and two publishers later, *Electric Word* is independent." But it was not independent, and there was never another issue. Keizer sued for recovery of the expenses involved in producing the last issue, which he said he had not authorized, and attached his ex-employee's bank account. Louis and Jane countersued for ownership of the name *Electric Word,* and for payment of Jane's advertising commissions, which the publisher withheld.

Louis and Jane were living in close quarters in Louis's tiny walk-up on Wilhelminastraat, which cost them about $150 per month. The front door opened onto a narrow living room; a few feet toward the back of the apartment, it widened enough to hold a bed. This was hardly Jane's idea of happiness. Louis disagreed.

"It's just like in the old days," he told her, "when families would farm together."

"Back then they had no choice," said Jane.

But Louis was a fighter, and for his sake Jane was untiring. She made hundreds of calls seeking a new backer, and when he brooded and grew angry she maintained her mask of cheerfulness and picked up the phone again.

Of course, Jane found it distressing that they now had no office, no income, and nobody to pay their enormous long-distance bills. Each move from here would be dependent on the charity of friends, which they were often forced to stretch beyond the limits of good manners. But their faith in the coming change, which they carried with them like a blessing, served to justify the hospitality they sought and took.

CHAPTER 3

PILGRIMS

In the winter, cold rain soaks through the clothes of bike-riding Amsterdam dwellers and brown moss insinuates itself into the crevices of their windowsills. One year Jane's feet were so swollen that she could not put shoes on. This is a condition known in Dutch as *wintertenen,* or winter toes; in English it is called chilblains. The impression Louis and Jane gave when they came to New York was of refugees from a damp European exile. They wanted their next magazine to be launched in America, but they did not know where to begin. Old acquaintances gossiped about their plight with pity and amusement.

At the mention of Rupert Murdoch, Michael Wolff, who was one of Louis's main American contacts, suppressed a groan. Wolff did a lot of favors for Louis. Wolff sympathized with Louis. On certain rare days, in fragments of minutes, Wolff even liked Louis, but the last thing he wanted was for social chatter to link his name to a clueless ex-hippie parading around New York with a pamphlet about "Hacking the Brain" and a fantasy about a partnership with the famous publisher.

Wolff was a devoted observer of the New York media elite. His reaction exactly forecast the response Louis would get from every magazine expert to whom he appealed for help.

Their initial meeting had been pure charity. In 1988, after Ink cut off support for *Language Technology,* Louis had gotten Wolff's number from a mutual friend. Perhaps Wolff could give him some advice? Wolff knew something about magazines. His father had been in advertising, and his wife was the in-house counsel for Ziff Davis, a leading publisher of computer magazines. However, by occupation and temperament Wolff was actually closer to Louis than to the professional colleagues of his wife. Like Louis, he was an ex-writer turned entrepreneur. Like Louis, he was still looking for his first business success. And like Louis, he wanted to own a magazine. In 1986 Wolff had tried to buy *National Lampoon,* but having no money of his own with which to buy it, he failed.

They met in a bar on the Upper West Side. Wolff found Louis baffling. He was too old to be a dropout. He was too fixated on business to be a bohemian. He had an otherworldly quality that seemed incompatible with serious employment. And his ideas about magazines suggested he was completely in the dark about the realities of the computer-publishing industry. American computer magazines gave their readers lots of hard facts. But Louis was not interested in reviews of hardware and software. He claimed he was telling the story of a new society to the most powerful people on the planet. Wolff did not believe a word of it. He was immune to Louis's charisma. He had too much experience, and besides, the genuinely powerful New Yorkers he watched from a distance absorbed all of his capacity for fascination. They shook hands and parted.

Two years later Louis was back. When he called, Wolff was distressed. He struggled to find the right words or phrases that would send his unwelcome visitor away. Unfortunately, there was something in the man's character that seemed to shield him from polite abuse. Wolff had never met anybody who presented himself so silently, so hungrily—as if any bit of advice he could offer was just the nourishment that would keep Louis from perishing. Finally, Wolff gave him a few numbers of media insiders he knew, just as an apology for breaking off the meeting. Only later, when Louis had walked away, did Wolff feel the full force of his potential embarrassment. Louis's ideas were ridiculous.

Later, in the wake of Louis's success, Wolff would found an Internet company, drive it to insolvency, write himself a check with the last funds in the bank account, and savage his ex-partners in a brutally funny book called *Burn Rate*. But at the time he met Louis, Wolff still hoped to earn the trust of businesspeople. To their meetings, Wolff wore an Armani jacket. Louis wore his regular jeans, and carried his regular daypack, and sported his old-fashioned white sneakers with green stripes. He looked as hopeless as he sounded. "Louis wanted to be in the computer-magazine business," Wolff later said, "but he did not have a goddamn clue."

John Plunkett was dismissive also. This came as a surprise, because Louis had recently taken John on an inspiring trip to San Francisco. Over the years, the two men had kept in touch, and Louis's constantly evolving schemes played upon John's imagination. John occasionally supplied Louis with little bits of free design work, faxing suggestions to their Amsterdam apartment. When John had work assignments in Europe, he spent many hours in Louis's company. They browsed the racks at local newsstands, poring over every new thing. In 1989 Louis and Jane had been guests at John's wedding to Barbara Kuhr, who was also a designer and who became John's business partner.

"One day we'll do a magazine together," Louis told Barbara and John.

"Well, okay," John answered. This did not mean that he agreed. When Louis said something to John, and John responded with an intake of breath that widened his already wide chest and a wince that widened his already wide face and said "Okay," drawing the word out slowly, it meant only that he refused to commit himself. But Louis would often mistake his sarcasm for polite agreement. There was something strangely powerful in his failure to take offense.

With the terminal issue of *Electric Word* in the hands of readers, Louis had invited John to meet him on the West Coast for Macworld. Macworld was a computer trade show with evangelical highlights. In January 1991, hundreds upon hundreds of fledgling entrepreneurs circulated among the crowd on the main floor of San Francisco's Moscone Center, carrying plans and demos on the three-and-a-half-inch diskettes that had become an icon of a new industry. Arguments over technical loyalties were known as *religious disputes,* and though the phrase was used humorously, the zeal was genuine.

One morning during the show John and Louis sat on a carpeted balcony above the exhibit floor with two other men: Randy Stick-

rod, the ex-publisher of *Computer Graphics World,* and Jim Felici, the managing editor of *Publish*! Both had been fans of *Electric
Word* during that magazine's short run. Neither felt, as Michael
Wolff did, that Louis was delusional. After all, Louis had been
putting out a magazine for three years, which made him mani-
festly less delusional than at least 50 percent of the competing
businesspeople in San Francisco that weekend. Now Louis was
saying that he wanted to make a larger, slicker, and more popular
version of his magazine in America. John Plunkett would be the
designer.

Randy Stickrod was immediately optimistic. He had been working on the West Coast for many years and knew many wealthy
investors, known as angels. Angels could coax companies into
existence by writing personal checks for tens or even hundreds of
thousands of dollars. This was not philanthropy; the common notion of a fair reward for an angel investment was 1,000 percent
over four or five years. Still, angel investments had a certain miraculous quality, because they could transform ephemeral chatter
into the raw materials of a durable enterprise.

In this friendly atmosphere, it was easy for the four men to
speak as though they were already partners. Louis had a vivid
image of living and working with Jane, John, and Barbara in the
perfect Victorian house he had found while walking around the
city that weekend. Since neither he nor Jane had jobs in America
or any sort of checkable credit history, Louis gave the rental application to John to fill out and sign. John was doubtful. There was
something in Louis's gaze that bothered him—the way he showed
no uncertainty when he set down the application, which John had

never seen before, and explained why John had to sign it. "I am completely happy to do anything I can as a designer," John explained, "but I cannot finance this venture."

John and Barbara had been thinking seriously about leaving New York. They had enough money in the bank for a down payment on a house somewhere far from Manhattan. But John did not want to be entangled financially with Louis and Jane. "Whatever we do," he told his wife, "we are not letting them get their hands on our down payment."

Louis returned to Holland from Macworld and prepared to emigrate. John, keeping in touch by fax and phone, came up with a name. Their new magazine would be called *DigIt,* which could be pronounced either "digit," in which case it represented computers, or "dig it," in which case it represented an interesting and fashionable phenomenon that you suddenly grasped, or *dug.* Jane knew the name *DigIt* was laughable. She preferred her own idea: *Wired.* John was unconvinced until he realized how effective it would be in the imperative mode: Get *Wired.*

For traveling money, Louis and Jane sought help from a long-haired, countercultural business owner and former *Electric Word* advertiser named Eckart Wintzen. Louis spoke to Wintzen frankly; he said that he was going to America to start a magazine and needed cash. The Dutch entrepreneur peered back through tiny, brightly tinted eyeglasses and explained that while an investment in a new magazine would suit his general inclination to diversify his technical consulting firm, he predicted that if he got involved in magazine publishing he might lose track of more important affairs and then he would have to reorganize the company, and this would mean that he would have to cut Louis off again. Wintzen said he preferred to just short-circuit this whole painful process and not invest in the first place.

On the other hand, since he had read and respected *Electric Word,* and since the amount of money they needed was not large, Wintzen offered to just give Louis and Jane a little cash to help get the first issue off the ground. He did not want any stake in their business. His money would simply be payment in advance for an advertisement in the magazine's first issues plus a few thousand promotional copies to give away to clients. If the first issue came out as planned, he would supply them with a second payment equal to the first.

Before the shock had worn off, Wintzen gave them forty-five thousand Dutch guilders, about twenty thousand dollars. With this money in hand, Louis and Jane flew to New York. On the way they stopped in London and Louis bought a dark blue Ermenegildo Zegna suit, which he hoped would be perfect for doing business in. They let their acquaintances know they were on their way.

That winter, the New York publishing community could hardly have been in a less credulous state of mind. The financial downturn coincident with the Gulf War was short-lived and soon forgotten, but it lasted long enough to cause advertisers to cautiously restrict their spending, which meant that thriving magazines shrank, and struggling magazines perished. More than five hundred titles had been launched in 1989, and less than half had lasted out the year. Many were small, specialty publications, but knowledgeable publishers suffered along with the rawest neophytes. Mainstream casualties included *7 Days, Manhattan, Inc., Fame, Wigwag,* and *Egg.* The founders of *Spy,* the most celebrated new magazine of the eighties, were desperate for cash by the end of 1990. In February 1991, after five years of publication, *Spy's* owners sold a 90 percent stake in their monthly for just four and a half million dollars.

When Iraq invaded Kuwait in August 1990, Michael Wolff had been trying to start a travel magazine called *America*. He was sharing offices in a building on Fourteenth Street with *Smart* magazine, *Mother Earth News,* and *Psychology Today.* Soon the cash flow dried up and the lights started going off a circuit at a time, and then the locks were changed and the repo man appeared. By the end of the year all of these magazines, including Wolff's, were dead. When Wolff heard that Louis and Jane were choosing this moment to give up their threadbare but comfortable Amsterdam life for a new American venture, he laughed.

Abandonments began immediately. As soon as he touched down in New York, Louis called John Plunkett and discovered to his dismay that his designer was not going to move to a large, comfortable flat in the Cole Valley district of San Francisco, in which they could reproduce the quaint communal atmosphere of the era of the magazine they so much admired, *Rolling Stone,* but rather to Park City, a touristy, ski-plagued ex-mining town about forty minutes outside of Salt Lake City and a good, safe twelve hundred miles from Louis and Jane. Louis was astounded to have been let down so quickly.

John thought he had been clear about his intentions: he would gladly help if Randy Stickrod found an angel. But Randy hadn't. Besides, there was another problem. There had never been any written documentation of the Macworld discussion. When John said to Louis, "What's the deal with the partnership?" Louis just stared at him with that blank, intimidating, melancholic gaze and waited for a full minute before answering, as if from all the way across the room, "What do you mean, what's the deal?" John would answer, "What do you mean, what do I mean?" Then the two men looked at each other, just like in the movies, though they were unarmed.

Louis felt it was absurd to commit to specific terms when there was no real business to be owned. But in that case, John was certainly not going to move to California with Louis. In fact, John was not going to do a single additional page of design for Louis without a written partnership contract. John and Barbara already had their car loaded up for their trip out to Utah, so they had no place to work even if they were willing to help, which they were not.

Afterward, John was not able to explain to himself what happened next. For three more days he and Barbara stayed in Manhattan, working around the clock in a studio they borrowed from a friend to produce a good-looking pamphlet for Louis, and they did it for free, with no formal agreement about any sort of partnership at all. Steve Jobs, the cofounder of Apple, was said by his employees to possess a *reality distortion field* that bent their will to his ends. Louis had a similar power over John. It may have been produced by Louis's strangely affecting combination of certainty and vulnerability. John later remembered Louis saying something like, "If you leave now, you will kill our dream." John supposed he was motivated by compassion.

There was no time to make a complete representation of a new magazine, for which, in any case, there was no content. Instead, they created what Louis called a manifesto, giving a taste of *Wired*'s mission and design. The manifesto was sixteen pages long, in a squarish format. Inside there was a short, dramatic statement by Louis warning that technology was less a tool of convenience than an irresistible force capable of disrupting the most intimate relationships. "You, the information rich," he wrote, "are the most powerful people on the planet today. You and the information technology you wield are completely transforming our lives, our families, our neighborhoods, our educations, our jobs, our governments, our world." There was a sample table of contents, a list of potential writers and editors, and the first page of a story titled "Kamikaze Kapitalists in the Land of the Salaryman." But the main goal of the manifesto was to convey what the magazine would look like, and Plunkett used a color photocopy and hundreds of images cut from other magazines to simulate the possibilities of computer illustration. After more or less ransacking the borrowed studio and going so far beyond the limits of his friend's hospitality that John eventually wrote him a check for thousands of dollars out of his own pocket to make up for it, John and Barbara drove away in their packed car toward Utah with multiple sighs of relief and a feeling—slow to fade—of manumission.

The shock Louis felt at being abandoned by John Plunkett was multiplied by other blows. Jim Felici, partner number two, moved to France. Notwithstanding his enthusiasm for Louis's magazine, he decided not to put off the fulfillment of his own dreams; besides, he did not need the headache. Randy Stickrod, while still optimistic, had not raised a cent.

Louis and Jane bought a used Honda and drove west, staying in cheap motels along the way. Through a wealthy shoe manufacturer Jane had grown friendly with at an industry conference, she and Louis met a San Francisco real estate developer whose beauti-

ful home in the Berkeley Hills was temporarily empty; he offered
to rent the place to them for only a thousand dollars per month.
They could not refuse such a bargain, though it was more than five
times what they had paid for housing in Holland. Jane knew that
Louis had scraped his way through many uncertain situations and
that he called this necessary combination of scrimping and free-
loading *living close to the ground.*

Every morning that fall and winter Louis and Jane drove together to a fragment of an office in San Francisco near a park
shaped like a tiny racecourse. South Park, by Rincon Hill, had
once been the most fashionable neighborhood in the city, but the
mansions had burned in 1906, and by the time Louis and Jane arrived every trace of its first incarnation was gone except the old-
fashioned oval of grass among blocks of warehouses and small
buildings. The offices surrounding South Park were cheap, which
made them appealing as headquarters for unremunerative endeavors. For instance, the well-known type foundry of Andrew Hoyam
was here, and the great printer must have stepped over to the park
a few times for air while composing his celebrated *Inferno.* On the
northeast edge a seismically questionable four-story brick building
held a publishing business devoted to the Commodore, Atari, and
Macintosh platforms. Times were hard, however, and the operation had shrunk to a single floor. The owner sublet a small street-
level office to Randy Stickrod, who donated a corner of his corner
to Louis and Jane.

Randy drove a silver Porsche but was himself in the process of
going broke. He had sold his computer-graphics magazine for a
tidy sum and sunk his new money into a vineyard in Sonoma
County and a duplex on Nob Hill, after which a drought killed his

vineyard, a divorce took his duplex, and a tax problem consumed the rest of his ready money. Still, Randy generously offered Louis and Jane the benefit of his expertise. Along with two battered desks and two phone lines, he let them use his fax machine.

Louis first saw *Wired*'s new office in June. The week after they moved in a bullet came through the window and lodged itself in the wall near Jane's desk. Soon afterward, somebody shot up the front door. These were not vendettas, as far as anybody could tell, for Jane and Louis's angriest enemies were far away, in Europe, where the contributors to the last issue of *Electric Word* had never been paid. They were merely an outward expression of social problems unfamiliar to the couple, who had lived in Europe for a long time.

For month after month they ran down their bank accounts and tried to find angels and failed. Soon after the turn of the year, Louis and Jane were not speaking to each other about any social topic, because just when things were at their most tenuous, Jane had impetuously gone off for the weekend to Belize with a well-built, dark-bearded purple-prose specialist named John Perry Barlow. Her choice in this affair, while terribly damaging to Louis, was not as inexplicable as it might have seemed, for while Barlow was irredeemably affected, he was also intelligent, unconventional, and sincerely in love with Jane.

They had met in 1989, at a garden party in Amsterdam. Barlow was a rancher and lyricist who owned a spread in Wyoming and penned songs for the Grateful Dead; he was also a leading activist on behalf of the civil liberties of computer users and, with software pioneer Mitch Kapor, a cofounder of the Electronic Frontier Foundation. His photo had graced the cover of Plunkett's manifesto for *Wired*. Shown in three-quarter profile, he wore a cowboy hat and glared obliquely out from under its brim while a mass of pink and blue clouds gathered behind him in the western sky. His gloomy, defiant expression showed the digital revolution in its Byronic mode.

In early winter he and Jane had begun a private e-mail correspondence, which quickly became torrid, and it bothered John Perry Barlow that these letters, which he prized, were probably written while Louis was sitting just a few feet away. They got themselves into what he described as a state, and the result was five nights in the tropics under a full moon.

"There is a lack of emotional inertia in cyberspace," Barlow said later, by way of an explanation. By the end, Jane was aware of what she risked losing, or had already lost.

They returned embarrassed, and Barlow wrote a long e-mail to Louis full of contrition and bombast. Its main purpose was to outline why Louis would do best to choke down his rage. Louis was a pilgrim in this part of the world, Barlow implied, and he could not afford to make enemies. "I suspect you would prefer I simply disappeared from this part of the galaxy and are desperately trying to imagine that I already have," Barlow wrote. "But unless you redefine Wired pretty fundamentally, you will encounter either me or my warm trail every time you go back out on your beat. It is a rare Digital Visionary who has no current truck with me. Can you imagine how rugged it's going to be if we have to go through the same anxious gavotte every time we encounter one another?"

Barlow acknowledged that in some communities he knew, violence would have been the only possible reply, but he urged Louis to keep his eye on his goals, and not falter out of anger or misery:

"Recent experiences aside, I will be a lot safer to you as your friend than as your adversary. A friend is what I would greatly prefer (and still consider myself) to be. Besides, a grudge always becomes, eventually, a self-inflicted wound."

This was the lowest they fell. Jane and Louis were together all the time. *Wired* was the only outlet for the intensity of their feelings, and a return to Holland was impossible. They had taken money from Eckart Wintzen to accomplish this task, and they had burned many bridges with *Electric Word*.

Fortunately, the city where they were trapped had a long history of transforming heartbreak into legendary success. "Gold rush" was a phrase still uttered by San Franciscans in tones of admiration and wonder, even if the fate of a typical forty-niner had been to arrive from his trip around Cape Horn sick from dysentery and near mad from narrow confinement; to march in his weakened state toward the mountains; to find no gold, and to die of starvation—if he was not murdered by one of his friends. A hundred and forty years later, dreams of a big strike still lingered, especially among the hundreds of technical entrepreneurs who shared offices near South Park and who would one day be known as *the new forty-niners*. All of them were better situated than their predecessors, for survival if not for success, and the risks Louis and Jane faced upon taking over their donated space in Randy's office were not of starvation and death—despite the bullets, which missed. What they risked was merely an undramatic dissolution into the modern San Francisco ambience of wasted potential, provincial gossip, and crackpot politics. People who knew Louis before his arrival expected him to fail in exactly this manner. In South Park, he blended in.

—

CHAPTER 4

FEEDBACK

On the night before Easter, Kevin Kelly fell asleep in front of the Church of the Holy Sepulchre in Jerusalem. He had returned to his youth hostel past curfew and the proprietors had locked him out. The night was cold and he was wearing thin clothes, so Kevin had wandered around the Old City until he could barely pick up his feet, then sat down at the entrance to the church. In the morning the sun and commotion woke him up and he joined a group of pilgrims walking toward the tombs where the body of Jesus was said to have been interred. Kevin followed the crowd without knowing why, except that as an aspiring photojournalist he was used to trailing along in the wake of things.

Kevin was a reflective and vaguely religious twenty-seven-year-old who had traveled the world on a shoestring and who, like Louis, could almost have been mistaken for a hippie except that his personal sloppiness lacked a floral motif and he did not use drugs. For the sake of his photos and his curiosity Kevin was willing to go along with just about anything that did not require aggression; he was very peaceable. But one thing Kevin never expected, when he sat down to listen to the Easter service, was to realize that the story of the Resurrection was true and that Jesus was available to him as a personal savior.

Resting under the warm sun and surrounded by strangers, Kevin wondered what he ought to do, given that he had just been converted. The answer came by means of a voice. The voice, which was not regularly audible but rather a direct communication into his understanding, told him that he should be *ready to die* in six months.

Kevin returned to New Jersey to see his parents. Without telling anybody what had happened, he quietly began ridding himself of his possessions. He sold his camera equipment and gave away his meager savings in anonymous gifts. After a few months he began a trip around the country and visited his brothers in Idaho and Arkansas for the last time. He rode his bicycle and slept in campgrounds or on lawns. Every day he wrote a haiku and made a sketch, pressing his hand, greasy from fixing his bike chain, onto the paper for a palm print, or drawing the individual bricks of a storefront bar in Alamosa, Colorado, over the natural haiku of its signs:

MEXICO CAFE

NO SHIRT   NO SHOES   NO SERVICE

ICE COLD BEER WELCOME

By the time Kevin got back to New Jersey it was Halloween night. His six months were over. All through the summer and fall he had warded off fantasies of getting married or learning a profession by reminding himself that he would soon be dead. With practice, he had severed himself from his future. This heightened his immediate pleasure but also made him sad. On his last night alive he went to bed early. He did not want to die. The next day, when he woke up, Kevin had a feeling of gratitude that would stay with him for decades. Not to be dead was part of it, of course, but there was another gift: he had his future back. He was free to plan meetings with his friends, to buy books in anticipation of later reading, to wonder what kind of job he would be good at. For years afterward, Kevin held on to the joy of a person who regains his life after thinking he lost it, and for whom the future has the special value of a gift from God.

Though a Christian, Kevin was no narrow fundamentalist, and he enriched his point of view through wide research. He worked as a producer of scientific films at the University of Georgia, and his presence on campus gave him access to an up-to-date computer network. He wrote travel articles for *New Age* magazine, and he started a journal devoted to recreational walking. Some of the poems he wrote during his cross-country bike pilgrimage were published in an eclectic journal called *CoEvolution Quarterly.* When the magazine's founder, Stewart Brand, decided to rename and relaunch it as the *Whole Earth Review,* he convinced Kevin to move to California and become the editor.

The brown-shingled office of the *Whole Earth Review* was hidden down a bayside street in Marin County called Gate Five Road.

Northern California in this era seemed to prefer its centers of influence to be invisible. The region's tallest buildings, the Bank of America tower and the Transamerica pyramid, represented the imperial hopes of an older generation. Though city officials still spoke about a *gateway to the Pacific Rim,* the real business of San Francisco was tourism. Slow-growth advocates had won a limit on new office construction during the last boom, but there was plenty of room under the cap because there was no profit in building. Meanwhile, famous technology companies performed their miracles out of sight. The bigger ones, such as Hewlett-Packard, in Palo Alto, and Apple, in Cupertino, had private campuses of their own. The smaller ones, the little investment firms and consultancies and research labs, could be found, if you had an address, directions, and a map, at the end of Santa Clara cul-de-sacs and alongside Marin County piers and behind the high, grassy banks of Peninsula throughways like Sand Hill and Page Mill Roads.

The navigational entanglements of a trip to someplace like the Foresight Institute, where Eric Drexler was envisioning transistors made of single molecules, or to Gate Five Road, where Kevin worked, invited obvious comparison to the origins of the enterprises themselves. In the two and a half decades since the invention of the microcomputer, local millionaires had formed nonprofits that had spun off businesses that had recruited engineers who had funded new companies; simultaneously, programmers and propagandists for the new technologies shuttled from big firms to small ones and back, establishing elaborate threaded mats of co-nutrition and support. Louis, with his Amsterdam-based magazine, was part of this network without knowing how to use it. There was no recognizable hierarchy of power such as Michael Wolff described to him in New York.

Louis first met Kevin Kelly on a research trip to the Bay Area during the last days of *Electric Word*. Kevin, sitting among crazy piles of books and papers that reached from the floor to nearly his shoulders, cheerfully told him that he ought to move to San Francisco if he wanted to succeed, but at the time this struck Louis as a little reckless. Move to San Francisco and do what?

A year later he and Jane made the leap, counting on Randy's angels to catch them, and down they fell, further and further, with Jane on the phone pitching the magazine two hundred times, and every time a failure. As seen by a man who was plummeting, Kevin's advice, which he had delivered from his comfortable seat in the *Whole Earth* warren, near the New Agers' houseboats and the retired surgeons' sailboats and the by-the-hour kayak-rental shop, seemed, if not smug, then somewhat discreditably risk-free.

But Kevin was right. The evolution of San Francisco's counterculture and its boom-and-bust history, plus the Santa Clara Valley's computer talent and its invisible supplies of capital, had created new cultural resources that had not yet been claimed. Louis, as the last of his money disappeared, was wracked by contradictory fears: that nobody would understand his idea, and that somebody else would beat him to it.

In fact, it was not that simple. Others had worked the same territory, to little effect. For instance, Kevin Kelly had already edited a visionary do-it-yourself catalog, called *Signal,* which had something to say about every facet of the nascent revolution. *Signal* reviewed hacker manuals and computer bulletin-board systems, word-processing software and robot supplies, copy machines and the cyberpunk novels of William Gibson. *Signal* had even noticed Louis's *Electric Word,* calling it "a thrilling journal."

Signal was published by the nonprofit Point Foundation, created by Stewart Brand with the profits from his 1968 best-seller, *The Whole Earth Catalog.* In the sixties Brand had been one of Ken Kesey's Merry Pranksters, traveling around the country on the Pranksters' famous psychedelic bus and throwing huge parties that helped introduce LSD to the masses. Along with starting the magazine Kevin now edited, Brand had helped build one of the first important general-interest online networks, known by what even its members acknowledged was a stunningly lame acronym, "the WELL," which stood for "Whole Earth 'Lectronic Link." But though they were successful on their own terms, many of Brand's projects were avant-garde, nonprofit efforts. *Signal* was threatening not because it duplicated Louis's idea but because it circulated so much raw material freely, putting it out for any observant entrepreneur to grab.

A different competitor was outwardly more dangerous. Up in an enormous, ramshackle mansion in the Berkeley Hills a constantly shifting set of editors, hackers, designers, and hangers-on were working together on a glossy magazine about technology and culture under the direction of an independent publisher named Queen Mu. In the fall of 1989 Queen Mu, whose given name was Alison Kennedy, had relaunched a magazine called *Reality Hackers* as *Mondo 2000.* Mu's magazine far outdid Louis's *Electric Word* in the range of its preoccupations and the extremity of its speculations. The very first issue featured interviews with Richard Stallman, a well-known hacker who had founded the Free Software Foundation; interviews with science fiction authors Bruce Sterling and Rudy Rucker; a review by Terrance McKenna of *The Letters of Marshall McLuhan;* and a charming rant by Lee Felsenstein, the inventor of one of the first microcomputers, who asked: "Why can't we have a few personal computer magazines with the feel of gun magazines?" These were the very people Louis intended to profile, and they were coming together under somebody else's banner. By the time Louis moved to San Francisco, even Kevin Kelly was contributing to *Mondo.* Randy Stickrod, Louis's fund-raiser, was *Mondo*'s chief advertising consultant and salesman.

And yet, despite its apparent success, *Mondo* was strangely out of touch. Or maybe it was too in touch, too exact a translation of the Bay Area's mix of technical genius and personal eccentricity. The guiding spirit at *Mondo* was Timothy Leary, the ex–Harvard psychology professor whose slogan "Tune In, Turn On, Drop Out" had been replaced, in a later work, by "S.M.I2.L.E.," an acronym for "Space Migration, Intelligence Increase, and Life Extension." Inside, a typical article proclaimed: "Good news! Researchers have found some more opiate receptors." In the days of the Merry Pranksters, drugs had nourished a nationwide movement, but this method no longer worked. *Mondo* did not resonate. Everybody who read it got a kick out of it, and there its effect seemed to stop.

Louis regarded *Mondo* warily, but its existence was also a good sign. New opportunities, still ill defined, were attracting local attention. Fred Davis, a well-known trade editor, had begun throwing regular parties where scores of writers, artists, designers, and programmers mingled. Later this mix would be common; at the time it was strange. One night, at Davis's house, Jane and Louis met a slim, leather-clad young man named Eugene Mosier who worked in the production department at *MacWEEK*. Eugene had a morose, outwardly unimpressible quality, but after listening to their ideas he asked how he could help. "We don't have a budget yet to pay you," Jane told him.

"That's not what I asked," said Eugene.

At first Jane didn't know what to do with his offer. Eugene obviously was not rich. Eventually Louis figured it out. Without money to take his magazine much further than a copy shop, Louis fell back upon the improvised methods pioneered by amateur publishers around the country who managed to get time on somebody's office equipment after the business day ended. At a trade show, Louis had seen a new type of copy machine from Canon that made high-quality color prints directly from digital files. Through a Canon representative, he learned that one of the machines had recently been purchased by a copy shop in Berkeley. They had not yet figured out how to get it running. Louis called Eugene, who was an expert in digital production, and in exchange for free technical assistance plus five dollars per page the owners gave them access at night. In October and November 1991, Louis finally made his first issue of *Wired*.

He called it the "zero" issue. Printed on pages that appeared to come from an expensive, multicolor press—but that were really just output from the remarkable Canon—the issue opened with three double spreads, from Apple, Sony, and Infiniti. Then there were eight uninterrupted pages of digital collage, including images of a young man and his father in front of a wall-sized television screen; a robot family, and a computer model of the earth. Next came a series of well-written stories that showed the proposed magazine's range, including a profile of the chairman of the Federal Communications Commission, a report from one of Silicon Valley's most famous research laboratories, and a call by former attorney general Eliot Richardson for an investigation of the suspicious death of an American computer journalist. Shorter articles mixed technology previews with travel tips and book reviews. The cover was a black-and-white collage of a man plummeting from an immense height, the city streets beneath him surreal in their networked clarity. At the top, in red capitals, it said WIRED.

None of the articles or photographs were original, and none of the advertisements were real. They were cribbed from every type of publication that touched on parts of the story Louis and Jane were trying to tell: *The Wall Street Journal, SF Weekly, Scientific American, Outside, MacWEEK, Microtimes, Bay Area Computer Currents, The New York Times, Sports Illustrated, Nature, Business Week, Details.* But the borrowed stories seemed bolder here than they had in their original publications. Bound together, they radiated a sense of fanatical self-assurance, as if united in expectation of technological wonders and tremendous social changes. The fact that the stories were taken from mainstream sources strengthened rather than softened the effect, for the credits page offered evidence that the revolution Louis believed he was chronicling had already been widely noted; only the context was new.

Jane obtained the other tools they needed using every persuasive method she could think of; mostly, she stayed on the phone and begged. With a donated monitor, donated scanner, and donated hard drive, they made something that, while very much a computer magazine, was exactly what Lee Felsenstein had called for in *Mondo 2000:* a computer magazine with the feel of a gun magazine. They spent the last of their cash on tickets to Amsterdam so they could show it to Eckart Wintzen.

"We do not have two thousand copies," Louis told Wintzen. In fact, they had only one. But they promised to fulfill the agreement if Eckart would advance them more money. The businessman turned the pages one by one, peering at them through his tinted glasses, and at the end he granted their reprieve, in the form of forty-five thousand guilders, enough for six more months of survival.

That winter Louis and Jane kept their poverty well hidden. They were living in a big house, and the origin of their support was a topic of speculative gossip. At the hillside redoubt of *Mondo 2000,* Alison Kennedy presided over strategy meetings from the gigantic bed in front of the mansion's main fireplace, and she informed her staff that Jane and Louis were bankrolled by CIA-connected drug dealers, as a counterforce against her outlaw publication. Her theory, while entertaining, failed to take hold. Most people thought that Jane's family was paying the bills.

Mu had a real magazine; Louis did not. Nonetheless, in the competition for local strength, for immediate resources and support, for what Louis, who enjoyed mixing revolutionary and business jargon, called *cadre* and *mind-share, Wired* slowly gained ground. They contacted Mitch Kapor of the Electronic Frontier Foundation; Paul Saffo, a futurist at the Stanford Research Institute; Jaron Lanier, the virtual-reality pioneer. They were looping around these interconnected circles again and again, spending Eckart's money and trying to find the right formula, the right contact or catalyst.

So far, only one person had ever turned what was more and

more indisputably a *scene* into a successful business. His name was Richard Saul Wurman, and his approach was exactly the opposite of Louis and Jane's.

Wurman was a designer who had trained as architect. He was the founder of a conference in Monterey, California, called TED, which stood for "Technology, Entertainment, and Design." While Louis and Jane's goal was to broaden the definition of the digital vanguard to include hundreds of thousands of readers, Wurman, for the purposes of TED, had compressed it to a narrow circle, and he charged high admission. He admitted about seven hundred people, and the price per ticket was a thousand dollars. The third TED conference was scheduled for February 1992.

Jane and Louis paid up. They could not afford anything like this amount, but Jane knew better than to beg for a discount. Wurman was a gregarious, imposing man, with a nearly round silhouette and an engaging, almost comical aggressiveness that made argument seem futile. "You don't know me, but you owe me," was one of the ways he asked for a favor. John Plunkett and Barbara Kuhr had been turned away from the last TED because they tried to get tickets too late. This time they had registered a full year in advance. In the opening moment of one of the sessions, sitting in the darkened auditorium, John got a glimpse of Jane and Louis coming in through a side door.

"Oh, fuck," Plunkett said, "they're here."

After their weekend together in New York, John and Barbara were extremely wary of Louis and Jane. For the rest of the day John strained to avoid them, moving to the other side of the room whenever either one appeared. At last, tired of feeling childish, he put aside his bad feelings and said hello. Louis showed him the prototype and gave him some interesting but perhaps not entirely believable news: Nicholas Negroponte was on tap as a big supporter.

There was not a man in the world more expert at unearthing money for academic research into media and technology than Negroponte, the founder of the MIT Media Lab. Back in 1968 Negroponte had written a book called *The Architecture Machine* that sketched a future in which computers and people intimately cooperated. Back then, only scientists and technicians had computer terminals on their desks. Now the situation had changed, and Louis was proposing to offer a general audience monthly updates on what had once been Negroponte's wildest speculations. During one of the breaks Negroponte allowed Louis and Jane to sit next to him in the auditorium and show him what they had been working on. He paged carefully through the prototype and when he got to the end he surprised them by asking frankly how much money they needed and how much he could invest.

Negroponte only had seventy-five thousand dollars; in return he wanted 10 percent of *Wired*. This was a big chunk of their business in exchange for not very much money, but they asked him to commit himself to writing a column for a year and took the deal. They believed his approval would have a contagious effect.

They were right, and the first to feel it was Plunkett. For John, Louis's sense of conviction was powerful even when he was speaking from a position of weakness—when he was broke and new in the country and in need of help. Once he had allies, he was even harder to resist. John found himself daydreaming about how *Wired* might look. He had been a student in Los Angeles back in the seventies when the impact of psychedelic art was at its height.

Jamie Odgers, one of his charismatic instructors, had shown what could be done with collages of popular images. Now the mixture of real and artificial, of photos and illustrations, no longer required painstaking work with scissors, pens, and paints. It could be done on-screen. With the right approach, *Wired* could refer back to that exciting time while also making a grand claim about the future of design.

While John was thinking things over, Negroponte's support helped seal an agreement with a software entrepreneur named Charlie Jackson, who agreed to become *Wired*'s second angel. Jackson paid $150,000 for his 10 percent. Louis and Jane now had nearly a quarter of a million dollars in the bank. They hired their first employee, Will Kreth, who had been working for the Apple Multimedia Lab. Will started in April and worked for free until June, after which he began receiving a hundred dollars per week. His friend Kristen Spence, a former receptionist for Apple, joined him soon afterward. Spence was interested in feminism and magic, and she told Louis she wanted to help wrestle technology away from the powers of darkness. She bargained with Jane and got two hundred dollars a week, but she supplied her own computer. The four of them moved from the tiny corner of Randy Stickrod's office up to the top floor of a building on Second Street, clearing out piles of junk left by the last business to expire there.

Louis was a compelling leader and took steps to bind the founding team to him tightly. He tried to make them understand *Wired*'s larger significance. He said the curve of history was at an inflection point, which meant that their actions today could affect human destiny far into the future. It was impossible to overestimate the importance of such moments. He told Will and Kristen about the eight-hour-day agitation of 1886, which ended when a bomb went off in Chicago's Haymarket Square. The mystery of who planted the bomb was never solved, but the eight-hour movement was crushed and several anarchist leaders were hanged. The outcome of history is not preordained, Louis said. If the anarchists had won and their success had inspired similar triumphs in Europe, communism might never have arisen; without communism, there might never have been Nazism. These were the stakes they were playing for at the dawn of a new century.

Louis had been a libertarian since his first years of adulthood, but even libertarianism—which was still, after all, a political doctrine—seemed too confining for him now. The answer could not be another political revolution that would simply repeat the mistakes of the past. Instead, *Wired* would advocate what Louis called *spontaneous order*. Spontaneous order was a more benign mode of human civilization that was inherent in digital technology. State authorities always depended upon media to manipulate the population; but when computers democratized media, governments would lose their control.

"I could totally see the flame within him," remembered Kristen later. One night, when he and Kristen were at the office late talking, Louis offered her a small stake in *Wired*. He repeated this offer to all the employees who joined him before the magazine's launch. As coinventors of what Louis liked to call *the mouthpiece of the digital revolution,* they would also be part owners.

In midsummer Kevin Kelly dropped by the new office. He shared Louis's interest in making a better future, but his temperament was entirely different. Where Louis was choleric, Kevin was sanguine. He had an innate optimism that he tried to extend into a rigorous philosophy, and he was interested in exposing the hidden processes that were likely to make the world better. He had recently taken a leave of absence from *Whole Earth Review* while finishing a large, ruminative book about the implications of cybernetics, called *Out of Control: The Rise of NeoBiological Civilization.*

Kevin's topic had been out of fashion for a long time. Originally, cybernetics was an attempt to understand complex phenomena using mathematical tools invented by Norbert Wiener. The most important concept Wiener worked with was *feedback:* the output of one iteration of a cybernetic operation was fed back into the system as part of the input controlling the next iteration. Cybernetic analysis quickly proved useful. For instance, a colleague of Wiener's at MIT, Jay Forrester, successfully applied it to problems in industrial production.

In 1970 Forrester was invited to a conference in Europe on "the predicament of mankind." The theme of the conference reflected the anxieties of the era, and Forrester was inspired to construct a computer simulation of the world using cybernetic techniques. He plugged in data for food production, natural resources, industrial growth, population, and other key indicators of progress. His conclusion was that the earth would reach the utmost limit of its capacity within a hundred years. *The Limits to Growth,* a popular description of the model by Forrester's colleagues Dennis and Donella Meadows, was a best-seller in 1972, and its baleful news expressed a growing sense that contemporary civilization was self-defeating.

When Steward Brand had begun publishing the *CoEvolution Quarterly,* he had been in full save-the-world mode, influenced greatly by Forrester and the social dimensions of cybernetics. But when Kevin joined the *Whole Earth Review,* a subtle change was already under way. The end of civilization was not progressing as quickly as anticipated. Apocalypse remained stuck in that psychologically frustrating category of always-just-about-to-happen, and *Whole Earth* helped to lead its small segment of the movement into the more immediately fruitful areas of alternative health, private entrepreneurship, and do-it-yourself media.

By the time Kevin stopped by to visit Louis at *Wired,* he was already convinced that *The Limits to Growth* had failed to predict the future; all its estimates were too pessimistic. Kevin believed humankind was likely to survive and even thrive. But in sharing his optimism, he had become sensitive to cultural resistance. Among the well-read, critically minded people he considered his peers, bad news was more intellectually comfortable than good news. The twentieth century, with its genocides and global wars, its thalidomide babies and poisoned lakes, and above all with its fifty-year threat of nuclear annihilation, had trained the educated public to regard optimism as infantile.

Kevin did not doubt the strict conclusions of the various studies inspired by *The Limits to Growth.* He accepted that continuous progress along known lines was ruinous. But continuous progress along known lines was exactly what did not happen in life. Instead, there were unexpected innovations that shocked all observers. What happened when a hitherto unnoticed phenomenon expanded and doubled back into a feedback loop that changed everything? When increased literacy among girls and women led to declining birthrates and made a mess of population models? When innovations in logistics made shipping costs plummet?

When instant communication via electronic networks routed uncensored news across national borders?

Kevin's faith was in the dynamics of complexity, in the unexpected and the impossible-to-predict. Once, at a large academic meeting on religion and science, Kevin asked the audience if they could imagine an event that would disrupt their religious faith as much as Darwin had disturbed their predecessors'. A non-Christian in the audience, in an attempt at humor, called out, "Aliens landing!" Kevin was not rattled. He punched up his next slide: it was E.T., the extraterrestrial. "Exactly!" he exclaimed.

In the summer of 1992 his big book on cybernetics was nearly completed, and at first Kevin thought he had only a passing interest in Louis's activities. He was very busy, and besides, he had grown tired of tiny magazines. But when Kevin got to the *Wired* office and looked at the prototype, he changed his mind. Louis, he could see, was not making a tiny magazine. *Wired* was treating the digital revolution as if it were the main event for everybody. One of the best examples of feedback is when an amplifier recycles small sounds—little ambient rustlings—until they become a roar. *Wired* might be an amplifier.

Louis offered him a job as executive editor. When Kevin accepted, *Wired* ceased to be a vanguard computer magazine and became something even stranger: a radical attempt to reacquaint its audience with the prospect of a happy future. His arrival also changed the atmosphere. When the two men cooperated, Kevin's metaphysical confidence worked upon Louis's pugnacity like oxygen on a fire.

CHAPTER 5

FASCINATED, REVOLTED, MESMERIZED

Andrew Anker was the son of a successful Philadelphia physician, one of four affectionate siblings who grew up cheating each other at cards. After graduating from Columbia in 1987 with a business degree Andrew joined First Boston Bank, one of the most innovative companies in the junk-bond field. Andrew was confident, good-natured, and generous with his friends; at work he was humorous and guileful. With his broad face, tall but unmuscular build, and deceptively easygoing air, Andrew could seem easy to fool, and he was perfectly willing to be underestimated.

When Andrew signed on, First Boston Bank was earning huge investment-banking fees, including hundreds of millions of dollars from just one of its many clients, the Campeau Corporation, but soon after he arrived the music stopped. Engorged by acquisitions, Campeau faced bankruptcy. Meanwhile, many of First Boston's best junk-bond salesmen were hired away by a competing firm,

Drexel Burnham Lambert, which was busy arranging the deals that would result in its own bankruptcy, criminal indictments, and a national banking crisis.

"Capitalism is messy," John M. Hennessy, the First Boston CEO, told *The Wall Street Journal* that year, in reference to the company's losses.

"We're all consenting adults in this market," explained another top executive.

Andrew enjoyed shouldering the responsibilities of his profession. "Banking," he once explained, "is about people who are way too young and way too inexperienced exercising way too much power—and that's the fun of it." But he was interested in hands-on management. After leaving First Boston and spending a short time at an unsuccessful media start-up, Andrew joined a boutique banking firm in San Francisco called Sterling Payot. Bob Smelick, his boss, encouraged him to use Sterling Payot as a launching pad. He could survey the new businesses coming to the firm and perhaps join one as a top executive. Like John Plunkett, who had missed the extremes of the sixties and was sometimes wistful, Andrew had come along too late to enjoy the excesses of the American financial system during the junk-bond, mergers-and-acquisitions, savings-and-loan debacle. But when he met Louis and Jane he was just twenty-seven years old and undiscouraged.

In the summer of 1992 Louis and Jane had been utterly humiliated by their encounters with bankers. The climax of their search for support in the sophisticated financial community came in July, when Negroponte met Louis and Jane in New York to pitch the magazine to Veronis, Suhler & Associates, one of the most powerful New York banking firms specializing in media. John Suhler met with them in a conference room whose walls were decorated with Lucite trophies, known as tombstones, that commemorated huge deals. Suhler could see from the spreadsheets forecasting *Wired*'s circulation growth that Louis had absolutely no idea how the magazine business worked, and he picked the plan apart in detail. He asked Louis archly about various circulation ratios that ought to have been familiar to anybody who fancied himself a media entrepreneur, and he elicited expressions of ignorance in response. Truthfully, Louis did not know what Suhler was talking about. It was a terrible hour.

Louis had been prepared to discuss the fundamental concept of *Wired*. He wanted to talk about a magazine that would exemplify a new global culture. But the meeting never budged from the topic of these arcane circulation formulas, which Louis could not discuss. Louis was reduced to silence, and by the end he was shaking with rage.

"I wanted to kill him," Louis said afterward. "I wanted to disappear."

A few minutes later all three of them were out on the New York street, where the trucks and taxis blew dirt onto Louis's only suit. "Do you want your money back?" Jane asked Negroponte.

To their relief, he said no. Louis may not have been an expert in the technical details of circulation that John Suhler quizzed him about, but Negroponte could see that he possessed something substantially more valuable. He knew his audience intimately. If the world he described was not yet generally visible, well, this was an additional strength, for *Wired* would serve as a beacon, and the border territory it illuminated would be all their own. Negroponte phoned a New York friend. They borrowed his office and began calling other people he knew. "Dialing for dollars," he called it. Unfortunately, his efforts were fruitless.

Soon it was August. Jane and Louis had begun the summer with $225,000. This was a vast sum of money compared with their previous balance but a minuscule one in relation to their task. Established media corporations regularly blew tens of millions of dollars starting new magazines. Louis and Jane were working in a different style, but even they had to write checks now and then. Just getting a commitment from distributors to put the magazine on newsstands looked like it was going to require money up front. One major distributor asked for seventy-five thousand dollars in advance, to cover expenses in case the magazines did not sell. This was an impossibility.

Even if the magazine won distribution, the return on investment was terrible. Successful magazine companies often sold less than half of the magazines they shipped to retailers; the rest were chopped into pulp. Each copy brought in about a dollar after all the middlemen took their cut. Printing costs were high, and publishers lost money on every newsstand sale. It took millions of dollars to build circulation through direct mail, advertising payments were minimal until the readership increased, and in the meantime sickening amounts of cash disappeared. The experts whom bankers like John Suhler felt comfortable with often made enormous errors; a few years later Tina Brown, the famed editor of *Vanity Fair* and *The New Yorker,* and Harvey Weinstein, founder of Miramax, would blow more than fifty million dollars launching *Talk*.

Louis did not think highly of traditional magazine economics. Not only did it take forever to build an audience, but the industry was structured in such a way that editors were encouraged to be conservative and servile. His proposed remedy was to charge an unusually high price for *Wired*. Single issues would be five dollars, and subscriptions would be forty dollars per year, which was two to three times the normal price. He wanted *Wired* to make money, not lose it, when readers bought a copy.

Wired had some advantages in going directly to its readers for support. In the spring of 1981, writing in *CoEvolution Quarterly,* a countercultural businessman named Paul Hawken had taken a dry bit of economics jargon—*disintermediation*—and made it the touchstone of an argument about the power of nonhierarchical and informal networks to challenge mainstream business. This became one of *Wired*'s core ideas. By disintermediation, Hawken originally meant the reduction of the economic role of middlemen. The *Whole Earth Catalog* had been a harbinger of this trend, as it was filled with the addresses of businesses that would sell their products directly.*

Technical people already used and maintained well-established informal networks of communication. There were, for instance, tens of thousands of local electronic bulletin-board services serving uncounted numbers of members. Among the most influential of these was the WELL, where journalists and software program-

---

* Hawken had cofounded an important mail order company: the Sausalito-based garden-supply catalog Smith & Hawken. Curiously, Smith & Hawken functioned not as a direct producer but as a middleman. It turned out that opening new channels between producers and consumers encouraged the formation of new layers of marketing and sales. Disintermediation pointed to a genuine phenomenon, but contradicting its name, the result was not the removal of middlemen but rather the creation of more middlemen.

mers mixed with punks and old hippies. One of Will Kreth's first contributions was to create a conference on the WELL through which this motley group of experts could contribute their thoughts to *Wired*. Many of the WELL's most respected participants had already encountered Louis and Jane during their relentless fundraising efforts; therefore the magazine, before printing any issues, began to develop a reputation.

The WELL was not typical. Most computer bulletin boards consisted only of a personal computer attached to a single phone line that often greeted callers with a busy signal. However, in 1984 Tom Jennings had created a program called Fido that allowed these services to share a single e-mail addressing system, so that a subscriber to one bulletin board could get a message to a subscriber at others. Using the WELL, FidoNet, and the networks running at universities and government-research sites, Louis could advertise *Wired*'s existence.

By the end of August, *Wired,* which until recently had been a crusade and a charity case, was beginning to look a little more like a legitimate business, but the quarter million was diminishing steadily, and Louis and Jane had to admit that their original plan was obsolete. Soon their angel money would be gone and their fragile infrastructure would vanish. Instead of slowing down, they chose to accelerate. They would operate as if publication were assured. They planned to spend everything in their bank accounts by the end of the year. If, at the end, they were broke, they would at least have a better prototype, and they could return to the floor of Macworld in January and begin trying to raise money again.

Louis called Park City. He offered John Plunkett and Barbara Kuhr four thousand dollars a month, plus airfare to and from

Utah, in exchange for spending three full days in the office each week. He also presented them with an ownership share of 3 percent.

Three percent! This was disgusting! He had originally been a full partner. So many times, expressing himself angrily to Barbara, he had vowed never to be taken advantage of by Louis again. But Barbara calmed him down. She had heard John talk about Macworld, and *Wired,* and the potential to make something new in the world of design. She knew he wanted to do it. "Why don't we assume we're going to get fucked over," she said. "Take that for granted. Aren't there still reasons to do it?"

In early September John arrived at the new office. "What are we going to do with all this space?" he said, when he first saw the empty loft, with a few lingering piles of junk in the corners. It was nearly ten thousand square feet and seemed impossible to fill.

John took the main burden of the graphical work for *Wired,* while Barbara kept the rest of their small design business going. The real state of *Wired*'s finances became apparent to them quickly, and the idea of producing a magazine in three months before the cash ran out served as a good litmus test for other potential hires. "No you're not," laughed one otherwise qualified candidate for managing editor, when informed of the plan to publish by the new year. "You simply cannot do it; it's impossible." He may have felt that he was already assisting the inexperienced staff with his professional advice, but they quickly cut him from the list.

Kevin did not understand the concern. "What's impossible about it?" he asked. Kevin liked flying by the seat of his pants, and he had never worked for any mainstream publisher.

On Labor Day they interviewed a long-shot candidate for man-

aging editor named John Battelle. To Kristen Spence, who described herself sometimes as a techno-pagan and sometimes simply
as a witch, and who liked to think of *Wired*'s employees as a team
of mutually supportive freaks and nonconformists, Battelle did
not seem to fit in. He was a twenty-six-year-old graduate of the
school of journalism at the University of California, Berkeley, and
he had worked at *MacWEEK,* one of the computer industry's
most respected trade journals. He reminded Kristen of a grown-up
Jimmy Olsen, the eager copy boy in the Superman comics. After
their first meeting with him Louis and Kevin looked at each other
happily. They could tell he would work like a maniac.

For the first time, Louis and Jane had a staff. Louis was editor
in chief and publisher. Jane was the president and, for now, advertising director. John and Barbara were listed together as the creative directors. Kevin was the executive editor, John Battelle was
managing editor, Eugene Mosier would handle production, and
Will and Kristen would run errands, write some of the smaller stories, manage the databases, open mail, buy furniture, and handle
hundreds of other major and minor tasks involved in publishing a
magazine, albeit a magazine that might only exist in the form of a
single copy.

In October Louis was introduced by a friend of Stewart Brand's
to the bankers of Sterling Payot. Compared with other Bay Area
banks, Sterling Payot was an utterly unimportant firm, but it had
one virtue: it was at least aware of and loosely linked into the West
Coast network. Jane and Louis went in on a Friday and sat across
from Andrew Anker and Bill Jesse, one of the lead partners, in the
firm's office on Sutter Street. The custom-made conference table
was huge, and Louis noted curiously that they were sitting at a ter-

rific distance from one another. Jesse had another engagement and had to excuse himself two thirds of the way through their first meeting, but Andrew Anker politely stayed on and listened closely.

Jane's first impression of Andrew was that he was startlingly young; her second was that he ought to come work for *Wired*. Unlike so many others who had heard their pitch, he understood what they were trying to do. He had even done some amateur computer programming himself. Andrew talked up the project at Sterling Payot. Bill Jesse agreed *Wired* was interesting, but the deal was small. "You only need a million dollars?" Jesse said to Jane during one of their follow-up conversations. He believed he could get this amount from his personal acquaintants, and Sterling Payot proposed raising what Jesse called the *friends and neighbors* round by the end of the year. A million dollars would not be enough to see the magazine through to profitability—this could take four or five years. But it would support them for a year, and when the concept was proven, they could raise a second round. Bill Jesse was upbeat. It seemed that they had finally found a banker with faith.

The contrast between the thrill of the work and the marginal nature of their enterprise peaked that winter. An intentional leak to the *San Jose Mercury News* about a new technology monthly brewing in a South Park loft had resulted in a burst of press coverage. CNN sent a camera crew, and their story was picked up and replayed on the canned-news programs shown to captive audiences on transcontinental flights. The footage showed a ragged group in a bizarre setting. John Battelle appeared in a white bandana with Japanese characters on it. Louis had bought one for each staff member, to give them a feeling of unity. John Plunkett had taken to sleeping on a mattress on the floor of the office. Despite his vow to handle things with detachment, he was already feeling bitter. He felt that he and Barbara were the only real professionals in the office, which gave them enormous responsibility, while Louis and Jane retained all the control. "My worst nightmares had come true," he later said. "I was their slave."

Abnormal currents in the Pacific Ocean created weeks of bad weather. Constant wind rattled the dirty windows of *Wired*'s raw Second Street office, while buckets of rain flooded the streets. John Plunkett noticed that Jane and Louis had nice little personal heaters running next to their desks. He looked at them with envy. The creative director had no heater by *his* desk.

Editorially, the main recipe for *Wired* was worked out between Louis and Kevin. Kevin had a shoe box full of ideas from his days at *Whole Earth Review,* but Louis rejected most of them. They were too old. "This feels like months ago!" he said.

"So what?" Kevin replied. Kevin always liked to pile up his newspapers and read them weeks later, which sort of automatically filtered out the trivial stories that bubbled up and disappeared without effect. The hardcover anthology of articles from *CoEvolution Quarterly* had been subtitled *News That Stayed News.*

Louis rejected more story ideas. He said he wanted *Wired* to feel just minutes old.

They talked it over. "If something was interesting a few months ago, it's probably still interesting," Kevin argued. Kevin liked stories that the mainstream media missed, and he pointed out that there was no chance people would be tired of them because they would never have heard of them. What was the use of things that were only a few minutes old if, as in the case of most media trendlets, these few minutes comprised their entire lifetime of relevance?

In the end the idea of a magazine that felt just minutes old was replaced by a clearer and more original concept. One day, still struggling to explain what he envisioned for the magazine, Louis mentioned that *Wired* should be a message mailed back to the present from the future. Suddenly, Kevin understood. "*Wired* would be like a reverse time capsule," he later said. "It would sail back through time and land at people's feet, and they would stare and wonder and not be able to stop themselves from picking it up. They would be perplexed, fascinated, revolted, mesmerized."

Kevin had once heard the cyberpunk writer William Gibson say, "The future is already here—it's just unevenly distributed." This became his motto for *Wired*. He figured he knew something about where to look for the erupting future, as they came to call it, and soon *Wired* would be sending reporters to India to see how independent rural engineers set up pirated satellite television networks, and to Singapore to analyze high-tech authoritarianism, and to Redmond, Washington, to live for weeks among the Microsoft millionaires who slept on mattresses on the floor of their communal houses.

But at the beginning these far-flung assignments were outside their capacities. The feature stories they worked on that fall were modest. They included a profile of a digital special-effects studio in Hollywood; a book excerpt about Japanese fans of violent computer games; an account of the army's use of high-tech simulations; a survey of advanced projects for electronic libraries; an entertaining exposé about cell-phone hacking; a low-quality rant about abolishing all public schools and replacing them with computer-oriented education companies; and an interview by Stewart Brand with the already overexposed academic provocateur Camille Paglia. This list completely fails to capture the excitement that grew as the first issue came together, an excitement that owed almost nothing to journalistic quality, narrowly conceived, and yet was evident to anybody who glimpsed the pages or fragments of pages appearing on John Plunkett's screen.

Plunkett's design told *Wired*'s story more explicitly than any list of features. He made almost every page from scratch. Even the look of the letters altered as you went; one piece was typeset in sober, well-spaced lines in a classic font, the next had thin, sans-serif characters, the next had copy running sideways, so that you had to flip the magazine ninety degrees to read it. The magazine was wider than the standard; it was almost square. But most important, Plunkett had an idea about where to find unusual colors.

During his time as a corporate designer Plunkett had watched color production change. Traditional methods for matching the printer's work to the designer's wishes were just beginning to give way to digital prepress systems. Output was difficult to control, for the actual look of a printed page depends on dozens of variables, from the thickness, absorbency, and whiteness of the paper to the consistency and opacity of the inks. Most magazines were printed on a four-color press, and most magazine production departments had limited time and money to check the output and make changes.

John had limited time and money too. The total design budget for the first issue was ten thousand dollars. He was used to spending as much as that on a single photograph. How could he apply his experience with high-end production to the primitive world of magazines?

John turned to an old friend in the printing business, Bill Sherman, who worked for Danbury Printing and Litho, in Connecticut. Danbury was a commercial printer, and the company had just acquired a six-color Heidelberg press from Germany. This was the last thing you would imagine printing a magazine on—too expensive. But business was slow, and John got Bill Sherman to price the job at about what conventional printers would charge. *Wired* would be the first project off their new press, just as Louis's prototype had been the first pages off the new Canon on Shattuck Avenue.

The Heidelberg press gave *Wired* access to brilliant fluorescent and metallic inks. The Day-Glo hues were both a self-conscious reference to the optimism of an earlier era and a futuristic celebration of the capacities of print, capacities that John would push to their farthest limit. With its extreme colors, large size, and unrelenting, page-after-page design, *Wired* transformed expectations of what a mass-market magazine could do. For the first cover, John created a logo in glowing orange and green, with alternating serif and sans-serif type representing the binary foundation of the digital revolution. The magazine was perfect-bound, which meant it had a flat spine. Along the spine John put vivid squares of alternating color that looked like an LED display running down the edge; *Wired* would be instantly recognizable even when only the thinnest strip could be seen.

In November their money was nearly gone. Though John extracted the best price possible from Danbury Printing, a press run of 125,000 copies would still cost about $130,000. Bill Jesse said the money was coming, but it did not come.

It was time for their bankers to share in the risk. Jesse had arranged for his firm and its investors to receive 15 percent of *Wired* in exchange for raising one million dollars. At the time of this promise, *Wired* barely existed; it was little more than a proto-type and a small cash balance supplied by Charlie Jackson and Nicholas Negroponte. But by Thanksgiving, *Wired* was close to publication. They had even sold some ads; Jane had recruited a vet-eran Ziff Davis sales director named Kathleen Lyman, who took 2 percent ownership of the company, flew in from Australia, and in a few weeks sold about ten full-page and double-page spreads. *Wired* had begun to look like it might succeed, and it would cost less than $150,000—the printing bill plus a few sundries—to find out. Bill Jesse offered a personal guarantee to Danbury. He would pay for printing himself if the first investment round failed.

Louis and Jane spent the last of the angel funds on a small mar-keting campaign consisting of wall posters and billboards on buses in a few cities, including Manhattan. The buses drove up and down Madison Avenue. They said GET WIRED, in bright colors. Mi-chael Wolff saw them and was amazed.

In December issue number one went to the printer. *Wired*'s first pages were advertisements: double spreads from Origin (Eckart Wintzen's company), Seagate, and Apple. Next came a visual mani-festo that John and Louis hoped would brand the idea of *Wired* in-delibly into the minds of its readers. The manifesto went on for six pages. It was designed by Erik Adigard of the San Francisco studio M.A.D., and it introduced the motifs that would soon become unavoidable icons in technology advertising: the upraised hand, the schematic brain, the fluorescent overlays of text against bright circles. Over Adigard's images were the magazine's first words. They were taken from Marshall McLuhan's 1967 book *The Medium Is the Massage,* and they stretched across four pages:

The medium, or process, of our time—electric technology— is reshaping and restructuring patterns of social interdependence and every aspect of our personal life. It is forcing us to reconsider and re-evaluate practically every thought, every action, and every institution formerly taken for granted. Everything is changing: your education, your family, your neighborhood, your job, your relation to "the others." And they're changing dramatically.

On the fifth page, Louis explained his mission. "Why *Wired?*" he wrote.

Because the Digital Revolution is whipping through our lives like a Bengali typhoon—while the mainstream media is still groping for the snooze button. And because the computer "press" is too busy churning out the latest PCInfoComputing-CorporateWorld iteration of its ad sales formula cum parts catalog to discuss the meaning or context of social changes so profound their only parallel is probably the discovery of fire.

Louis had finally created the platform from which he could make his Promethean claim, and on January 2, 1993, his message found a small circle of technologically oriented readers who were eager for it. At a time when the country was just emerging from recession, when the Communist collapse had ended the cold war and raised the possibility of a different kind of future, *Wired* announced that a salutary global transformation was already under way.

Louis and Jane had decided that the magazine would appear at Macworld, and that they would have a party to celebrate it. They asked Bill Jesse for three hundred dollars to pay the band. Boxes and boxes of magazines arrived on the day of the show. When Will and Kristen brought copies into the lobby they were snatched from their hands. Everybody wanted one.

Perhaps the best acknowledgment of their success came from the protests of their critics, who complained grievously that *Wired* was hard to read. Louis liked to torment John a little bit by forwarding him e-mail from readers who disliked the design, but on the whole he respected his partner and understood his audience very well. They were autodidacts and know-it-alls. If something was a little beyond them, they were all the more eager to catch up. John hated to hear that his design was unreadable, but he knew the reaction was evidence that their provocations hit their target.

Looking back at the first issue with all the complaints in mind, it is strange to notice how many of the words were printed in black characters on white paper. The extreme colors were used mainly in headlines and illustrations. True, John allowed himself room to experiment, running a few stories on top of vivid backgrounds and layering smaller pieces on top of multihued illustrations. But the first issue of *Wired* was hard to read not only because some of the pages had clashing colors or unusual fonts. Louis insisted on treating the technical people profiled in his magazine as celebrities, enforcing a casual and allusive style that assumed vast knowledge. This flattered readers, but it also frustrated and challenged them.

"Everyone even peripherally involved with computers agrees that object-oriented programming (OOP) is the wave of the future," wrote Steve Steinberg, in what would become a regular feature called Hype List. This was not true. Many people peripherally involved with computers had never heard of object-oriented programming, which was a passion mainly for engineers. And while engineers might find OOP old hat, they still had to cope with the narrow band of type running across many pages that contained chummy but insular accounts of social news and gossip written in the collective voice of the editors. In and around this message to readers, called Flux, were insider references to new fiber-optic systems; news of lawsuits by *Playboy* magazine against pirate porno bulletin boards; kudos to John Gilmore, "our favorite anarcho-hacker," for badgering the U.S. government to release old cryptography texts; an analysis of the implications for copyright law of a legal battle between two competing taco stands in El Paso, Texas.

Nathan Myhrvold, the chief technology officer at Microsoft, considered himself well informed, and yet the magazine managed to make even him feel left out. "I've been asleep at the switch!" he thought when he saw *Wired* for the first time. This was exactly the reaction the editors hoped for.

Louis included his e-mail address at the bottom of his manifesto, and he was soon drowning in responses, which came in batches of hundreds. On the WELL, long threads of conversation about *Wired* scrolled down the screen. Richard Saul Wurman sent a copy of the magazine to every attendee at TED, with a note that compared the first issue to the premiere of *Life*.

On the other hand, all this was praise from the choir, and it failed to prove that Louis had been right, and the publishing establishment wrong. *Folio,* the leading trade journal of the magazine industry, interviewed some well-informed analysts after *Wired*'s launch. The fact that Louis and Jane had managed to take their publication from concept to copy shop to printing plant to Macworld might have earned them an A for effort, but it meant nothing, businesswise.

"The definition of a good magazine is a magazine that makes money," said Peter Craig, president of the Los Angeles–based Magazine Consulting Group. "My impression is that people want service and information—they are not interested in the lifestyles of computer nerds."

Dan Orlow, president of Periodical Studies Service in New York, was equally honest. "I don't see it as the wave of the future," he said. "It's more of a trial balloon. Frankly, I don't think they have a prayer."

CHAPTER 6

VICTORIES

The walk to South Park from the large and newly remodeled Rincon Hill branch of the United States Post Office took fifteen minutes, but Jane could not do the trip on foot due to the sacks of mail that came in daily. There were two of them, regular as sunrise, each barely liftable, so she ferried them in her car, which she had to move every two hours anyway to avoid overstaying her parking space.

Ed Anuff, who had an office nearby, watched her come and go out his window. Ed was a pale, thin-limbed, twenty-five-year-old computer programmer with a bleakly cynical laugh he had been perfecting ever since he sold his small company for shares in a larger firm whose stock was traded in Canada. Ed was forbidden to sell his shares for cash until a year after the sale, and before this period elapsed their value evaporated. Later the company's CEO, exposed as a thief, perished from carbon-monoxide poisoning while resting in a Rolls-Royce in his closed garage. A suicide, said the police. Ed would have preferred it to be murder. By the time of Jane's daily mail runs the young engineer had almost resigned himself to the fact that his new Miata with his lost company's name—VISION—on the vanity plate was all he would get out of his first adventure in entrepreneurship. The rest had vanished on the Vancouver Stock Exchange, a notorious labyrinth of fraud.

Jane dragged the sacks of mail across the sidewalk, past the closed door of Randy Stickrod's office, up four narrow flights of stairs, through the chain-link security fence that surrounded the fourth-floor landing, across the not-very-clean wooden floor, painted black, and over to the desk of Amy Critchett, a naturally cheerful person who had spent her college years in Santa Barbara on tequila and roller skates but whose buoyant disposition had been weighed down, in recent weeks, by the constant addition of responsibilities. She was the person in charge of filling subscriptions. As this was the end of the mail run, Jane had no more need to harbor her strength, and she raised the bags high, like a figure of justice with overloaded scales, then slammed them down on the desk, which was made from a door lying flat on two sawhorses. The door jumped, but Amy did not move. In her thoughts she measured the circumference of the bags, then the length of the coming weekend, and concluded that the former would completely fill the latter, with a few dozen letters leftover.

Amy had been hired to help in the late fall, and her payment had been the standard intern's salary of $100 per week, but in January it had been raised to $307.69, in acknowledgment of the sacks, among other burdens. Her rent was only $250 a month, and she had a handful of housemates to defray the costs of groceries, and she had been thrilled to help with the launch of *Wired*, unloading boxes out of the back of her car during the heady premiere at Macworld. But as she stared at the sacks it took her a few seconds to escape from a clinging sensation of unfairness.

"Subscriptions!" Jane cried, inviting the occupants of the dusty office to come see.

The sacks were signs of their instant success. A few weeks after the launch of *Wired*, newsstands in New York and Los Angeles had sold out of magazines. By March, copies were rare in most cities. The high price of $4.95 did not seem to scare anybody off. Sightings of the last few unpurchased *Wired*s at the back of an obscure bookstore ten miles out of town were noted on local bulletin-board systems wherever there was a small circle of technophiles, and in an hour the copies were gone. This added to the rush of mail, as disappointed would-be readers put in their reservation for issue two. It was a precarious moment, and Louis was determined not to lose his balance.

Louis wanted to give *Wired* the same principles of flexibility, openness, and instant gratification that he understood as the essential qualities of the society-in-the-making. *Wired* would be, he later said, "a modern organ that showed what was possible and necessary at that time." On the other hand, he never anticipated instant acclaim. He expected to have some time to grow and learn.

Normal magazines never saw any sacks of mail. All they got were reports from a distant company called NeoData Services, whose employees opened the subscription envelopes in Boulder, Colorado. Amy had never heard of NeoData. "They are the biggest bunch of idiots that you ever could possibly imagine" was Louis's assessment. They admitted it could take up to *six weeks* to process subscriptions. Louis felt that in the age of Federal Express, such delays were intolerable.

In his cover letter to members of the Electronic Frontier Foundation, who had received the first issue free, Louis promised that subscriptions would always be processed in the San Francisco headquarters. And at first they were. Amy, along with some recently recruited friends whose salary demands were also small, opened every letter and looked at every postcard that came in. Soon they were alarmingly behind.

The piles of cards and envelopes grew, and with them the burden of the fledgling magazine's startling popularity, and the promise of its eventual prosperity, and the temptation to capitulate to proven methods. Louis resisted. Operational complaints were funneled to Jane.

One day that spring, a neighborhood and a half away, Amy was wheeling a cart through the aisles of a discount store. The store was on Potrero Avenue, near the bread line at Saint Martin's Kitchen. In her cart was a large amount of printer paper, some miscellaneous supplies, and no pens. She was under strict instructions to return without pens.

"Pens just disappear," said Louis. "Give a person ten pens, and he will lose ten pens."

He was not just being frugal. The pens—or rather the absence of pens—had a meaning: hold on to your independence; do not get lazy; do not lose your identity; do not merge with the group.

"The meaning was 'buy your own fucking pens,'" said Amy, years later.

Amy approached the counter with a full cart, minus pens. She gave the clerk her account number, and he said that he was sorry but she would not be permitted to leave the store with any office supplies, due to a history of nonpayment. She asked the clerk to call the manager, and she asked the manager to call Jane. He did. Jane spoke with him briefly, then he politely rang up the supplies. Amy admired Jane's ability to be reassuring under pressure. Thanks to Jane, there was paper. Thanks to Louis, there were no pens. As more and more sacks were hoisted up the stairs, this equilibrium was maintained, but under a growing strain. Jane and Louis shared one of the only offices, which was useful, since without an office there would have been no door, and without a door, nothing to slam.

A month after the launch, the sacks were bulging with checks and credit-card orders. The final draft of Louis's written plan had predicted three thousand subscriptions in the first year, a number that was reached in February, ten months ahead of schedule. A survey showed that most readers were young, and they bragged of good salaries and high degrees. Median income was eighty-five thousand dollars Three fourths were under forty-one. The newsstand sales pointed to a 100,000 circulation by December, and there had not yet been any mass mailings.

On the other hand, Jane still had to sweet-talk suppliers into extending their credit. Why was the company penniless?

After meeting some resistance Bill Jesse and his partner Bob Smelick had reduced their fund-raising goal to eight hundred thousand dollars. The original deadline had been December 31, 1992. Twenty-four hours before this date they extended it another month. The second deadline had also passed. Meanwhile, newsstand payments would not start arriving until after the second issue appeared. Money had flown out the door for mailing, for publicity, for travel; even the staff's small salaries made a dent. The printing bill had not yet been paid. There was something persistently frustrating about the immensity of those sacks of mail and the smallness of the windfall that spilled out.

The disproportion of sacks and cash was not the only contrast between outward success and inward panic. Congratulations poured in, as did certain critiques that, for an obscure monthly in far-off California, were nearly as valuable as congratulations. *Newsweek* welcomed them with a headline reading: "Propeller Head Heaven: A Techie Rolling Stone." This hit the spot, even if the article's author, John Schwartz, was put off by the self-important tone of the magazine and quoted an anonymous industry analyst saying: "It's just hard to continually watch people breathe their own exhaust and not wonder when they'll asphyxiate."

Invitations for interviews came in from CNN, from ABC's *Good Morning America,* from Connie Chung at CBS. Louis and Jane's allies and friends saw a huge triumph and expected them to be liberal in victory. Everybody who had touched the magazine, in large ways and small, waited for their acknowledgment and reward.

The principals were exhausted, and small errors swelled into fights irrationally. Peter Rutten had been overlooked when invitations for a New York launch party were sent—he faxed an angry letter. Randy Stickrod, whose usefulness was now months in the past, had been eased from his position of executive publisher before the first issue appeared, but he resented being listed on the masthead under the general heading—"tea and sympathy"—that Louis and Jane used for helpful friends. He put his complaint in writing just after the launch, following a tense and discouraging meeting with the founders. Gerard Van der Leun, a contributor to the first issue and an ex–staff member of the Electronic Frontier Foundation, also failed to get a party invitation. Van der Leun was an experienced prankster on the WELL, where he used the name Boswell. The WELL had deep links into journalism, business, and technology circles, and Louis and Jane saw every mistake they made—a missed invitation, an issue delivered late to a subscriber or not delivered at all, a dumb spelling error—broadcast to everybody listening. The boost they got from their passionate core of supporters had a predictable price, and each ripple of success generated counterwaves of intimate hostility.

In the spring even their employees got angry. The proximate cause was the long-delayed arrival of money from Sterling Payot. The full amount had proven too difficult to raise, but the firm's top bankers, Bill Jesse and Bob Smelick, finally convinced their friends and neighbors to accept 9.6 percent of *Wired* and to pay $640,000. The implied value of the magazine, after one issue, was now four million dollars. Jane and Louis, who owned more than half, were millionaires, but the millions were figurative, existing only by extrapolation from the optimism of their bankers. The cash, absorbed by creditors and new bills, was scheduled to be gone by June.

The Sterling Payot investment involved a restructuring of the company. All of the earliest employees had been given a small share in *Wired*. Just as the magazine was launching, Jesse had an idea that promised to disencumber the new investors from the consequences of Louis and Jane's too generous policy. Wired would be split into two parts. *Wired* magazine was set up as a new partnership, Wired USA, Ltd., and most of the ownership of Wired

USA, Ltd., would be transferred into the hands of another company, called Wired Holdings, Inc. Wired Holdings would be the *general partner* in Wired USA, which meant that it would control the magazine's future, and it would be owned only by Jane, Louis, Charlie Jackson, Nicholas Negroponte, and the Sterling Payot group of investors. All rights to the Wired trademark and to any future extensions, ancillary products, and licenses would remain with Holdings. The magazine would even have to pay Wired Holdings for the right to use its own name. The employees suspected a trick. "I came here in the same boat you did," said John Plunkett, speaking for them all, "and I am going out in the same boat, or I'm leaving today."

After some vehement argument and a written threat of a lawsuit, Louis and Jane gave in—the employees would remain full partners. Whatever the bankers might have intended, Louis, upon examining his motives, found no shred of selfishness. He expressed contempt for what he called the paranoia of people who knew nothing at all about business. John Plunkett, in particular, frustrated him. He believed that John was paralyzed by his suspicions. Moreover, John seemed obsessively attached to Bill Sherman, the account executive at Danbury Printing, whose bill was still unpaid. John complained that his friend was being hung out to dry.

John's plea to pay Danbury did not seem right to Jane, either. The goal right now was to survive. The magazine had not flopped, and if it did flop, Bill Jesse would clear their bill. For now, they merely had a cash-flow problem. If Wired paid Danbury, or caught up on payments to the stationery store, or succumbed to any other passing, subsidiary pressure, then everything would begin to fall apart.

John never agreed with these tactics. "If it works, it's called bootstrapping, but if it fails, it's called fraud," he complained.

Editorially, *Wired* sympathized with outlaws. The cover of the magazine's second issue—also printed on credit by Danbury—showed three masked men holding an American flag, under the headline: REBELS WITH A CAUSE: YOUR PRIVACY. The masked men were programmers who called themselves cypherpunks. By distributing free, powerful tools that encrypted digital communications, they stymied the government's effort to preserve its eavesdropping capacities.

"If privacy is outlawed, only outlaws will have privacy," said Phil Zimmermann, who had written the first popular implementation of the newest cryptographic techniques and released it to the world, thus inviting prosecution under federal law. Steven Levy's story had an even, expository tone, but it gave full room to the cypherpunks to explain themselves, and implicitly supported their theory that when it came to choosing what computers would do, engineers, not legislators, moralists, or policemen, would be the deciding voice.

In headlines and cover lines, Louis laid it on thick. A few issues later, the cover showed a dramatic quote from futurist Alvin Toffler, who in answer to a question about whether the future was as shocking as it used to be, answered: "How does a constitutional crisis in the United States, the breakup of China, a global revolt of the rich, and niche wars with personal nuclear weapons sound to you?"

Each feature story in *Wired* was amplified by multicolored pages of illustration. Since original photographs were often too expensive, Plunkett used stock material and put his freelance computer artists to work. The cover story about rebel cryptographers was printed on a background of red-and-white stripes, some vertical, others horizontal. As if in response to the early criticism that *Wired* was unreadable, Plunkett pushed things further and further. "You are going to take it and like it," *Wired*'s pages seemed to say.

The second issue had more than twenty full-page and double-page advertisements. The rate was $7,200 per page. The ads were sold over the phone by Kathleen Lyman. She sat at her desk as if pegged there, making two hundred calls a day, selling to any technology company that would buy. When an order was placed, she whooped like a banshee. But the money went out faster than it came in, and as Wired's bank balance dipped toward zero, rose with a few advertising payments, and dipped toward zero again, Jane's job was to not bounce any checks.

In August, Danbury refused to print another issue. Bill Sherman was squeezed between Jane, who could not pay, and the owners of the printing plant, who wanted him to explain again just why he had been so eager for the business of this unprofitable and demanding client. Without some money coming in, there was nothing he could do.

Nori Castillo, Wired's young bookkeeper, sat with Jane as she wept a couple of nights later, when the crisis had passed. Salvation had come in the form of incompetence. Overwhelmed, one of the circulation assistants had been layering unbanked subscription orders in the drawers of his desk for weeks. Out of sight, they caused less shame. Nori had wondered why so few credits were being posted to the magazine's account. After all, the sacks were still regular, and there was now an eight-hundred number as well. Inside the drawers were a thousand orders. The orders were worth forty thousand dollars. Like a mother who drags a toddler from the middle of a busy street and alternately hugs and spanks him, Jane was crying with anger and relief. She quickly made partial payments on their bills.

Under pressure from the owner, who wanted his home back, Jane and Louis had moved out of the house in the Berkeley Hills and rented a little cottage in Oakland. They were bound to each other more closely now than before the launch; theirs was the type of link that is strengthened by hammering.

One Saturday morning, very early, three months after the hidden subscriptions had won them a temporary reprieve, the phone rang and Jane picked it up. It was John Veronis, partner of John Suhler, the supercilious banker whose scorn for them had been so devastating a year before in New York. Veronis wanted to talk to her about making an investment in the magazine. Louis and Jane had used their slight margin from the hidden subscriptions to continue to shop the magazine to big investors who would not demand control, and the magazine's popularity, which had never stopped growing, helped them. Through careful delay of payments to creditors, they had retained a positive balance in their bank account.

On the advice of a London friend with experience in business, Louis and Jane were now asking for $3.5 million in exchange for 15 percent of the company; this meant an astonishing $23 million valuation for a magazine that was less than a year old. They expected to give a good deal of ground before the deal was signed. In November 1993 they were booked on a flight to New York for face-to-face negotiations with several potential partners. Veronis told Jane he had a client who would like to participate.

Any offer was welcome, but this one came from a firm that had humiliated them during their hour of need. She covered the receiver and said to Louis, "It's John Veronis."

"Tell him to go fuck himself," Louis replied. He was not really a morning person.

Jane did not pass on the message but demurred politely. She listened for a minute more, then covered the handset again.

"They have what they describe as a major media player who wants to take the whole round," she said.

Louis repeated himself, and added, "We're going to be making money by the end of the year!"

Jane returned to the telephone, refused the offer, and listened again. She covered the receiver. "The media player is Si Newhouse at Condé Nast."

"*Tell John Veronis to go fuck himself!*" Louis said. His bad mood had now entirely lifted.

Jane refused to translate or convey his sentiments. Instead she said something civilized, and turned back to Louis for the fourth time.

"John Veronis says if you don't want the money, you should at least meet Si," she told Louis. "He wants to meet you, he's an important person in the magazine world, you might want to do something with him someday."

"Okay," said Louis happily, and early one November morning Louis and Jane went to 450 Park Avenue for the second time. With John Veronis, they walked along Forty-fifth Street to Madison Avenue.

Si Newhouse's office was not what Louis expected from a media tycoon. He owned some of America's most glamorous magazines, including *Vogue, Architectural Digest, Vanity Fair,* and *The New Yorker,* but there was beige carpet on the floor and wrapped around the two pillars that held up his oval desk. The walls were covered with old editorial cartoons. Newhouse was wearing socks without shoes and a sweat suit, and his physiognomy suggested, to Louis, an intelligent turtle. His face sloped forward toward his mouth, and his head rose alertly from a scrunched-up body. He seemed shy but glad to see them. Several times Louis suspected that Newhouse was about to laugh out loud. With Veronis and Jane sitting quietly by, Louis and Newhouse discussed other magazines for over an hour, conversing as readers and fans.

"You know why we're meeting," Newhouse finally said. "We would like to invest in your magazine."

"We're very far along," Jane answered. "We're here in New York for final negotiations."

"I know you've made an offer," said Newhouse. They had faxed John Veronis their maximum proposal, with its grand valuation. "And we accept it," he said.

Louis looked at Jane, and Jane looked at Newhouse. It seemed premature to say thank you.

"You understand the terms?" This was Jane, filling the space.

"I understand, and we accept them," said Newhouse.

Jane looked at Veronis. He seemed to want to say something, but it was too late for counteroffers.

Back in San Francisco, Louis called a staff meeting and said: "We're done raising money for this magazine." The Condé Nast money arrived in January 1994. The bill with Danbury was settled, and Louis planned his first mass mailing to potential subscribers.

The office was soon drowning in response cards, queries from writers, and letters from its thousands of fans. Almost all were men. Michael Ovitz, then at the height of his power in Hollywood, ordered thirty issues every month; President Clinton's communications staff displayed it to reporters as a sign of their familiarity with the latest thing; Negroponte spread it around the Media Lab; bankers set it out on reception tables to intimidate visitors, and computer programmers and software managers and engineering students all over the country refused to loan their issues to friends out of fear they would never be returned.

That spring, Amy received a call from a representative of the American Society of Magazine Editors, inviting Wired to purchase a table at a yearly awards banquet to be held at the Waldorf-Astoria. Jane and Louis considered the invitation trivial and ignored it, but after repeated phone calls they relented. It would be their first break since the magazine's launch. They rode in a rented limousine from Kennedy and stayed at the New York Helmsley, and the next day, at the banquet, they received a National Magazine Award for general excellence.

The audience at the ceremony proved that they had been right to come. It included most of America's top editors and publishers. Having been unable to gain admittance to this circle upon his arrival in America, Louis had run in the other direction and then, by one of the least traveled routes, captured its top prize. He gave a very short and grateful speech, shocking Jane by offending nobody.

After dinner, a man Louis recognized as Jann Wenner came up to offer congratulations. Wenner, who had seen in rock music a cultural shift with connections to nearly everything, was still the editor in chief of *Rolling Stone,* a magazine that had sustained him as an independent publisher for three decades. His cultural influence may once have been larger, but he was legendary in San Francisco, which had never seen a repeat of his success. Coming close, Wenner said, in a tone that could have been flattery, or irony, or even regret: "Ah—here I am—at the white-hot center of things."

PART II

—

THE GROTTO

Martha Baer came to San Francisco from New York in 1991 and took a job at the night copy desk of the Alameda Newspaper Group. She earned five hundred dollars per week and apprenticed with a master of the craft as it was then practiced, learning to size up headlines with a pica pole and adjust the borders of a photo with a proportion wheel. At the end of every shift, around midnight, her mentor, who had worked in the newsroom for four decades, would put his pica pole away, lay both palms flat on his desk, and say, "There's thirty!" This was a leftover reference to the numerals used by typesetters to signal the end of a job.

Baer's next paper was a step up; she was hired by the *San Francisco Examiner,* an afternoon daily owned by Hearst. She worked in silence from 5 A.M. to noon, sitting on the periphery of an uneven circle of desks (the rim) and taking handoffs from the senior editor in the center (the slot), receiving reprimands if a headline scheduled to take three and a half minutes took four minutes instead. She was good with words, but her heart would race when she was missing a verb as the time counted down. At the *Examiner* she saw other refugees she knew from her days at the Alameda papers, including union men who had worked in the layout room and were artists with their Exacto knives; they could slice twenty lines apart in a moment, respace them slightly to fill out a column, and finish with a period carved from a comma. You let them know you liked their work without speaking, because the layout men could not hear you. A tradition of skilled print work had long been established among the deaf.

These were people Martha admired but could not hope to imitate. At the *Examiner,* somebody would call out to the most senior copy editor a question like "What's the population of Ottawa?" and the old man would pick up his pencil, suck air through his teeth, and answer. He was eighty. The ranks of his juniors were being regularly thinned in response to shrinkage in both advertising and circulation, and there were regular rumors that the paper would be closed or sold. Most cities had only one daily, which gave San Francisco a surplus, since it had two. Affluent readers had moved to the suburbs, paper costs were skyrocketing, and major retailers had gone bankrupt, making ad accounts vanish without hope of return. Martha knew that whatever the *future of journalism* might be, it was unlikely to entail many more years of this, and the dirty white button on the cracked intercom outside the door of 210 Second Street—ten minutes by foot from the Hearst Building—was a welcome promise of a thorough change of scene. She buzzed, and heard a voice say something through the static.

"Uh, hello," she answered. The door clicked.

In the spring of 1994 Wired offered visitors the ambivalent welcome of a party where the hostess had gone to bed hours and hours ago and there was nobody to stop you from wandering in and making yourself at home, but where the revelers were preoccupied by matters too immediate and too personal for you to ever unravel. Martha was hired as a copy editor, and she remained an outsider for months. Even so, long before she was introduced to the complicated quarrels and hatreds that had taken root in the office since Louis and Jane's brilliant success, she had an intuition that she had finally arrived at the right place. The poor light and the loud music and the raucous, very large gray bird at the top of the stairs who was wrestling a swinging corncob with his beak and, above all, the extreme youth of the people gathered into little clumps around the room told her that here, for once, she might be tempted to participate wholeheartedly instead of merely donating her competence in exchange for a paycheck and the chance for antiquarian observation.

She was given a desk against the east wall, overlooking Second Street. Triumph had sent the founders scattering. John Battelle was on his first vacation in a year and a half. Kevin Kelly was on a publicity tour for his book, *Out of Control,* which had just been published. Meanwhile, John and Barbara were holed up in their quiet canyon home beneath the town ski lift in Park City, Utah, trying to regain their calm. A recent scene had destroyed their plan to cooperate intelligently with Louis while putting their personal feelings to the side; this plan depended upon the success or quick failure of the magazine, followed by, in the case of success, some well-deserved credit taking and cheery good-byes. They had been caught off-guard when called into Louis's office and greeted by Jane, who had a bottle of champagne. Jane asked them to join her and Louis in celebrating the inauguration of the magazine's first foreign edition, which would be published in a joint venture with *The Guardian* of London.

To John the sudden entanglement of their new asset was crushing news. "Why not just ship over American copies?" John asked. Jane pointed out that *The Guardian* was offering to pay 100 percent of the cost, in the form of a loan to the joint venture. A British *Wired* would thus be a source of cash, which they could put to use on riskier projects. Also, the British edition would put the world on notice that *Wired* intended to lead the revolution everywhere. They were getting similar invitations from possible partners all over the world. "We're only going to be this hot once," Louis said.

Being hot—this had huge dangers. John saw them clearly; why couldn't Louis? John thought of *Wired* as a pirate ship. Their goal was to ambush the old media companies, not join them or imitate them.

John's analysis was superficial, as far as Louis was concerned. Authority abhors a vacuum. *Wired* had created an international demand, and if they didn't stretch to fill it, a host of knockoffs and competitors would.

There was reason to be confident. The quality of *Wired*'s features had steadily improved, and they stayed in front of stories that grew more important by the week. In April 1994 *Wired* exposed the likely outcome of the first Department of Justice attack on Microsoft. In June they used a bright yellow-and-green cover, a take-off on *Mad Magazine* (SPY VS. NERD!), to inflame widespread protest against the National Security Agency, which proposed a system that would allow it to eavesdrop more easily on computer traffic. In July they put cable executive John Malone on the cover in a *Road Warrior* costume and broadcast his facetious request for the assassination of Reed Hundt, the head of the Federal Communications Commission, whom Malone accused of standing in the way of the deployment of broadband networks. This produced a very satisfying stir.

Wired was hardly the only magazine to take note of what was happening. Philip Elmer-DeWitt, a *Time* reporter and a member of the WELL, wrote a series of major stories in 1993 and 1994 about the implications of new technologies. He was burdened by the responsibility of explaining the basics to *Time*'s readers, many of whom had never touched a keyboard. Still, in his lengthy reports he hit many of the highlights; he reviewed current privacy debates, warned about easily accessible pornography, and described how amateur and independent writers used their computers to route around the traditional gatekeepers of the mainstream press. "In this paradigm shift lie the seeds of revolutionary change," he wrote. This was Louis's theme, exactly.

Barely a month went by without some chart or essay or full-length feature in *Wired* that purported to show how mainstream companies, and especially mainstream media companies, were dinosaurs headed for extinction. In February 1994, *Wired* had two well-known New York admen on its cover, posing in blindfolds along with the Pillsbury Dough Boy before an execution squad whose hands held remote controls instead of guns. In the next issue, reporter John Heilemann took aim at the BBC, and predicted in passing that "ABC, CBS, and NBC will all be on the verge of terminal unprofitability in four years." Novelist Michael Crichton went further. "To my mind," he wrote, "what we now understand as the mass media will be gone within ten years. Vanished, without a trace."

Wired had leapt to notice while other magazines and newspapers were struggling, and for a moment this seemed sufficient evidence that the editors' theories were true. They were not just talking about the transformation of the press, they were demonstrating it. *Wired* had more than a hundred thousand subscribers, and the responses from the first mass mailing were just beginning to come in.

Josh Quittner, one of Louis's favorite writers, took it upon himself to call McDonald's and warn them that their Internet address, mcdonalds.com, was unregistered and available for the taking. He was unable to convince the corporation that this was important, so he registered the name himself, and invited *Wired* readers to submit suggestions about what he should do with it to his new e-mail address: ronald@mcdonalds.com. The fact that McDonald's, so notorious for protecting its trademarks, was vulnerable to this prank is evidence of *Wired*'s free rein.

But soon the contradiction inherent in trying to lead an anarchist revolution began to be felt. That spring, the magazine published a story by John Perry Barlow under the headline "Everything You Know About Copyright Is Wrong." Barlow, using the house style, wrote that conventions governing ownership and wealth were changing "more fundamentally than at any time since the Sumerians first poked cuneiform into wet clay and called it stored grain." *Wired* was an appropriate test victim, and what happened next was utterly foreseeable: two computer engineers in Singapore copied all of *Wired*'s back articles and presented them on the Internet in a format of their own creation.

This was not what Louis had had in mind. The Internet was still an obscure domain; nonetheless, the pirates were not just consuming *Wired* for free, they were appropriating its identity. You could try to pressure them, and *Wired* did, but it would hardly be politic to actually sue them; plus it would be time-consuming, plus others could replicate the archive and it would escape forever.

The Singapore engineers were not trying to make problems for *Wired*. Copies of the magazine had been hard to get in their country ever since *Wired* had published a darkly comic travelogue by William Gibson that described Singapore as "Disneyland with the death penalty." Because print copies were rare, it seemed logical to republish the magazine online.

"You can't stop people from copying stuff," Louis acknowledged in a newspaper interview. *Wired* was getting plenty of press attention now. All spring, the magazine's booklet of flattering clips grew thicker and thicker. But if competition from below had arrived, so had competition from above. *The San Francisco Chronicle* ran a front-page business story on the growth of the Internet before *Wired*'s third issue came out. By the end of the magazine's first year, John Markoff at *The New York Times* was writing about a new system of publishing and reading documents called the World Wide Web. Time-Warner soon announced an online program, called Pathfinder, that would republish content from its magazines.

Meanwhile, *Wired*'s success among its core readers had been so fast and so universal that it was no longer clear whether the magazine was leading its audience or merely amplifying thousands of ongoing conversations. That spring, riding across the Bay Bridge to the *Wired* office, Louis and Jane could have turned on their radio and heard George Gilder, one of their favorite futurists, chatting with the host of a local public-affairs show. "We have an obsolete mass media," said Gilder. "The mass media, with their centralized systems, broadcasting to millions of people, necessarily seek the lowest common denominator: our morbid fears and anxieties. . . . A computer culture will supplant this broadcast culture." Gilder was a contributor to *Forbes,* where he was the star voice of a technology supplement called *Forbes ASAP.* A revolution in media was the hot topic everywhere.

The demands upon Louis were severe. He closely controlled editorial development at *Wired,* reading every word before publication, marking up copy liberally, and approving—when not writing—every headline. The staff was growing, and the copy chief was a woman whose very name, Constance Hale, foretold difficulties for the irregular and feverish editorial group. "God damn it, where are the editors?" she would ask, after Louis and Jane and John and Barbara had disappeared behind closed doors or out of the office as a deadline approached.

Hale was an experienced newspaperwoman and a strongly built, somewhat bellicose person. She did not like to back down; this made for exciting afternoons. Having decided not to yell at Louis, who truly frightened him, John Plunkett often found Constance an attractive target, and the conniptions, shit fits, fights over music, improvised feature stories, and overall atmosphere of desperate improvisation made Martha Baer feel right at home, at least at first.

One afternoon, with Kevin Kelly still out on his book tour and

John Battelle away on his vacation and Constance Hale yelling "Where is everybody?" with the sound of murder in her voice, Martha looked down to the floor and noticed a pair of brown hands gripping the soles of purple high-top basketball shoes. The shoes—and the hands—belonged to me. Battelle had asked me to sit at his desk temporarily and pretend to do his job. As soon as I met Louis, I accepted. I had been earning my living as a reporter for the weekly papers and the computer trade magazines; but here was a man trying to turn the world upside down. Martha caught sight of me doubled over, leisurely stretching my back and looking between my legs at some bit of hysteria in the rear of the office. She stared and laughed, and we became friends. Like her, I was happy to take a small paycheck and root for chaos.

One day, soon after he returned, Battelle sent me off to Mountain View, California, to write a profile of another young person for whom the digital revolution had offered a welcome promise of career advancement. Marc Andreessen had come west after the Internet-browsing software he had developed at his university was taken over by his bosses, and he was now trying to make a competing version that he could sell commercially. His software was called Mosaic, but since the National Center for Supercomputing Applications at the University of Illinois owned the name Mosaic and also owned his original code, Andreessen was starting over again, with the welcome assistance of a Silicon Valley angel named Jim Clark, plus most of Andreessen's fellow programmers from Illinois, whom Clark hired away in a lightning raid. The name for their new software was Mozilla.

I quickly discovered that to the nebulous collection of self-appointed experts known as net old-timers, Andreessen was not a hero. The situation in cyberspace was disorganized. Computer users with modems could dial up local bulletin boards, where they could leave messages, play games, and download software. Universities and research labs had access to a publicly funded high-speed network; this was the Internet, and it was resolutely noncommercial. The four biggest, pay-per-minute commercial online systems—CompuServe, Prodigy, AOL, and Delphi—used e-mail systems that did not work together, and all the leaders lost money.

The newest Internet trend, the World Wide Web, had the potential to supplant these confusing networks with something everybody could easily use. On the other hand, the most notorious effort to build a popular, universal network of linked documents—Ted Nelson's Xanadu Project—had been ongoing for twenty years without success. Consensus among reasonable people favored a modest, decentralized effort to develop the web. The web's inventor, Tim Berners-Lee, imagined it would gradually evolve into a global tool for collaborative work. Then Marc Andreessen developed a point-and-click web browser, and modesty vanished. The web was cheap, quick to learn, and enabled a person to publish electronic documents into an open system that nobody owned or controlled. It could be like desktop publishing, only better. Fortunes had been made selling publishing software to the personal-computer market; the industry braced itself for another ride.

While Andreessen and his colleagues worked to release a new browser over the summer, his old employer, the University of Illinois, began issuing Mosaic licenses to other commercial developers.

In the heated discussions among programmers, many anxieties

were expressed. Would the Internet choke on all this new traffic? Would Andreessen's rapid pace of development help break the web into gated communities, with certain documents readable only with certain types of software, thus destroying the system's utopian universality at birth? Would Mozilla, which allowed users to publish images using a controversial function called the *image tag,* unleash a flood of trivia, inundating everybody with dopey pictures of kids and pets?

When I arrived in Mountain View, I found a suite of dull offices strewn with pizza boxes and bowls of M&M's, under the supervision of a very young and very wary engineer. He was wearing a white T-shirt that set off his indoor complexion, and his face had the determined, almost pouting expression of a technical person who has grown tired of querulous and ill-informed commentary. Andreessen waved off the old-timers' concerns, and he did not concede any territory. He boldly insisted that his browser was destined to become the standard interface to electronic information. "One way or another," he said, "Mozilla is going to be on every computer in the world."

His claim was absurd. Andreessen's new browser did not yet exist; and even if it had existed, there was almost nothing to browse; and if there were, the only entity plausibly able to monopolize it was nearly a thousand miles away, in Redmond, Washington, at the peak of his powers, and watchful. But the long-term outcome of the battles between Bill Gates and Mark Andreessen, which would soon be dubbed the browser wars, would prove of less consequence for ordinary users than the weapons of choice: web browsers, more web browsers, and still more web browsers, aggressively distributed to an eager public, usually without any charge. The idea behind the browser wars was that the company with the most popular browser would eventually be able to set the agenda, decide on the fees, and gain full control. The strategy of both parties was to give their product away, then take advantage later, after people were addicted. Therefore, though browsers often had a nominal price, payment was intentionally easy to evade. Before long, everybody had one.

After visiting Andreessen, I undertook an afternoon of field research in the poorly lit southwest corner of the *Wired* office where a small group of online editors worked in close quarters; they were knee to knee. The fifteen-by-twenty-foot area was called the Grotto. The group's leader was Jonathan Steuer, a recent Stanford Ph.D. who had been giving *Wired* technical assistance since its early days. The chief technical administrator was Brian Behlendorf, a nineteen-year-old who ran a large, popular electronic mailing list devoted to music. Steuer and Behlendorf had run into each other at a costume party with a hallucinogenic-mushroom theme, and Steuer—a long-haired, stocky man, dressed that night as a Catholic schoolgirl—invited Brian to come help out at *Wired*. Brian wrote a tool that served electronic copies of *Wired* articles to anybody who requested them via e-mail, as long as that issue had been off the newsstand for thirty days.

Right after Andreessen's new browser was released, Brian had a copy. Before long, he was one of the web's greatest developers and advocates. "If you are not on the web," Brian told Louis, "you do not exist." The Grotto dwellers argued that there was only one effective answer to the Singapore engineers who put *Wired*'s archive on the Internet for free. *Wired* must offer its own web archive, with better features. That way, they could at least hold on to their readers.

This was a plausible rationalization, but a rationalization was all it was. Nobody was working in the Grotto for long hours and low pay because of a profound desire to protect *Wired*'s intellectual property. They were there because the web held promise. The web was exciting. The web felt like the fulfillment of a prophecy. *Wired* had been saying that someday anybody could speak to everybody; now it was true.

Pure enthusiasm of this sort posed a challenge to Louis's philosophy. His theory was that social change would come through the medium of new businesses built on new technologies. But nothing that reached him from the insular Grotto inspired him with any confidence that business was something they bothered themselves about. It was easy to notice the division in the office. Moving back toward the Grotto I was aware not only of a reduction in light, as the windows got farther away, and of a reduction in space, as the desks crowded in, but also of a diminishment of the magazine's influence, or the influence of its editors, who were hardly understandable from here even when they were yelling at each other.

Jonathan Steuer felt, as front-line officers invariably do, that he had insufficient matériel. Wired was linked to the Internet via a primitive dial-up modem connection. Upgrading to a faster hookup would cost more than two thousand dollars per month. But Louis would not agree. He said that there would be no cash for better connectivity without an explicit statement of how this new type of publishing might someday become profitable. When he got no satisfaction from Jonathan Steuer, he called upon his young banker friend, Andrew Anker.

Jane had been trying to hire Andrew since their first meeting. After the large investment from Condé Nast came through, their discussions picked up again. *Wired*'s success was now proven, and the rising excitement over Internet media suggested that its growth had just begun. Andrew and Louis talked about the effect of the web on the commercial online services. The web was making them obsolete. This was only one of many opportunities becoming visible. Andrew prided himself on his realism, but when he talked to Louis he had a sense that this was one of those rare moments in history where a willing suspension of disbelief could pay huge dividends down the road. Andrew resigned from Sterling Payot and became the chief technology officer of Wired. His title paid homage to his longtime interest in computers, though he was hardly any sort of engineer. His first important task was to come up with a business plan for the web.

Andrew quickly decided that he would need to take full control of the online operation. For a few months he bided his time. "There was stuff that Steuer knew that I didn't know, so I couldn't blow him out immediately," he later confessed. He made friends with everybody and worked on his plan.

Apparently, just about all the web workers agreed on a short-term solution: sell ads. Andrew understood the power of round numbers. If a full-page ad in *Wired* cost nine thousand dollars, then a small banner on one of Wired's web pages would cost ten thousand, with a three-month minimum. And if nobody ever saw it—since an audience was one thing that could not be promised— the first sponsors would get a look at the new technology, and a good amount of hand holding, and their names in all the publicity. Wired's new advertising-supported website would be called Hot-Wired, a name Louis liked because it hinted at the possibility of additional extensions of the Wired brand, as the revolution broadened into other media.

Nobody expected the sponsorships HotWired would palm off for ten thousand dollars apiece to survive for long. The computer screen was low-resolution; the ads themselves were tiny, and they disappeared as soon the user scrolled down. For the sponsors, the ads were merely admission tickets to a demonstration of the new medium. Once the lessons were absorbed, they would need a better reason to continue.

All Louis and Andrew had to offer was a promise. The February 1994 issue of *Wired* had featured the ideas of Martha Rogers and Don Pepper, authors of a popular 1992 business book, *The One to One Future*. Rogers and Pepper argued that the demise of mass media had its counterpart in the demise of mass marketing. As publishers multiplied, audiences would split into smaller and smaller segments, and advertising would become minutely precise. Louis and Andrew favored building a membership-and-password system for HotWired that would give sponsors exact information about viewers and eventually allow targeted advertisements to hit specific users. Targeted advertising on the web would be the ultimate example of disintermediation. Since every buyer could find every seller, capitalism on the web would be both ultramodern and, in a sense, primitive.

But while Louis and Andrew were concocting a plan to harness the grass-roots energy of the web to *Wired*'s doctrine of antiestablishment entrepreneurship, the workers most familiar with the medium had no such idea. The thing they liked best about the web was its open, noncommercial nature. They liked to browse and explore among the growing number of personal pages that contained résumés, family albums, and little amateur essays about topics of interest. They argued that *Wired* should encourage its readers to create content for the website, and they hoped to design a casual environment for electronic conversation. The notion of user registration, which was key to Louis and Andrew's advertising plans, did not sit well with the Grotto. A registration system would only serve to wall off *Wired*'s website from the wider network.

The leading exponent of the Grotto's philosophy was Howard Rheingold, whom Louis hired on the recommendation of Kevin Kelly. Howard, who became the executive editor of HotWired, wore bright purple clothes, a fedora, and shoes he painted to match the sky from a Van Gogh painting. A small college in Portland, Oregon, had awarded him a bachelor's degree in 1968 after accepting a senior thesis titled *Mind Blowing and Its Methods;* the thesis had involved extensive self-experimentation, and since its completion the author had continued to pursue an adventurous sort of participatory journalism, mostly in the field of consciousness expansion. Howard was not a linear thinker. He liked to quip, and pun, and select examples from distant disciplines to illustrate life's inspiring switchbacks. "Our contributors are our audience," Howard said. Another of his slogans was "HotWired uses the net as a medium for a worldwide jam session."

Howard had been an editor of *Whole Earth Review,* and he was a major force on the WELL. He had extensive experience with computer networks, but if, like Louis, you were very impatient to get a real business going, or if, like Andrew, you had a hidden ambition to destroy your rivals, you could easily find fragments of Rheingoldian rhetoric to quote sarcastically. Andrew began this game immediately, and soon Louis picked it up. Meanwhile, there was division of responsibility and confusion.

Relations between Louis and the Grotto grew worse with each passing week. Barbara Kuhr hired Max Kisman, the graphic artist who had given *Language Technology* its look, to develop a set of icons for HotWired. Kisman's large, neoprimitive graphics would take forever to appear on the screens of users connecting with standard dial-up modems, but they reproduced beautifully in newspapers and magazines, giving a sense of identity to a medium that had not yet seen anything bold.

Kisman's huge graphics upset the Grotto dwellers. Louis laughed at their anxiety. "Fuck slow-modem users," he said. When his employees pointed out that Wired itself had been a slow-modem user until very recently, Louis was unconcerned. By creating a site that clogged their line, HotWired would give its audience a reason to upgrade.

News soon got out that HotWired would be aggressively selling advertising on the web. It was widely believed that Internet users would not tolerate advertisements. They would rebel, they would boycott, they would send thousands of angry e-mails. Louis paid no attention to this fantasy.

In August Howard Rheingold and Jonathan Steuer called the Grotto dwellers together for an unofficial meeting. Howard's house in Marin County provided an ideal site for an open exchange of ideas, for, like the other Grotto dwellers, Howard was interested in drugs, and at his house there was no chance of a crackdown on these stimulating allies. Even Chip Bayers, HotWired's new managing editor, was glad for a meeting away from the office. He was a bit more straightlaced than his colleagues, and he had been spinning his wheels ever since his arrival. He had moved out west from New York, and he was very curious to know whether he had made a mistake.

The staff members carpooled north. San Francisco's summer fog sometimes makes the city feel like a beach town abandoned in bad weather, but a quick run down Lombard Street puts you onto the Golden Gate Bridge, and if there's no traffic, you're in Marin in ten minutes. From the top of the headlands the fog looks like you can walk on it. A minute from the summit is the junction for Mount Tamalpais, then comes a worn-looking shopping center, and just past the shopping center is Howard Rheingold's street. On the day of the HotWired meeting, a half dozen cars lined the strip of damp dirt between his wide chain-link gate and the pavement. Guarding over Howard's little home office were several small statues of Ganesh, the Hindu elephant god who overcomes obstacles. An orange power cord snaked across the grass to a tree out back, where it was tied to a low branch. Howard did his best work under the tree, while sitting in a blue canvas chair.

At Howard's house, Jonathan called the meeting to order. Notes were taken by the Grotto's youngest member, a friendly blonde on leave from Swarthmore who loved personal exposure and whose web pages included popular links to pornography sites and a photo of the lithe author in nothing but a garter belt and panties. Justin Hall had been trying to get work at Wired since the magazine appeared, but his direct offer to put Louis in touch with "the hacker-pirate underground of Chicago" had not succeeded. Only after Mosaic was released and Justin's web page, Links to the

Underground, began to attract visitors did he hear back, at last, from Julie Petersen in the online department. Julie was in charge of Wired's relationship with America Online. She was a fan of the Grateful Dead, of Walt Whitman, and of Justin's pages, in which she recognized an unfettered egoism as pure as that of her heroes.

A joint was rolled and passed, and nearly everybody present took a hit, including Chip, who figured it was not his funeral, and Justin Hall, who took two, and finished his first beer. In the years since Howard's graduation from college, a change had taken place in American agriculture: marijuana was green now instead of brown; it was also seedless and very strong. Soon another joint was going around. Some people took a hit, and some people waved it off this time, and Justin took two, and the sun warmed the tops of their heads as the grievances and tension that had festered in the cramped Grotto for months were aired out and exposed.

Howard had put some of his principles in writing a few weeks earlier, and the answer from headquarters had been cold. Louis did not like the idea of a global jam session. He rejected Howard's airbrushed portrait of the rabble who tried to impress one another on the amateur bulletin boards, the Internet hobby sites, the middlebrow commercial services. Louis was no vulgar democrat. He believed in rigorous selection. He did not want a free-for-all. He wanted a meritocracy under the civilizing discipline of a competitive market. The naïveté of people who spoke in the name of the masses was sickening to him. When he said that the digital revolution was coming from the bottom up, he meant that powerful visions for a new society would more easily rise from obscurity to visibility, not that all notions of value would be erased.

"The net is as selfish as it is cooperative," Louis told Howard.

"What people want from HotWired is our point of view, our mix, our insight, our personality."

This response had baffled the Grotto dwellers. Their knowledge of Louis's history was hazy.

At Howard's house, the Grotto dwellers dreamed and complained, and a joint went around again, and most people passed this time, but some took a hit, and Justin took two, and finished his latest beer, and his notes began to trail off, and then he wandered away, and Chip was just deciding that the situation was probably hopeless, and asking for some kind of sign, when Justin reappeared on Howard's porch and vomited over the edge. Soon afterward, the meeting broke up.

Louis demoted Jonathan on Friday, September 8. Louis told him he could stay on in an advisory role; his title would be *information architect*. HotWired's launch date, scheduled for eleven days away, was delayed until October. Louis took a desk among the web workers, and another half dozen young adepts joined the project, selected from the hundreds of e-mailed offers to work for nearly nothing. John Battelle also helped recruit writers and editors from the magazine to help with the launch; for instance, he convinced me to start calling all John Plunkett's contacts in the design world. I asked them to donate digital work to help get the experiment off the ground.

Andrew and the magazine's sales staff sold the first ads, closing deals with Volvo, Club Med, Zima, AT&T, and MCI. Soon Andrew hired Rick Boyce, who had been the vice president of a well-known San Francisco advertising agency. The advertisements Rick would pitch would run on the top of a handful of editorial sections, including a column of industry gossip; a gallery of digital pictures and tiny animation clips, a travel feature, a column about Internet technology, and a web-based discussion area. By means of savvy discounting, Rick found buyers for all the remaining banners. By mid-autumn Andrew was able to announce that the site was completely sold out.

For the launch of HotWired, Louis produced an outrageous press release that, like nearly all of his communications, was brilliantly tailored for hostile quotation. HotWired, said Louis on October 27, is the *live, twitching, real-time nervous system of the planet.* His words were widely broadcast.

"Is HotWired, Wired magazine's Web site, too cool to live?" teased *Newsweek* magazine. Then they more than compensated for the put-down by republishing an entire paragraph of Louis's most aggressive claims.

Soon after the launch both Howard Rheingold and Jonathan Steuer resigned. Facing the outside world as a staunch revolutionary, Louis Rossetto had shown the Internet idealists the other side of his nature. "The era of public-access Internet has come to an end," he said. He commanded his staff to speak with authority and establish order.

A photographer came to take a picture of Andrew, flanked by Louis and Jane. The picture appeared prominently in *The New York Times,* and Andrew's phone starting ringing with requests for quotes and speeches. But the attention did not seem to go to his head. He retained his humorous, unprepossessing demeanor. Net old-timers protested that they had never elected this leader, but their worry was a sign of his success. Advertisers clamored to join, and other publications raced to catch up. HotWired was leading a new industry.

As a provocation, at least, the launch was phenomenal. If Louis had wanted to panic the newspaper and magazine publishers who had once failed to take him seriously, he had found a way that was more effective than feature stories on their upcoming extinction. *Wired* had been a prediction, but HotWired was an insurrection—not a break in the future but a break occurring right now. Acceleration was rapid from this point on.

CHAPTER 8

CARL

A rural youth of extreme intelligence is almost certain to be unhappy. Among other deprivations there is nobody to talk to.
Carl Steadman's rustication was extreme; ditto his misery. If there
were 356 residents of Dent, Minnesota, aside from Carl, then to
355 of them, at least, the short, thin, wispy-haired, round-headed
teenager inspired either indifference or irritation. This number
included Carl's father, Luke Steadman, who made his feelings
plain with open-handed slaps, attempts at strangulation, closed-
fist punches, and harsh words. The private feelings of the 356th
citizen, Carl's mother, were difficult to ascertain. Carl suspected
her of tenderness, but marital pressures made her mute.

Carl had the kind of misfortunes that beg for accompaniment
by lone violin or twangy guitar: there was violence, drinking,
paternal adultery, a bankrupt farm, and Herculean after-school
stable-cleaning chores. Unfortunately Carl, though he lived on a

farm, was not a country type, and overt pathos was ill suited to his analytical nature. Since he could not become a low-voiced maudlin country singer, he learned to express himself indirectly, and developed a terrifying sense of humor, the trick of which lay in his tone of voice. Carl could answer nearly any inquiry, no matter how drunken, narcissistic, or absurd, with deadpan condescension. His technique was to echo, phrase for phrase, the required commonplaces while making very slight syntactical alterations or allowing his voice to catch momentarily before a particularly oleaginous construction, which made his reply sound like an open insult. His father, who was mentally ill and an alcoholic but not stupid, wanted to kill him at these moments and sometimes tried.

In 1981 Luke Steadman bought an Atari 800 at an auction. This was standard alcoholic behavior. There were always random, never-asked-for gifts Carl ended up with and could not use, such as a gas-powered toy airplane and a horse. But the Atari had one powerful virtue: it was operated in silence and alone. The machine dropped a curtain of privacy around Carl.

There were also disadvantages. Carl's Vivarin habit, which he started at age ten as an aid to reading all night, soon became an aid to playing with his computer all night. This enraged his father, who was counting on a farm-fresh early-rising adolescent to help with the cows. That Carl, pale-faced and Vivarin-tweaked, writing programs as a freelance, was making more money for himself than was earned through all his father's inept husbandry did not make Luke more tranquil.

When Carl was sixteen, he wrote the software that managed the *Knowledge Bowl* quiz-show competitions, for which he was supposed to receive a third of the publisher's revenue, but this was written into his contract as a specific cash amount whose value stayed the same as prices rose. This gave Carl his first lesson in commerce. Still, every time he wrote a program for *Uptime,* an experimental magazine-on-a-disk that was sold in ComputerLand stores, Carl got two thousand dollars. With this money he bought a Dodge Omni to drive on recreational trips to Fergus Falls, Minnesota, population fifteen thousand, near the mouth of the Pelican River. The good thing about the Omni was that as long as Carl kept the gas tank less than half full, he could lift the back of the car out of a ditch unassisted. Barreling down the unlit farm-to-farm blacktop on a subzero midwestern night, Carl liked knowing that he would not have to wait for rescue if he hit a patch of ice. A police interview would be embarrassing and also dangerous, because Carl had graduated from Vivarin to methamphetamine, the easily available drug of choice among assembly-line workers at the local chicken-processing plants whose shifts ran late into the night and who, like Carl, were desperate for an antidote to tedium.

Carl was in high school during these escapades, but his teachers seldom bothered him. He had learned early that authority figures were just ordinary human beings like him, only less intelligent, and at school he made an explicit bargain: you will not mark me absent, and I will not disrupt your class. He got a hall pass and laminated it.

Negotiations on the home front were harder because his adversary was not sane. One day when Carl was riding the tractor down a paved road trying to get his chores done as quickly as possible before retiring to his room to learn things and make money, Luke pulled up abruptly in his Chevy, jumped out, climbed into the tractor, and grabbed him around the neck. Fearing murder, Carl shoved the tractor into first gear, popped the clutch, and sent his father sailing to the pavement headfirst. There was some dispute later as to whether Carl also ran over him. For a time, Carl wondered if he should worry about retribution and take protective measures such as wearing a motorcycle helmet around the house, but he solved the problem by moving out and living in his car.

Around this time Carl became depressed and ate fifty sleeping pills, a fatal dose for such a small person except that it was summer and he was lying in a cemetery where there was a mosquito infestation. The incessant stinging got him up and wandering around, hallucinating and ringing strangers' doorbells.

At the mental hospital he raised his skill at mimicry to the highest level of perfection. In order to get out of the hospital, which was organized like a prison, you had to mime the symptoms you were accused of having; this made you *cooperative* and improved your prognosis. There was something about the way Carl said cooperative that made you want to smack him, if you were paying attention.

If Carl had not been so distracted during his senior year of high school, he would have realized what the other kids were doing with the forms that they handed to the most popular teachers. They were asking for recommendations to college. Nobody had mentioned anything to him about this. The University of Minnesota required only a signature and a transcript, so he moved to Minneapolis and arrived at the height of the craze for cultural studies, a stimulating discipline that applied literary and anthropological theory to current affairs.

Carl did not have to learn that the world was an arbitrary collection of signs; he already knew that. What he learned was that he was not alone, and among these academic extremists he soon established himself as an admirable intellect. He published a cartoon commentary on the work of Jacques Lacan, called *Kid A in Alphabet Land,* and received a prestigious contract to write the text of a popular guide, *Lacan for Beginners.*

He also fell in love, an experience that led him to reconsider his conviction that emotions were mere theatrics. For the first time he detected states within himself that matched what others described as *happy* and *sad.*

Carl's experiences as a teenager had rendered him permanently unafraid of computers and computer programmers, so he introduced himself to the developers of Gopher, an early tool for browsing files on the Internet. When he spoke in praise of Mosaic, with its controversial image tag, their response was predictable: *Bah, eye candy!* they said.

Carl, who was sensitive to ridicule, did not persist.

When *Wired* appeared Carl got a call from a technical friend so excited he could barely articulate anything except that Carl had to go out in the snow and get one. From the moment Carl opened it, he knew he would eventually have to move to California. In the meantime he built an online archive for *Critical Theory,* the scholarly journal for cultural studies, which became one of the first nontechnical publications on the web. He wrote an epistolary novel in e-mail, for which he received invitations to be interviewed on the radio, and the year he graduated he took a job at the new online division of the *Minneapolis Star-Tribune.*

Carl realized that no academic rebellion was a tenth as powerful as these disruptive tools, connecting writers and readers in a network of links that no authority could control. When HotWired appeared it made Carl angry. It was what he had been waiting for, but he was still far away. Worse, he could see that they were making a terrible mistake.

When you hit HotWired, you got a white page with a question and two answers. The question was: "Are you a Member?" The answers were "Yes" and "No." *Wired*'s archives, which had been available for nearly a year, were now buried behind this gateway.

If you were a member of HotWired, you had to remember your member name and password. If you were not a member, you had to establish a new account. Carl almost never succeeded in looking at HotWired. He would decide to see what was happening there, and enter the address, and try to put in his name, and be denied access, and by the time he had requested and received a new password his mind would be elsewhere and he wouldn't think about it again for a week, by which time he had forgotten his password again.

That Louis Rossetto, the founder of *Wired,* would make such an error was baffling to Carl. He felt that there was no time to lose. Time-Warner had already threatened to charge for access to Pathfinder.com, its new website; this would mean another large domain fenced off from common use and hyperlinks.

Just before HotWired launched, Mark Andreessen's Mozilla browser had been rechristened Netscape and officially released. To the image tag Andreessen added the blink tag, a function permitting fanatics and advertisers to make parts of their page blink on and off for emphasis. But to Carl, the blink tag was merely an aesthetic offense. HotWired's password system was a fundamental threat. The web was nothing without links. Either the web would fail or Louis would. To see the creator of *Wired* back himself into this corner made Carl frantic. He decided to interpret Louis's errors as a cry for help.

But Louis was by no means as ignorant as the password system made him seem. The idea of a user-registration and member-authentication system had been as horrifying to the Grotto as it was to Carl, but Louis was not a kid and he was not fooling around, and he explained to his rebellious staff that winter that a revolution cannot be led from a position of bankruptcy. Part of inventing a medium was inventing a disciplined plan of attack, called a *business model;* mere high hopes and courage were not enough.

During the first two weeks following the launch, the young HotWired employees protested passionately against the registration system. At first Louis tried to quell their panic with forceful argument. When this failed he became sarcastic, then angry, then dictatorial, banning further discussion. None of these tactics worked. On November 9 and 10 there were more than twenty companywide e-mails, some in the form of lengthy essays explaining to Louis why he was ill informed and wrong.

Did the staff, young as they were, sense that the future was advancing too quickly for business logic to keep up? Ian McFarland, a twenty-two-year-old programmer who had been working on HotMOO, a chat system with a distant origin in electronic Dungeons and Dragons games, refused to back down, and chased his boss through endless arguments: user authentication was a hassle, it broke the web, and it was wrong in principle.

"Privacy is our defining issue," McFarland wrote in one of his messages. "Is privacy just hype at Wired, a part of the new hip-ocracy? Or does it really mean something?"

The accusation of hypocrisy rankled, not least because Louis had suffered for years from an inability to soft-pedal his beliefs. On the cover of *Wired*'s second issue he had published a photograph of three masked cypherpunks, but this did not mean that Louis had made privacy his dogma. The subjects of that story were fighting against the government. HotWired's registration system was a free commercial exchange.

Wired was one of the first publishing companies to provide e-mail to all employees, and one of the first to air out its conflicts in freewheeling, companywide electronic debates. From these innovative experiments Louis emerged with damaging wounds. He could easily have escaped. A dignified word of disapproval plus a threatening reprimand passed down privately via one or two layers of flunkies would have quickly silenced McFarland and the other protestors. If Ian had persisted, he could have been taxed with making technical progress on the MOO, which was probably impossible and would have occupied his mind for a time before he was given a subpar performance evaluation and fired. There was no need to invent these techniques of management; they had existed forever in well-run businesses where *respect*—as Carl might have put it—was paramount. But Louis never thought of subterfuge. He did Ian the honor of treating him honestly; i.e., he told him to shut up.

Out of the thousands of words traded between Louis and his unhappy staff, the excerpts below capture something of the intensity of these early battles over the invention of web publishing.* Ian first appealed to principles, then turned to practicalities, and

---

* They have been severely condensed here; also, some punctuation has been added and obvious typos corrected.

slipped in some ad hominem remarks. Louis rejected the principles, waved off the practicalities, and returned the remarks sharply.
Each e-mail was sent, at the moment of completion, to everybody
in the company.

IAN: The metaquestion then becomes: Is Wired progressive, or
has it become merely the marketing of the progressive?

LOUIS: The metaquestion is: what are you smoking?

IAN: Oh, please, Louis, must we resort to personal attacks? This
is not a naive question.

LOUIS: It is an absurdly naive question. I have a very non-naive
question: Do you have another business model which will
allow us to pay your and everyone else's salary while sup-
porting your absurdly abstract sense of what privacy really
means? All five million subscribers to closed online services
are fully identified. All members of the Well are identified.
Are they all dupes? Fools? Exploited?

IAN: How likely is it that someone somewhere will create a link
to an article of ours? With authentication, the likelihood approaches 0.

LOUIS: I don't know what the likelihood of creating a link is,
and I'm sure you don't either.

IAN: Well, Louis, I can tell you that I'm not going to point people off at some page they probably don't have access to.

LOUIS: When we started Wired, we got a ton of shit about the
design. It was a "hassle," it was "user unfriendly," it was
"pretentious" etc. We persisted, because we knew what we
were doing. I feel we do now as well. The only real issue is:
do the vast majority of the people who visit, do our advertis-

ers, and do we think we are doing a good job? And I think the answer so far is clearly yes.

IAN: The question is not "are we doing a good job." That's pretty easy this far ahead of the curve. The question is whether we couldn't do a better job. I think it's a little early for laurel-resting. You have surrounded yourself with creative, enthusiastic people with a real grasp of net culture. Why did you do that, if not to ask their opinion?

LOUIS: Thank you very much, Ian, for your lesson in the Net, media, advertising, and how to run a business in general. Whenever I want to start a new business of whatever sort, I will be sure to consult with you before I take even the smallest step. I now consider this discussion closed. If you have anything further to say to me about this topic, I will take your answer offline.

After so public and so painful an exchange, the young idealists began keeping out of his way as much as possible. Louis had invited anybody who wished to discuss such topics further to please schedule some time with him privately. Few did. Louis soon had almost no idea of their latest personal projects, which were carried on with little thought of profit. Nearly all of them were publishing web pages of their own, some of which garnered substantial traffic. When asked to manage a simple piece of editorial business, Justin Hall agreed in his nicest manner, but the request vanished from his thoughts as soon as he was left alone. Links to the Underground was growing by leaps.

Having defended himself against the unbusinesslike idea that an aggregation of happy freeloaders constituted a commercial success, Louis took steps to structure his companies more rationally. First, he untangled the website from the magazine. HotWired was spun out as a separate company called HotWired LLC; this was a partnership in which Wired's original shareholders owned the majority, with a small stake—about 10 percent—being handed out to select HotWired employees.

Andrew controlled the distribution of the employee shares. As the in-house banker and, after the reorganization, chief executive officer of the new company, he estimated that his portion should be predominant. When this first priority was taken care of, he spread the remaining fractions equitably among the others. Andrew's goal, he said, was to grow HotWired into a company whose value exceeded one hundred million dollars, at which point every tenth of a percent would be worth—and here the conversation would pause so they could all do the math together—*a hundred thousand dollars*. For most of his young employees, a hundred thousand dollars seemed like riches; the subsequent madness was still unthinkable. Andrew set about trying to raise seven million dollars to fund HotWired, far more than had ever been invested in the magazine. The Grotto was no more. That fall Wired and HotWired together had finally outgrown the corner loft on Second Street. Both companies moved to an old warehouse building on the other side of South Park, where they took adjoining spaces.

The management of his fledgling empire imposed terrific burdens upon Louis, which distracted his attention and allowed him to imagine, when he stepped across the hallway from the magazine and entered HotWired's unmarked doors, that the atmosphere was alive with devotion to his cause. The entrance smelled of smoke, fermented fish, and burned fabric; in November there had been a fire in the enormous trash bin used by the crowded sewing shop next door for the disposal of scraps. Garment manufacture was still the building's main business, and the smell of fish sauce lingered from lunch, which the seamstresses brought from home in metal tins and ate on the staircase.

The transit from the gray reeking hallway into the glare of the HotWired space always held the possibility of amazement. Newcomers experienced it every time, and even Louis enjoyed it when he was not preoccupied. Banks of high warehouse windows facing south and west diffused the light in such a way that many of the computer monitors were unusable without shades constructed from cut-up cardboard boxes and resembling the hoods of portrait cameras. Enormous bundles of electrical cables the color of Pepto-Bismol spread out and subdivided across the ceiling and down the pillars to three dozen closely crowded door-and-sawhorse desks. On any given day at least one of the desks was occupied by a young person in tears, and the music was very loud.

Louis escorted visitors across the hall when he wanted to give them a vivid impression of the new medium. Since most potential investors did not have time to investigate the web directly, a glance into the confusing and overwrought office provided a visual substitute. But Louis himself was also deceived by this substitute, for his employees, while extremely active and even ragged from long hours and extraordinary efforts, were not achieving his goals, and in some cases were not even trying to achieve them. Justin Hall's Links to the Underground was the most popular site on the HotWired servers, followed closely by Bianca's Smut Shack, another unofficial project devoted to personal exposure and off-color storytelling run by three recent recruits from Chicago.

Justin Hall was more of a mascot at HotWired than a contributor, and this was too bad, for what Louis really needed during these months was to get angry and argue his positions deeply, giving the teenager one last chance to inform him that he was derided as an ignoramus by most of the web experts on his staff. Louis was urging them to seize leadership in this new medium the same way *Wired* had seized leadership of a new niche in magazine publishing. But what did leadership mean in a medium that routed around leaders? The issue flared up again in April, with another series of angry e-mails. The idealists referred to the traditional ethics of the Internet when it was dominated by amateurs, when content was there for the taking, and when anonymity was assumed. Louis was having none of it:

> A gift economy outside a small tribal setting doesn't work, period. The idea that the Net was, is, or can be a gift economy is the real nonsense in this discussion. . . . Furthermore, I reject the idea that anonymity itself is actually an overriding benefit to users. . . . Anonymity is not the good, privacy is. Confusing the two is ahistorical knee-jerk ideology that is going to look damn foolish in very short order, along with a lot of other wishful thinking about the Net. In the end, reputation, reliability, reality—those will dominate the virtual world, as they rule the real.

Louis was the better futurist, but all the registration system was doing at that moment was keeping users out. The argument over user registration had gotten lost in an ideological thicket, when the real issue was not privacy, or anonymity, but simply convenience.

Louis was sacrificing today's market share to tomorrow's business model. He needed to pause for a minute, to *mellow out,* and Justin, who had an ideal combination of courage and charm, was just the person to get him to do so. It is easy to imagine the two of them conversing late into the night and then, in the wee hours, smoking a bowl of Humboldt County's finest, justly famous for encouraging reflection. But at the moment Justin was gaining vast traffic for Links to the Underground, *Wired* was suffering its first backlash from external enemies. His boss's patience was extremely limited.

The political hostility Louis confronted in 1995 had taken a while to develop, for at first nobody outside his base of fanatical readers took *Wired* seriously as anything but a computer magazine. But through circulation growth, predictive success, and relentless provocative editorializing, *Wired* had finally managed to attract attention to its wider philosophy. As always, the editors had help from the outside world. The same month *Wired* launched, a new president took over in Washington. Offering himself as a trustworthy manager of economic and technological disruption, Bill Clinton was an advocate of free trade and an enemy of the old-fashioned liberals in their party. His vice president was famous for his enthusiasm for the Internet. Both had an interest in emphasizing the power of computers to change society.

Then, just after HotWired's launch, Newt Gingrich became the speaker of the House of Representatives. Gingrich's tone closely matched *Wired*'s millenarian fervor. Anti-statist ideas that had seemed extreme in the eighties, when Ronald Reagan had to use a fair quantity of his patriotic folksiness to put them over, were now the victorious dogma of the new Republican majority. Citing his influences, Gingrich often credited his friends Alvin and Heidi Toffler. The Tofflers' theory was that human society had been transformed three times, by agriculture, by capitalism, and now by cybernetics. Gingrich believed that in the age of cybernetic revolution, government power should be radically cut back.

Louis had no party loyalties, for he opposed voting on principle. He never enforced a pusillanimous conformity in the magazine's pages, and the liberal opinions shared by many of his writers found numerous small occasions for expression. But in *Wired*'s choice of subjects for interviews and profiles, in its refusal to interject balanced caveats into stories about capitalist ambition, and in its editorializing on technology issues, it advocated unfettered competition and complete libertarian freedom. Louis was proud that *Wired* had a worldview, that it was nontrivial. He had no problem with spirited debate—this was something of a pastime, and the more violent the better. But he never allowed ideological attacks to go unanswered, and as *Wired* gained prominence, so did arguments over its meaning and credibility.

Back in *Wired*'s second issue, Louis had published the magazine's first letter to the editor, and with typical bravado he chose one that painted *Wired* as a morally bankrupt purveyor of fashion trends. The author was Gary Chapman, director of a nonprofit group called Computer Professionals for Social Responsibility. "I sincerely wish you well," Chapman wrote. "It's just that it's irresponsible . . . to be 'fashionable' in the way that *Wired* seems to strive to be. It's yuppie bullshit."

This complaint about *Wired*'s fashionableness was a bit narrow, given the other things the magazine was giving the writer to dislike, and soon after the launch of HotWired Chapman published an expanded and more wounding critique in *The New Republic* that described *Wired* as a howlingly brainless gazette of right-wing propaganda, smoke-shoveling celebrity punditry, and adolescent consumerism. The WELL, which all the *Wired* editors read, picked up and amplified the attack.

Louis was furious. He understood that controversy was natural among a knowledgeable and rivalrous crowd, but he had specific fears about being misunderstood, especially by potential partners in Wired's campaign to expand. In England, the marketing director of *The Guardian,* David Brooks, was presenting *Wired* as a fashion and pop-culture magazine for technology-obsessed urban males, a mistake that came dangerously close to Gary Chapman's caricature and one that stood to ruin their joint venture. This sort of thinking horrified *Wired*'s founder. He had never intended *Wired* to be a policy journal, but fashion trends and cultural stories were interesting only insofar as they offered advance warning of social revolution. He often said *Wired* was a lifestyle magazine, but by lifestyle he meant *way of life*.

On frequent and exhausting trips to London Louis berated the staff of *The Guardian* until he won at least partial victories. Louis was happy with David Brooks's idea of who should grace the U.K. edition's first cover. They used a fluorescent pink-and-orange portrait of Thomas Paine under the legend: *We have it in our power to begin the world over again*. Louis believed Paine was the perfect icon for *Wired*: a revolutionary too radical even for the revolutionaries, and an enemy of every entrenched power.

To *The New Republic*, Louis and his fellow editors responded with their most direct statement of their mission thus far. *Wired*, they wrote, "reports on a Revolution without violence that embraces a new, non-political way to improve the future based on economics beyond macro control, consensus beyond the ballot box, civics beyond government, and communities beyond the confines of time and geography." Louis believed that only people who were actively using the new technologies could appreciate their power to change everything. So frequently compared during its first year to *Rolling Stone, Wired* was different from its predecessor in being aimed not at the fans of its favorite industry but at the creators and participants. It was always a vanguard magazine.

On the other hand, what did it mean to be the vanguard of something whose popularity was expanding so rapidly? In January 1995 Louis learned that the number of subscribers to the online services had grown from three million to well over five million in the past twelve months. Online access was spreading so quickly that it produced spontaneous successes. You could compare it to hydraulic pressure: the flow of new users coursing through the network would find an outlet—something *interesting*—and there would be a dramatic spurt of local traffic. There was even a subgenre of knowing satire on the web that made use of the latest techniques in the service of highly personal nonsense, and pointers to these sites would circulate by e-mail, attracting tens of thousands of curious visitors who could, if they wished, type greetings underneath a constantly refreshed digital photo of a house cat, or click repeatedly on a very large button that did nothing. The masses were coming, and they were looking for something to do.

Louis, while continuing to investigate new ways to magnify the influence of his magazine, made HotWired the primary instrument of his expansionist plans. He proposed a dozen new websites under the HotWired banner. Each would be separately managed, and each would serve a different segment of the online audience. There would be a visionary entertainment channel, an adventure-travel channel, an extreme-sports channel. He called this strategy *planting flags,* and it was premised on his conviction that the web, unfettered by print and broadcast expenses, would be the natural terrain for new forms of culture. He was looking for what he described as the "top 10 percent" of Internet users—the people who wanted not packaged tours but adventure travel; not baseball scores but windsurfing advice; not celebrity news but access to unusual music from all over the world. And they would want these things on the web, not in a closed environment like the older commercial online services. The fastest growing of these services, America Online, had more than two million members but still did not offer complete access to the web.

Louis was attempting to delineate the features of a new elite. When he recruited leaders for his online division he looked first not at a candidate's skills but at his temperament; he aimed to fill his staff with people who had no stake in proven methods. There was a bias toward inexperience, even ignorance, as long as it was combined with energy. I had been giving part-time help to HotWired since before the launch, and at the beginning of 1995 I replaced Howard Rheingold as executive editor.

Louis and I met often. Mainly, we discussed hiring people. Day after day, I left Louis's office with the light step of a person who has been given permission to be bad. I was on the phone recruiting staff every day. I called friends who were used to earning ten cents a word writing book reviews and offered them exciting contracts for a literary channel Louis was eager to launch. I scattered my largesse, and even the mistakes seemed to lead to happy results. A meek local editor who was overcome by the sudden prospect of a genuine paycheck (there had not been a commercial literary magazine in San Francisco in the memory of anybody living) worked for a few months as an intern, then flubbed his interview for a paid position by failing to remember the name of a single book he had enjoyed reading. A few weeks later he parlayed his association with Wired into a job in Netscape's publicity department. It was rumored he would soon be rich.

Rick Boyce, HotWired's new advertising director, was selling out advertising space as soon as new web pages appeared. There were no volume discounts—it was $120,000 for a year, $30,000 for a quarter. A few other commercial websites had followed Wired into the market—but so far not many. HotWired could not expand quickly enough to capture all the advertising business that flowed in, and Andrew ordered Rick to raise the price of a HotWired sponsorship. The price jumped to $45,000 per quarter. At this rate, HotWired was profitable, and Louis's boldness seemed vindicated. But only a few weeks after the price hike, the company's commercial sponsorships began to fall apart.

Rick's first warning came at the end of February 1995, when an ex-colleague from the *Wired* magazine advertising department named Bill Peck dropped by for a visit. Peck was now working at Infoseek, one of the Internet's first search engines. From Peck, Rick Boyce learned that Infoseek was serving hundreds of thousands of pages every day—many times HotWired's traffic. Next, Peck showed Boyce what Infoseek was preparing to sell to advertisers. For a generic advertising banner, the search company would charge twenty dollars for every thousand times the banner was viewed. But advertisers could also buy keywords on the search engine, so that people searching for "computer" might see an Apple advertisement, while people searching for "auto" might see Chevrolet. Targeted banners would cost fifty dollars per thousand.

After the meeting Rick walked over to South Park by himself and shed tears. He was attached to HotWired, and assumed that the experiment was now over. HotWired's best price for a thousand viewers came to about seven hundred dollars, but HotWired did not like to talk about cost per thousand. The advertisers were sponsors of specific sections; they were not buying traffic in bulk.

Andrew left HotWired promptly each day at 5 P.M., but he compensated for his short hours by making sophisticated predictions about effects of the rapidly changing business environment. Based on Rick's news Andrew predicted that if HotWired did not increase its audience and lower its prices, *advertisers would bail!* His tone, discussing this with me, was heated.

Soon the advertising agencies, still smarting from the 50 percent price hike Andrew had imposed on them, demanded concessions, and no amount of creative discussion of the merits of HotWired's loyal and affluent demographic could completely extinguish their complaints. Louis was loath to switch to cost-per-thousand pricing because it did not reflect the deep relationship that would soon be possible using imminent user-tracking techniques. Andrew was loath to switch because a report of the number of visitors to these sections was likely to surprise the agencies unpleasantly.

Until now, I had enjoyed a carefree attitude toward my job. It was fun to hire people and spend money, especially if you had never done it before. The Infoseek crisis ruined my good cheer.

While I was perfectly willing to risk the bankruptcy of third parties in the abstract, I hated to think the end would be so swift. My
new business cards had not even been printed.

Simultaneously, another deflating influence arrived on the scene.
Her name was Beth Vanderslice. She had been Andrew's colleague
at the firm of Sterling Payot and had been working for Bill Jesse
when he drafted the complicated structure that had almost succeeded in liberating the Wired employees from their founders'
shares. Andrew knew she was a hard worker and would remain in
the office in the evenings after he left.

Beth was a new type. She comported herself with dignity and
had worked briefly at IBM. She wore expensive clothes and held
business meetings at her elegant house on Russian Hill. With her
well-practiced stare of intelligent attention, she asked her staff at
least once a day: "*What* will we do about Louis?"

Beth argued that it made no sense to start new enterprises when
HotWired's current activities were so unprofitable. She mentioned
that we all could make a lot of money at HotWired—far more
than Andrew had ever suggested—but there was a catch. We had
to come up with a way to earn a profit. These encounters rattled
everybody. Had we somehow, mysteriously, become top lieutenants
in a legitimate enterprise?

Meanwhile, HotWired continued to expand. Chip Bayers, Hot-
Wired's managing editor, saw Carl's résumé in May and called
Minneapolis immediately. When he picked up the phone Carl said:
"I should tell you I'm quite inebriated right now."

Chip was undeterred. Drunk or sober, Carl had more expertise
managing the production of websites than all but a handful of

other people in the country, and most of these were already employed by Netscape or one of the competing licensees of Mosaic. He asked Carl to start in two weeks.

Carl was so eager to get to San Francisco he did not even bother to move his possessions or rent an apartment. He simply purchased a bunk bed and installed it against one of the walls of the open office. He worked until two every night and woke up at six; for the four hours in between he enjoyed complete solitude and quiet in his top bunk, rent-free.

Carl had no idea about the worries that beset HotWired's so-called executives. His information came to him more directly. He had access to the records of all the traffic that came into the site, and even without a sophisticated data-analysis package Carl could see clearly that most of HotWired's web-publishing efforts were meaningless.

Despite great surges of traffic and registration attempts when HotWired launched something new, the site's repeat audience was tiny. No section was seen regularly by more than a thousand people per day; most sections had fewer than five hundred visitors. A careful survey of the traffic records revealed that more than 50 percent of the people who hit the front door failed to make it through registration to the rest of the site. Of those that registered, most never visited HotWired again.

Carl resented Justin and the other idealists because their utopian arguments left Louis more wedded than ever to his registration system. Louis would never give in to them because he sensed that they cared little for business. But while Louis may have been right in theory, his timing was utterly wrong. Tracking individual movement through the web ought to be handled invisibly, Carl said.

Soon these capacities would be imbedded in the browser, and users would barely notice that everything they did online was tracked by savvy marketers who used deep databases to uncover personal information. Until that day came, registration was depriving Hot-Wired of the traffic it needed to establish itself. Their great experiment was being suffocated at birth. Carl and Andrew talked about eliminating registration, and Carl got to work on the technical issues. But how would they convince Louis without being lumped in with the ultrarevolutionaries whose counsel he had already rejected?

The pressure against user registration, and the manifest failure of HotWired's traffic to keep pace with the rest of the web, had worn Louis down, but he still clung stubbornly to the notion that a new form of publishing required a new form of revenue; otherwise it was simply dilettantism and a joke. He was very tiresome on this topic; it was always when his logic was incontestable that he was most unbearable. He refused to agree to cancel the cumbersome registration system. Andrew argued vehemently, but he was overmatched and finally reduced to silence. "What is *your* business model, then?" Louis said. It was an impossible question to answer. When Andrew gave him the bad news, Carl was very upset.

In mid-1995 everybody who knew what was really going on in the new web-publishing industry was waiting for the other shoe to drop. The search engines were crashing prices, and there was substantial doubt that all of this would ever be more than a business of pennies.

On June 29 Andrew celebrated his birthday by giving representatives of Orca Bay Capital Corporation and Burda Digital, Inc.—

two more potential investors—tours of the HotWired offices. Chip and I made a list of thirty-seven new hires and sent out thirteen new job announcements. HotWired's books advanced into the red. The question of revenue was bothering Andrew's potential investors, too. All July, they refused to commit any funds.

And still the web continued to blow up. Summer 1995 saw the transformation of the Internet frenzy from its first, subcultural, almost tribal stage to a national obsession. *Wired* got hundreds of e-mails from argumentative readers, and so did HotWired. Except for the fact that e-mail replaced postal mail, this type of communication was traditional. But HotWired also received an enormous number of queries of a different type, ones that began with statements like: "I'd like to start a site for information about llamas." These queries concluded with requests for detailed information on how to publish a web page, for guesses about how big an audience to expect, and for tips on how to attract advertising. The most popular sites on the web were the ones that supported this vast curiosity about the web itself.

The cost of publishing was reduced to nearly nothing, and hordes of voyeurs discovered legions of exhibitionists. As if in explicit rebuke to Louis's rash proclamation of less than a year earlier—*the era of public-access Internet has come to an end*—the web had quickly been recognized as a beautiful forum for individual self-expression. AOL was saturating the country with free computer disks, and, although AOL users still could not connect directly to the web, this feature was coming soon, meaning that two and half million more people—scratch that, by the beginning of July it was three million—would be in the game.

Justin Hall was one of the heroes of this movement. At the end of the internship he returned to Swarthmore College, and from his dorm room he produced an explicit diary and web guide that attracted three times as many users as all of HotWired's sections combined.

Before HotWired had launched, the *Wired* magazine pages were among the most linked-to pages on the web. *Wired* had always been a forum for the movement's leaders. Now, when Carl looked over an independently compiled list of the top twenty-five linked-to pages, *Wired* and HotWired were not on it. Netscape was in the top ten; so was a search engine called Lycos. The White House was number eleven; IBM was fourteen; Infoseek was sixteen. Almost every site on the list was a tool for searching the web, a technical site for Internet developers, or a list of useful links. In spot number twenty, with six hundred links to it from the rest of the web, was a beginner's guide to creating your own page. And in the very first place was a web directory run off a server at Stanford, whose student founders, David Filo and Jerry Yang, had recently scored nearly two million dollars in financing from Sequoia Capital, a famous Valley firm that had invested in Apple, Oracle, and Cisco Systems.

This was Yahoo. Andrew and Beth were familiar with Yahoo. They had recently taken a trip down the Peninsula to visit Jerry Yang in his new, colorless corporate offices, where the task of categorizing new sites was pursued with dogged tenacity. Yahoo, Andrew saw instantly, had no real business. While it was the top site at this strange moment when millions were discovering the web for the first time, Yahoo, in the end, was merely a utility, and therefore vulnerable to the first superior directory that offered better results. There was no loyalty, no emotion, no attachment. An-

drew pointed out that there could never be a successful Yahoo
magazine, or a Yahoo television show. The rates for generic advertising banners on the web were headed down. New search tools
were certain to come on the market. The best Yahoo could hope
for was to merge with or be purchased by a more vivid and popular media company. The HotWired executives, on their way back
to San Francisco, agreed that they felt sorry for David and Jerry,
whose conundrum was even more difficult than their own. At least
Wired was a strong brand.

If Yahoo did not have the answer, perhaps Justin Hall and the
other idealists did. Andrew quietly asked his lieutenants to scout
for more popular content. I invited Julie Petersen to lunch. Julie
produced her own website, called Awaken, which, like Justin's
pages, experimented with the extremes of romantic self-revelation.
Her devotion to the Grateful Dead, a band that famously tolerated
pirate tapes of its live concerts, struck me as somehow related to
all the ingenuous giveaways on the web. Was there a business
model there? Had Howard Rheingold been right after all? Was the
web a medium for a global jam session?

At the time of our meeting, Julie was living with her hus-
band, Jim Petersen, in a mobile home in San Francisco's only
recreational-vehicle park, two blocks away from the office. We
ate and talked under beach umbrellas on the outdoor patio of a
Caribbean restaurant on Townsend Street, next to a brick two-
story building, since demolished, that housed a bar where the
neighborhood's older residents took refuge. But if there was a
business model hidden somewhere in the peculiar economy of
sharing, I failed to uncover it, and we never had a second conver-

sation. Our search was about to be superseded by more important events.

On July 30, 1995, an Internet expert named Mike Walsh published a lighthearted analysis of Netscape. Walsh's essay quantified the growing excitement. Spyglass, another licensee of NCSA Mosaic, had sold shares to the public, and was now valued by Wall Street at more than two hundred million dollars. If Spyglass was worth two hundred million dollars, then Netscape, with its far greater success at giving browsers away, had to be worth more than a billion.

Morgan Stanley and Hambrecht & Quist, the bankers, were said to be pricing Netscape's public offering at eighteen dollars per share; if Wall Street really thought the company was worth what Walsh said it was, the per-share price would rise on the open market to thirty-five dollars. This was laughably rich. Walsh wrote jokingly that the Securities and Exchange Commission had asked Netscape to include in its stock prospectus a reprint of Charles Mackay's classic book about manias and panics, *Extraordinary Popular Delusions and the Madness of Crowds*.

Louis pondered this strange turn of affairs. Was Netscape a software company? Technically, yes, but anybody could write web browsers, and at least a half dozen Mosaic licensees now did. He was rooting for Netscape, but the logic of their business was obscure. In an attempt to gain market share, they were giving away more browsers than they were selling, and the inevitable entrance of Microsoft into the market would put intolerable pressure on revenue. There was not a business model for Netscape—yet. But Louis had faith that the right business model would evolve out of trial and error, for both Mark Andreessen's company and for his own. Investors were giving their money to companies that promised to be on the scene when light dawned, and there was nothing irrational about that.

In the end, Louis took the excitement about Netscape's stock offering as an endorsement not of its business but of its story. This was a common conclusion, and the companies whose business was poor but who sold shares to the public on the strength of a quality narrative at the height of the bubble would be known among financiers as *story stocks.* Louis saw markets as the ultimate decentralized authority, and he believed that the combination of countless independent judgments yielded a verdict that was correct by definition. In this case, the verdict was that there could be business, at least temporarily, without a business model.

Andrew redoubled his campaign against registration. At last, on August 4, his arguments triumphed, registration was removed, and HotWired finally joined the web mainstream, in which all material was given away to anonymous users for free. Five days later Julie Petersen was riding on a train back from a meeting in Silicon Valley when she had a premonition, or rather, a clairvoyant receipt of knowledge about an event that had already occurred. When she got back it was confirmed. Jerry Garcia was dead. In South Park, you could get a laugh for a brief period by asking, *What were Jerry's last words,* but the punch line, delivered while clutching your chest—*Netscape opened at what??!!*—was ruined by evening; everybody had heard it. Marc Andreessen's browser company, originally priced at twenty-eight dollars per share, had made its first trade at seventy-one. At this price, the company was worth $2.7 billion, well over twice Walsh's estimate. The market frenzy of August 9 was truly something new, and in the hubbub it created at HotWired Louis's renunciation of his business model, which he had so tenaciously and so wrongly clung to, went unnoticed. No major membership programs were launched, and no detailed user-tracking system was attempted.

August 9, 1995, was a happy day for Carl. Registration was vanquished. Besides, Carl had no affection for the sixties, and he did not care for the groovy type of father figure. Idealists, in his opinion, were hypocrites. He was glad Jerry was dead.

CHAPTER 9

A SHOWER OF MONEY

The Netscape IPO was a thunderclap announcing a shower of money; it also muddied the terrain and made a mess of all strategies planned in advance. But Louis had always thrived upon chaos. It was his special skill, and one for which Carl admired him. Carl's summer had been painful, but by fall things were looking up and winter promised one of those rare happy endings that seem so improbable when a desperate young man shows up in a comic book or movie: genius is rewarded, youth triumphs, et cetera.

The nascent victory of the Internet over established business methods had created a deep bond between Louis and his most devoted employee. At first this bond was felt only by Carl. On the mezzanine floor of 510 Third Street, in a chilly, unfinished space previously occupied by an Asian-import business specializing in tea and now slated for development as the headquarters of a new division of Wired Ventures devoted to publishing books, Louis delivered what he called *the creation myth* to a large gathering of employees. Attendance was mandatory. The purpose of the meeting was doctrinal; or, as Louis preferred, genetic. The conveyance of fundamental beliefs and the narration of formative experiences was known at Wired as a DNA transfer.

In practice, this meant that Louis recounted the story of his and Jane's daring repatriation, their dauntless faith and their refusal to compromise, their many setbacks and their eventual victories. This talk, videotaped for posterity by Steven Overman, Louis's personal assistant, took three hours. During the weeks that followed, Carl used his insomniac hours to watch the video again and again.

What Carl saw in Louis's speech was a step-by-step program for success in the new economy. Louis, at first derided among his professional acquaintances as an oddball, then stigmatized by various onetime helpers and hangers-on as ungrateful, was, with his growing celebrity, reviled among a much larger circle as an arrogant extremist whose radical politics and extravagant claims were simply publicity stunts for a growing business. Louis was no longer merely resented by ex-friends. He was now hated by complete strangers. Carl took this as a great achievement.

The issue of *Wired* that was on the newsstand when Netscape went public had the face of Newt Gingrich on its cover. Inside, Gingrich reported that he had composed his book, *To Renew America,* on his laptop computer, a notable achievement at this early date, when most members of Congress did not type. Gingrich named as intellectual influences a number of writers dear to the magazine's editors, including, along with Alvin and Heidi

Toffler, business guru Peter Drucker and science fiction writer Isaac Asimov. *Wired* stopped short of endorsing this ambitious man—Louis disliked all professional politicians—but the close-up shot of the Georgia congressman's sly face under the masthead signaled the magazine's hope that its probusiness, antigovernment sensibility might be the advance wave of a genuinely popular movement.

The Gingrich assault on Washington and the Netscape IPO were simultaneous and, in a sense, equivalent. Netscape had captured the imagination of investors not merely because millions of people were downloading it to browse the web, but also because it stood in for the Internet itself, and the Internet represented capitalism's power of creative destruction, just as electricity had at the beginning of the twentieth century, and the railroad had in the nineteenth. New productive powers were unleashed, and *Wired* expected them to undermine existing institutions. "The Net," Josh Quittner wrote in his *Wired* profile of the Electronic Frontier Foundation, "is merely a means to an end. The end is to reverse-engineer government, to hack Politics down to its component parts and fix it."

Referring to Al Gore, Newt Gingrich told *Wired:* "He's repainting the den; I want to build a whole new house. My project, frankly, is to replace his world."

This kind of talk made people angry. Political condemnations were issued by familiar adversaries: there was a feminist critique in *Mother Jones,* a liberal critique in *The New Yorker,* an anticonsumerist critique in *The Baffler.* "Tofflerism, as surely as Marxism, is a variant on historical materialism, wrote *The New Yorker*'s Hendrik Hertzberg. He continued:

The apocalyptic three-stage theory of history, the belief in inevitable progress toward ever higher forms of society, the conviction that we, the revolutionaries, know what is best for the masses because we know the laws of history—this is a set of ideas that is not exactly inhospitable to hubris. In the orthodox Marxist version, it led to Stalinism; in a hippie-student version, it led to the excesses that everyone remembers as the worst of the radicalism of the sixties. And there is no obvious reason that those same ideas about history and inevitability and the greater wisdom of those who "get it" should not lead to something unpleasant today—even if, today, the certitudes about three stages and historical inevitability and all the rest can be found on the right and not the left.

The greatest dismay was expressed by competing radicals, who disliked the way *Wired* used revolutionary vocabulary. "*Wired* is technology's hip face, an aggressive apologist for the new information capitalism," wrote Keith White in *The Baffler.* White's article was reprinted in the *Utne Reader* and circulated widely on mailing lists and Internet forums. *Wired,* he continued,

. . . is at once captious doyenne and encouraging confidante to aspiring members of a new, socially insecure elite. *Wired* works, on the most basic level, by tweaking its readers' anxieties, constantly reminding them that they are hopelessly behind the times on the latest developments in technology and underground hacker culture. It simultaneously offers careful instruction in vocabulary, name-dropping, thinking, and purchasing to allow readers to retro-fit their resumes, apartments and lifestyles in a manner more "on-line" with current techno-opportunities. *Wired* then calms advertisers wary of its "phreakish" posturing by penning gooey appreciations of Silicon Valley CEOs and paeans to the macho individualism of your local cable provider.

Normally, business-oriented revolutionaries are too busy banking the proceeds of their so-called sellouts to care about this sort of thing, but Louis was atypical. He cared more about revolution than about money. On the other hand, his theory of revolution put new business in the vanguard. "I'm not walking away from the idea that we are comfortable with change agents at any level of society," he said when he looked over these attacks. "Whether they are engineers and nerds down at the bottom or whether they are people in corporations at the top, or whether they are people like Newt Gingrich: if they are actually provoking change that is part of this large, historical trend, then we talk about them."

Twenty years earlier Marshall McLuhan wrote a letter to the editor of the *Toronto Star* in which he remarked, "There are many people for whom 'thinking' necessarily means identifying with existing trends." This calmly stated observation, by a man who was intimately familiar with corporate futurism, summed up in one sentence the most scathing criticism of *Wired*. But from the inside, things looked different. Everywhere Louis cast his gaze, he saw old institutions holding on to their power. Government still controlled American schools, huge chunks of money were siphoned out of the economy and shoveled down the insatiable maw of the Defense Department, people still turned on their television sets and saw barely a few dozen channels, all of them similar. If *Wired*'s tone was triumphant, it was triumphant in order to buoy the spirits of its vanguard in conflicts that were still to come.

To Carl, Louis seemed to be trying to make his company into a model of the Darwinian system that he envisioned as the ultimate means of social progress. Business solutions at Wired emerged from the natural selection of a few successful projects from many failures. Conventional management, which requires careful planning and top-down authority, might have inhibited the process of extravagant risk out of which real economic value would grow.

Carl took this lesson, which was hidden in plain sight, as the solution to the problem of his ambition. He had long been in a fury of resentment over not being invited to what he thought of as *the high-level meetings* where the company's major decisions were made. After all, he had known that user registration was wrong on the day he arrived. And the idea of planting flags was absurd! HotWired was so inefficient that it barely managed to archive the magazine's back issues online. There were not even decent reports on user traffic. Louis had no business starting a sports channel that cataloged surfing spots all over the world, a travel channel offering hotel recommendations, or a literary channel that reviewed books. But nobody listened to Carl. People thought Carl was just a production monkey. In the end it was only the combined effect of Rick Boyce's panic and Andrew Anker's opportunism—and the public market's enthusiasm for Internet stocks—that changed Louis's mind about registration. Why didn't he just talk to Carl?

Carl had been stewing for months, but by the time he had watched the video for the third time he had cheered up completely. He had figured out a new way to look at it. If the world was a Darwinian game, then the managers who attempted to get Carl to work on their ridiculous projects were predators, and Carl's task was to evade the predators and evolve. After all, what would have happened to Louis had he listened to Jaap van der Meer's ideas about *Language Technology?*

Carl saw that within every business plan lay a hidden opportunity for subversive success, just as there is a seed of parody buried in every romance. The new economy turned the corporate pyramid upside down. The purpose of Wired was not to exploit Carl's talent; rather, the purpose of Carl's talent was to transform the company into an instrument of personal expression. The young man's face was a study in innocence as he expounded his new philosophy to anybody he guessed would be irritated by it.

"Louis is my hero," he said.

After a period of relentless lobbying, Carl gained Chip Bayers's permission to hire an assistant, and from a dead queue of e-mail résumés he resurrected one whose subject line was, *"You can kill yourself..."*

This was a promising beginning, for Carl remained very interested in suicide. The e-mail continued:

... through the practice of auto-erotic asphyxiation, unless you're a character on a Spelling show. In such a case, an explosion involving an exotic motor vehicle works best. But why waste a perfectly good yacht when more subtle methods of attracting attention are at your disposal...

Did you mention something about an editorial, uh, production, uh ... um ... a job? May I assist you with something? ETP (Extra-Value-Meal Transfer Protocol)? Quality

Control? Cranial-Rectal Inversion Detection? Would you care to Super-Size that, sir?

The author of the breathless job request was a twenty-three-year-old ex–comic-book salesman from Puerto Rico named Joseph Anuff. Anuff earned money doing minor project management and animation tasks for local technology companies. HotWired, now firmly established in its role as local savior, appeared to offer something better.

When his new assistant arrived, Carl discovered that he had hired a skinny, histrionic intellectual with dark hair, a high-pitched voice, and a fascination with eliminative functions that expressed itself in an enormous range of vulgar metaphors and colonic euphemisms. Carl had selected Anuff for the job for two reasons. First, Anuff knew a little about the web at a time when most people knew nothing. Second, his résumé displayed a streak of immaturity and an attitude problem that made the applicant slightly less likely than the average so-called *web expert* to skip out on Hot-Wired and join the staff of another new online company whose wages were slightly less miserable.

Anuff, known by everybody as Joey in honor of his amusing puerility, immediately dominated his surroundings at HotWired in a manner that Carl never could. Where Carl's talents were sly and cruel, Joey's were overt and hilarious. Joey acknowledged Carl's superior knowledge of the web and admired his devastating tone of voice. He was eager to introduce him to his brother Ed, for Ed Anuff was still stewing over the ruination of his company on the Vancouver Stock Exchange and his bitterness was exemplary. One day when the weather was decent Joey arranged for Ed and Carl to have coffee together on a bench in South Park.

Carl had been a habitué of computer labs since he was a teenager. Nonetheless, Ed was the palest person he had ever encountered. This gave him a favorable impression right away.

When Carl met him, Ed was depressed. The theft of his fortune had left him at loose ends, and he was living by himself in an apartment building on Post Street not too far from a convenient Kentucky Fried Chicken outlet. Ed also had an account at a reliable pizza vendor, a cable-television subscription, and access to the somewhat sketchy technical documents created by Sun for Java, the new programming language they were promoting. Carl followed Ed back to his apartment, where he saw the pile of crusty old take-out boxes on the floor, and the mounds of open technical manuals, and the dirty clothes on top of everything. "At last," he said to himself, "here is somebody I can truly respect!"

Soon Ed was spending nearly every night at HotWired. When he was tired of pondering nonworking code late at night, he could drive ten minutes to Third Street for company. There was no risk of being disappointed; he would always find Joey and Carl more or less alone in what had become, with the successive knocking down of walls, a very large room. HotWired employed nearly a hundred people now, but most were gone by midnight. Carl and Joey were having fun. They were using their late hours to create what they thought of as "the anti-HotWired."

The days were over when any alert fan of the web could go online and steal "mcdonalds.com." All the words in the dictionary were being snatched up. For example, Procter and Gamble registered "diarrhea.com"; they also took "underarms.com." Hundreds of new websites were being launched, many by major media corporations. There were soap operas and quiz shows and sports-chat pages and the inevitable variety of pornography sites. Millions of dollars, perhaps even tens of millions, were now at stake. Profit, absent any replacement scheme for Louis's failed registration system, was only a distant wish. But with Netscape worth an unfathomable fortune, it made sense to roll the dice.

On August 23, 1995, two weeks after Netscape *went out,* Carl and Joey, with much assistance from Ed, launched a website called Suck. Each daily edition was a page of commentary on recent web-related events, usually published over an inane pseudonym. Joey's rich scatological vocabulary, Carl's deadpan irony, and Ed's schadenfreude and technical knowledge combined to create a style that was more entertaining that anything the web had yet seen. Among their original contributions was an expression of sarcasm by means of links. A word like *community* might link to a marketing survey; *integrity* to a news photo of a well-known man in handcuffs; *trusted mainstream content* to the front door of *Playboy* magazine.

Louis had labored for years to convince people that the digital technology would allow anybody, no matter how underqualified, underfunded, or poorly socialized, to compete on a level playing field with the largest and most professional publishers. Suck set out to confirm this thrilling notion. Suck became the insider's guide to the latest thing, a voice of bad conscience whose exaggerated admiration for success, especially undeserved success, quickly made it more popular than any of the sites HotWired was producing. Carl's goal was to surpass all of the HotWired sites put together.

The site's recurring motif was that by the time you heard of the latest outrageous scam, it was already too late to participate. For example, in early September, barely a week after Suck's debut, the Sucksters obtained a copy of a draft press release announcing that the National Science Foundation would hand over the task of registering Internet domain names to a private company called Network Solutions. Network Solutions planned to charge one hundred dollars for each name and fifty dollars a year for each renewal. There were thousands of new names coming online every month. With the stroke of a pen, Network Solutions now owned this business. *Voilà:* a new set of Internet millionaires.

It took Louis a few weeks to catch on to Suck. The first foreign edition of *Wired* was already falling apart due to myriad conflicts with the British staff, necessitating lengthy absences, and when Louis finally had a chance to spend some time in the HotWired offices that fall he was dismayed by what he found. His company seemed to have devolved into a college dorm. Although he had always encouraged his employees to play loud music while they worked, he still expected them to display a certain level of common sense and respect. There was trash on the floor, toys scattered across the desks, and the faint smell of old bedclothes from the Suck headquarters, where Carl now slept for only an hour or two each night in his bunk bed.

Suck was growing more popular with each leap in the popularity of the web itself. The identity of the Sucksters was a secret. But it had been an axiom of Carl's academic studies that concealment is only a more subtle variety of publicity. The creators of Suck were famous for being unknown, and they passed as leaders by imitating the most credulous dupes.

On October 3 Carl noticed some strange links coming in to his server, and when he followed the trail backward he found an early prototype of a new competitor to HotWired and Suck, launched by Time-Warner. The largest media company in the world, whose flagship magazine, *Time,* was always careful to maintain its balanced skepticism about the Internet, was nonetheless making a play for the web audience with a daily program called the Netly News, edited by Josh Quittner. Afraid of being left behind, other mainstream publishers were also jumping in. In mid-October Condé Nast announced that it had secured more than a million dollars in advance revenue for its soon-to-be-launched websites Epicurious and Condé Nast Traveler, while Levi Strauss and Visa were ponying up a hundred thousand dollars each for banner ads on ESPN's website, called SportsZone. Next, a San Francisco–based cable-television channel devoted to the computer industry, called CNET, announced the beginning of a million-dollar advertising campaign publicizing its recently ramped-up web-content business. The entire sum was going to be spent buying banner ads, which made CNET's announcement a powerful endorsement of both the commercial and the editorial side of the web. A few weeks later some exiles from San Francisco's shrinking newspaper industry went public with a site devoted to literature and current affairs. The site, called Salon, would be supported by Borders Books.

The rush was on, but in no case had any of these newcomers solved the problem Louis had wrestled with earlier in the year.

How, in an environment of rising traffic but increased competition and plummeting banner prices, were the expenses of web publishing to be defrayed? Andrew was bold in his ridicule of his competitors' plans. He predicted a quick cash crisis, followed by a wave of mergers.

The sudden exuberance for web publishing on the part of mainstream corporate-media companies, venture capitalists, and software moguls with more money than sense sent a loud message to the young banker. The boom year of 1995 was coming to a close. In just twelve months the Dow had gained more than 25 percent and now stood above 5,100. The Nasdaq, home of many technology companies, had gained more than 30 percent and ended the year over 1,000. Over 1,000! This was too quick a rise—how long before it sank again? Perhaps it was time to consider a *liquidity event,* Andrew said, but only to a few people he trusted.

Louis saw it differently. The immaturity of his web employees bothered him. But at the same time he recognized that the dispersal of authority and proliferation of strategies inside his web company was an inevitable and healthy result of the digital revolution. As the market testified, such disruptions were happening everywhere. When he thought of the effect of these changes on the great structures of government and corporate power, he took heart. By late October, Louis was reading Suck every day.

During the next few months, major media companies would begin their coverage of the 1996 election campaign. Louis, who predicted that digital technologies were likely to make the United States government obsolete, asked John Battelle, at the magazine, and Chip, at HotWired, to coordinate a new kind of political reporting. To cover the campaign, he hired John Heilemann, who along with writing regular features for *Wired* had been working full-time for *The Economist*. Political coverage was the bastion of the mainstream press, and Louis intended to go at them directly. Cover the election, Louis told his editors, as you would cover a car crash. Treat it as a spectacle, a superannuated tangle of stupidity and ego that you watch with a mix of amusement and horror.

Louis did not blanch at estimates of roughly $200,000 for Heilemann's expenses, plus another $1.8 million for additional editorial and business costs. He called his initiative the Netizen. It would include a section in the magazine, a section on HotWired, and, if the right partner could be found, a weekly television series on a cable station that could be grown into a full-scale television network.

Andrew was concerned about how expensive the Netizen would be. His ideas about Louis were wavering. Sometimes he thought his boss was a visionary, sometimes he thought he was crazy. Louis clung to his arguments even when they contradicted the obvious tendencies of the industry. He had driven HotWired to the brink of failure with his insistence on registration. He did not seem to be interested in taking the company public, despite the fact that the market's enthusiasm for Internet stocks might end any day. But, on the other hand, when Andrew talked with Louis for a while, via e-mail or over the phone, he always gave in, partially convinced and partially bullied and partially just exhausted. In the evenings Andrew read books about famous capitalists, such as Henry Ford, looking for clues. Perhaps they were all like this?

Andrew was willing to take an intelligent risk, but he did not want to be an idiot. He was sure that the Netizen would never make money. However, it would raise their profile, quicken the pace of development, and accelerate the need for some kind of transformative event. The Netizen was sure to bring disaster under ordinary circumstances, but on the other hand, the environment had changed, and the change might not last, and Louis's need for money might be the catalyst of a stupendous finale.

CHAPTER 10

THE ROLL-UP

Wired had always been a place of meetings, and few employees went home at the end of the day. Junior members of the staff drank together at the Eagle Drift-In Lounge, around the corner, while the executives discussed their problems over dinners in nearby restaurants and in after-hours planning sessions that ran late. These ceaseless sessions, informal and without notes, lent a shifty reputation to the company's management. Decisions advocated forcefully in the afternoon were forgotten by sunrise, not superseded by events so much as dissolved in evanescent conversation. Young people would arrive for their first day of work and discover that the jobs they had been hired for no longer existed, but this did not matter, for better jobs had been invented in the interval.

Wherever two or three people gathered—in a conference room, out in the parking lot, on a park bench, at curbside—new theories about how to make money on the web were exchanged. The grass in South Park was tended more carefully now, and on sunny winter days there were hundreds of young people sitting on the lawn during lunch. One day I went so far as to scout the neighborhood, thinking it might be a good idea to open a bar, where, on crowded nights, a corner table might always be kept available for me. Though there were still dozens of empty storefronts in the surrounding blocks, I found nothing. Savvy investors had snatched up all the leases, speculating on a rise.

Meanwhile, down on the Peninsula, Yahoo had been awarded a free link on the Netscape home page, which all new users saw when they fired up their browser. This placement brought them millions of page views, and there were rumors that they would be the next web company to sell shares to the public.

A sense of bonanza coexisted with worry. Andrew had closed HotWired's first financing round just before the Netscape IPO, giving his company seven million dollars in the bank.* But what was HotWired supposed to do with seven million dollars that would turn it into eight million, instead of zero million? Perhaps we should create a new type of free chat system, or offer users their own home pages, or give people e-mail accounts ending in "wired.com," or set up an auction site for people who wanted to

---

* The seven million dollars came from a total of twenty-five large and small investors. The largest amounts came from Burda Digital and Orca Capital; the WPP Group, owner of the J. Walter Thompson and the Ogilvy & Mather advertising agencies, among others; the Pacific Telesis Group, a regional Bell operating company; the Tudor Investment Corporation, run by Paul Tudor Jones, a successful Wall Street investor; and NTT, the Japanese telecommunications firm.

buy and sell domain names. The credibility of each new concept, though it might shoot up precipitously in the morning, would inevitably plummet over the next days and weeks as intractable problems came to light. What kind of advertisers would put their banners on an uncensored site for free chat or free e-mail? On an auction site, how could we guarantee payments? There were scores of good plans for attracting traffic, but what was the business model?

The company's expenses grew out of control, and a whole new layer of executives joined up. To edit the Netizen I recruited a former vice president of the local public-television station, David Weir, who had also been a consultant for Salon. For the new health channel, I found an experienced magazine editor named Steven Petrow. To produce expanded entertainment programming, I called on a friend, Michael Small, formerly of *People*. Chip shocked the few remaining communitarians in the company by purchasing the name pop.com for the entertainment site for ten thousand dollars. "I could have registered hundreds of URLs, but I considered it immoral," marveled Dave Thau, one of HotWired's engineers. Thau's philosophy, back at the dawn of the Internet era one year earlier, had been that no one should register more names than he was likely to use.

Jane was dismayed every time she ventured over to HotWired from her office on the magazine side of the hall. She doubted the wisdom of this rapid growth. The number of employees was doubling every few months. She saw strangers everywhere, people who were not eager to talk to her about what they were doing. Some of them didn't even know who she was. While there were strong leaders at the magazine who reported to her—the advertis-

ing department, circulation, and accounting divisions all had professional managers—leadership at HotWired was chaotic. All any-
one talked about was "planting flags." Louis was relentless on this
topic. Rather than have the same fight again and again, Jane put
her main creative energy into overseas deals for the magazine. Besides England, there was a license for a *Wired* edition in Japan,
and plans for Germany and Brazil. Though her travel schedule
was brutal, and her battles with the staff of *The Guardian* exhausting, she at least felt more in control of her destiny when she
was away.

Andrew tried out his new strategy for dealing with his boss's
ambitions. Confronted by a detailed, two-million-dollar budget
proposal for the Netizen, he made a show of opposition, then accepted with a wave of his hands. Meanwhile, Louis recruited his
old colleague Peter Rutten to run a new book-publishing company, called HardWired, and he put John Battelle in charge of in-
vestigating opportunities in retail sales and television. HotWired's
head count passed 120.

Web traffic remained low. Nonetheless, the lack of enthusiasm
displayed by actual visitors to the HotWired website mattered little when the majority of potential customers were locked out for
other reasons: they did not yet own a computer, or if they had one,
they didn't have an online service, or if they had an online service,
it was walled off from the Internet, or if it was not walled off, it
made users pay by the minute, which discouraged browsing. Researchers from Morgan Stanley estimated that at the end of 1995
only 9 million people worldwide had web access, about 35 million
had e-mail access, while more than 140 million used a personal
computer. The potential for growth was huge.

HotWired, therefore, had two audiences: the audience of today and the audience of the future; the growing number of web users, on one hand, and another, much larger group of people who had heard of the web and perhaps even seen it once or twice but were not yet online. In creating a place for them, and publicizing that place, HotWired became both a medium and a symbol of that medium. The site's inaccessibility was part of its allure. AOL users— all four million of them—still could not browse the web.

Louis's magazine had a similar double existence. *Wired*'s status as the defining document of the Internet era gave it the luxury of publishing lengthy features that would never have appeared in a glossy monthly in ordinary times: thousands upon thousands of words of colorful reporting on the origin of the Java programming language, on the battle between the Church of Scientology and its critics over posting church documents on the net; on pirate software markets in Asia; on high-bandwidth asynchronous transfer-mode technology; and on how the *Star Trek* scripts are written, with tips on how to submit them yourself. The issues published in the months after Netscape went public swelled to more than 250 pages, and the circulation passed 300,000. At the same time there were indications that *Wired,* like a prizewinning novel or a weighty political biography, was one of those influential publications that are discussed by more people than purchase them, and purchased by more people than read them. In the words of Hunter Madsen, a Harvard Ph.D. who had written a dissertation on public opinion and had an expert familiarity with the history of propaganda, *Wired* was "a hazing brand." Madsen was an executive at J. Walter Thompson, the famous advertising firm, and Louis was thinking of hiring him to become Wired's director of marketing.

"Right now," said Madsen during their first meeting, "businessmen around the country are buying *Wired* magazines for their office waiting rooms. The magazines sit there, radiating their dangerous Day-Glo colors and signaling that this executive has crossed the chasm to the future." Perhaps they did not read every page, or any page; nonetheless, they wanted *Wired* in their lives.

The double nature of *Wired* and HotWired's reception was mirrored inside the company, where there was a schism among executives. Andrew, who knew that projects like the Netizen could never pay for themselves, was creating the shell of a business to which innocent onlookers could attach their fantasies of the future. He looked forward to a day in the near future when these fantasies would be translated into cash. Louis's purpose, as always, was to provide real leadership to a real vanguard. Their conflict was bound to cause innumerable small crises, which fed on one another and created an atmosphere of panic. Was our goal to gain traffic as quickly and cheaply as possible in a convincing simulation of real growth? Or was it to build a media enterprise beloved by readers that would someday be profitable? The former, since it involved no business model, ought to have been easier than the latter, but it required formidable nerve.

HotWired had combatted Infoseek's price war by a simple expedient. The home page had never had advertising. Even Andrew thought that banners on the home page might be going too far. "Does *The New York Times* have ads on its front page?" he asked rhetorically. But Louis understood the seriousness of the situation, and suddenly the home page had three small banners, side by side. This instant production of triplets, combined with an increase in traffic after the demise of registration, lowered the price from $700 to about $150 per thousand, and Rick Boyce was able to hang on to his customers.

One evening late in the fall, Carl asked Ed what he thought Andrew had in mind when he let drop hints—entirely calculated, Carl figured—about an *exit strategy*. Carl wondered how Andrew intended to benefit from the crazy expenditures. He must have something up his sleeve.

They argued about the problem all night. Soon afterward, they posted their conclusions on Suck. In an essay that claimed to answer the age-old question of "whether you should really leave 'alphanumerical filing skills' on your resume," an anonymous correspondent for Suck, writing under the name Corporate Lackey, offered a glimpse of the future:

> Brewster Kahle of WAIS, Inc. often jokes at his speaking engagements, "The only real way to make money on the Web is to sell your company." It may be more caveat than bon mot, but it's a truism for Mr. Kahle and many other former owners of companies quickly being swallowed by the ever-expanding America Online corporation.

Brewster Kahle's WAIS, which stood for Wide-Area Information Search, was one of the pioneering search companies. AOL bought WAIS in May. In June it bought another San Francisco company, called Global Network Navigator—one of the first web directories. Everybody would start making indices and directories now, Suck predicted. These were dumb, easy ways to collect traffic. And if the Internet was unlikely to be able to support dozens or hundreds of Yellow Pages, well, that's where AOL came in.

Why was AOL buying these companies? AOL's revenue derived almost entirely from by-the-minute online charges, and these were clearly threatened by the popularity of the web, which could be accessed via any number of low-cost providers who charged flat-rate monthly fees. If you made a traditional analysis based on business models, AOL was doomed. But the purchase of WAIS and GNN were nonetheless aimed at preparing the company for the day when its users were mainly interested in web access. And the currency AOL used to make these purchases was not cash siphoned from their user fees but rather shares of their skyrocketing stock.

AOL had gone public at $11.50 a few years earlier. In the past twelve months it had split two-for-one twice, and now it hovered at around $60 per share. A sale to AOL gave smaller web companies instant access to cash—that is, liquidity—while the purchase of smaller web companies assured the stock market that AOL was not going to be left behind, thus contributing to an increase in the price of the company's shares. Both sides benefited, at least temporarily. CompuServe was scouting for web properties, as was Prodigy.

Suck's theory was quickly confirmed, at least as it applied to themselves. The secret of Suck's anonymous authorship was blown by Josh Quittner at the Netly News, and as soon as their e-mail addresses became public, queries about buying them out began to arrive by phone and e-mail. Suddenly, Carl and Joey found themselves contemplating the possibility of abandoning Wired for a new corporate master. Carl liked the idea of a scorched-earth send-off that would enrage his colleagues, but on the other hand Suck was built in an atmosphere of chaos and improvisation, of brilliance combined with incompetence, of cynicism balanced by an almost blind hope in a miraculous payoff. They needed a special kind of owner, and Andrew quickly made them an offer. On November 21, in what would become the classic insider's essay on the dawn of the web boom, Joey, writing for all the Sucksters, lorded it over their readers.

The title of that day's piece was "The Suck New Media Autopsy":

Some things we thought you might like to know:
1. Suck is now a subsidiary of HotWired.
2. Suck is hiring.
3. Suck has some tips for would-be media jackrobbers.
It just ain't fair.

You sit on the digital sidelines, shaking your head in resigned horror as the Web derails with the momentum of an Arizona train wreck, from promising social experiment to bleak corporate welfare state. As you rub your eyes and pinch yourself to verify the irreality you see, the thought dawns on you: with all that luscious lucre slithering across palms and winding its way into Swiss bank accounts, what if there were opportunities for someone like you to play in the same economic sandbox as the new media Snuffleupagi?

The trick is to put down your crusty bong for ten minutes and draw up some sort of plan. The good news is that once your outline's been hashed out, you may actually be able to sell that—no further work required. . . . But if schmoozing vulturous creeps isn't your preferred modus operandi—and you have some time and a modicum of ability on your hands—your best bet might be to take the initiative and develop your idea yourself.

The Sucksters' advice was to fluff up a site, locate a rich, stupid buyer, and then run away fast before the concoction deflated. From the sound of it, you would think Carl and Joey had received a million dollars, at least. The least speck of idealism was understood to be ruinous:

Never lose sight of your ultimate goal: cash. There will come a time of reckoning, when you need to struggle or sell. Friends, you can't bank on net cred. Sell. Sell early and often. Rinse. Repeat. Now that you feel all dirty, you'll undoubtedly want to do it again.

In fact, Andrew had made them a terrible offer; less than thirty thousand dollars in cash. The noncash portion consisted of shares in HotWired LLC. But Andrew gave Carl and Joey enough information about his plan for the company's future to enable them to *connect the dots* and *do the math on the upside.*

The purchase of Suck functioned as a warm-up. The real value was elsewhere.

After six years of almost no pay, Louis and Jane had at last given themselves a reasonable salary, and they purchased a tiny Craftsman bungalow above Strawberry Canyon, with a view to the west partially obstructed by a giant evergreen. The road up to their house was so steep most people were afraid to drive on it, and the path to their front door traversed a beautiful hill of oaks. At the beginning of January 1996, Louis and Jane asked Andrew and a number of other close associates to join them at their Berkeley home, where they would discuss how to accept the great challenges of the boom.

Besides Andrew, the participants included John Battelle, Kevin Kelly, board member and Global Business Network cofounder Lawrence Wilkinson, and John Kao, a business consultant who had sometimes advised Louis and Jane on corporate strategy. Also present were Bill Jesse, the board member who had raised the company's first round of capital, and Kenn Guernsey, the company's outside legal counsel. John Plunkett and Barbara Kuhr, who could always be counted upon to balk at any bold scheme, were not invited. To advise on accounting and investment details, Louis had two chief financial officers: Rex Ishibashi, who worked for Wired Ventures, and Jeff Simon, whom Andrew had hired to handle the books for HotWired.

Rex, who was sociable and confident, had made a list of all the projects currently contemplated by Wired and HotWired. This list was copied and distributed in binders three inches thick. Plans included multiple foreign editions, new ideas for magazines, a television program that broadcast the Netizen's message, a publishing house for books, and, of course, a dramatic expansion of web-based programming. Rex had compiled this list to force some hard choices upon Louis and Jane, who did not have enough money to do everything at once. But Louis's ambitions were vast, and the task of financing the company's future was quickly transformed at this meeting into a simple matter of addition. The projected cost of all the contemplated projects, summed, was fifty-six million dollars. The question became not how to prioritize these many projects but rather, as Rex later put it: "How can we acquire this much money while still keeping control safely in the founders' hands?"

Andrew offered his solution in a nonchalant manner that allowed listeners to approach it at their own pace. The key word, that winter, in conversations about an Internet company's value on the public markets, was *multiple*. In banking, *multiple* was used to express the value of a company in relation to some key measure of its business. The most popular benchmark was the P/E ratio, where *P* stood for the price of the company's shares, and *E* stood for its earnings—that is, its profits. When, in January 1996, bankers spoke of Netscape's multiple, this was the sort of operation they had in mind, except that Netscape's profits were zero, and zero cannot be the divisor of any fraction. Therefore, instead of profits, bankers used revenues—the amount of money flowing into the company regardless of the amount of money flowing out. By this measure Netscape had a multiple of sixty.

The Netscape multiple was available only to an Internet company. Though *Wired* magazine had more than twenty million dollars in revenue during 1995, magazine values were governed by more conservative equations: three times yearly revenue would have been a stretch. Meanwhile, HotWired's revenues for 1995 were only a few million, and no matter what sort of fantastic Internet multiple was applied, its value would barely top a hundred million. If they funded the two parts of the company separately, they would have to sell a third or even more to get their fifty-six million—far too much to guarantee control to the founders.

But Andrew had been talking with a banker who worked for one of HotWired's investors, and the two of them figured that if HotWired was merged back into Wired, the whole enterprise could be pitched as an Internet company with more than twenty million dollars in 1995 revenue and a projected forty million in 1996 revenue. Multiply by some modest fraction of the Netscape multiple—say, by twenty—and the total valuation for the combined companies would be at least four hundred million dollars; thus, Wired could get away with selling only 10 to 15 percent.

The plan to combine the companies was called *the roll-up*. The roll-up would take the two opposing dimensions of Wired's business—the millions in magazine revenue, and the glittering future of the Internet—and make from them a third, far more valuable entity in which reality and dreams were intermixed. Andrew acknowledged that success would depend upon a certain mental pliability on the part of investors.

"This is a concept offering," he said. "The Netscape market is a psychological market, not a financial market. The only question is, how long does it last?"

His boss was not fooled. "His interest was so transparent," said Louis later. HotWired's shareholders overlapped with Wired's, but they were not the same. While the magazine was generating a lot of cash, HotWired was not. An IPO would take the pressure off Andrew, make his personal shares easily translatable into real money, and reward his investors quickly.

All the same, Louis liked the idea. The cost of capital on the public markets was low. Wired needed cash to expand, and the enthusiasm for Internet stocks was a threat as well as an opportunity. Other web companies were lining up to go public. They would be collecting money from Wall Street and coming right back at him to compete.

Andrew made sure to respect Louis's idea that his business would eventually flourish. "This is not about cashing out," he said. "It's about using the proceeds to build our company."

An IPO would take six to eight months. What would they do in the meantime? Bill Jesse suggested an intermediate or *mezzanine* financing round from private investors whose shares would convert to common stock when the IPO happened later in the year.

"Is there any way to expand at this rate without an IPO?" asked Kevin Kelly. He had never expected Wired to become a public company.

"HotWired is a rocket ship without fuel," Rex answered. "We're already operating like we have fifty million dollars in the bank."

"It all comes down to what Louis and Jane want," said Bill Jesse calmly.

Jane had been going full bore for eight years. "Our personal life was kaput," she later said. After the success of Wired, she and Louis had hoped to start a family, but their attempts to grow and finance the company always seemed to push this dream off into the distant future. "If I could live my life the way I want," Jane told the secret IPO group, in an outburst of frankness, "my living room would be filled with a lot more nice furniture and a lot fewer employees."

This was hardly the way to talk; it made the financing solution appear to be motivated by self-interest. Andrew summed up the discussion as casually as ever. "Let's do the mezzanine," he said, treating the debate as closed, "and take our time on the IPO."

The IPO project was named *Bengal,* in honor of Louis's comparison of the digital revolution to a Bengali typhoon. Rex agreed to lead the mezzanine round, but he had no desire to remain chief financial officer of Wired Ventures, as the combined company would be known, during the IPO phase. There was a top-level shuffle during the merger, and Jeff Simon—well organized, trustworthy, and quietly nervous—took control of the finances.

To Kevin the decision was an anticlimax. What he felt was not enthusiasm, he would later say; "it was surrender."

About a week after the IPO meeting, the number of HotWired employees made another leap. There would soon be nearly 150. An old brick building a block away was leased to house the growing enterprise. It contained forty-two thousand square feet, and would, if built out as planned, have a state-of-the-art commissary, a recording studio, and even sleeping capsules for people who worked late and didn't want to go home. Meanwhile, the word from the operations people was: *compress.* The only extra room in the office was over in the corner, where Louis kept a second desk. In the early months of 1996 this desk was frequently empty, as Louis tended to other responsibilities. For instance, the *Wired* U.K. edition was failing; constant disagreements with *The Guardian* and a poorly managed office had led to low circulation and a demoralized staff. The relationship with *The Guardian* was irreparably broken. Jane spent nearly all her time in London now. After months of wearying negotiations, Louis and Jane concluded that

Wired would shoulder the start-up's debts and carry on independently. Preparations for the IPO also required close attention.

The more Louis was away, the more Carl resented his absence.

"Here's your new desk, Ed," said Carl one day, guiding his friend over to the corner and sitting him down in front of the monitor that, to his extreme annoyance, was so rarely turned on. "You might want to change the phone message," Carl added.

Carl had played this trick on new employees before; it was designed to climax when Louis returned and violently reclaimed his property. Ed had just been officially hired, but he'd been hanging around the office for months and knew better than to go along. Besides, his time for goofing off was limited, as Andrew had hired him to quickly invent a search engine, with the goal of boosting Wired's traffic in advance of the IPO.

Ed made a good partner for Andrew. He was technically expert and resolutely opposed to idealistic time-wasting. Ever since the purchase of Suck, he believed himself to be clearly informed about his new boss's exit strategy, and he planned to follow Andrew's instructions to the letter.

There was a feeling that the clock was ticking, of a race against time. The price of banner ads was collapsing. HotWired was still attempting to charge $150 per thousand impressions, while the search engines were pushing prices below $20 per thousand. The staff of CNET, HotWired's rival website across town, were hard at work on a Yahoo-style directory.

HotWired's advertising revenues barely rose from the third to the fourth quarter of 1995. Average monthly revenue was less than $200,000 during this period—and HotWired was ranked sixth on the web. This was not the stuff out of which great industries were made.*

* This comparison is inexact because taken from two different sources. The HotWired revenue number comes from internal financial reports and is actual third- and fourth-quarter net advertising revenues. The rankings are derived from estimates by Forrester Research based on surveys conducted in October and November, assuming no discounts, and counting all advertising as paid and booked in the month it appears. The rankings as reported by Forrester were:

1.	Netscape	$1.8 million
2.	Lycos	$1.3 million
3.	Infoseek	$1.2 million
4.	Yahoo	$1.1 million
5.	Time-Warner's Pathfinder	$0.8 million
6.	HotWired	$0.7 million
7.	WebCrawler	$0.7 million
8.	ESPNet Sportszone	$0.6 million
9.	GNN	$0.6 million
10.	CNET	$0.5 million

The difference between HotWired's actual revenue and the revenue reported by Forrester suggests that the method was too loose to accurately distinguish between the bottom six sites, whose reported revenue ranges from $.5 to $.8 million, or between the second, third, and fourth sites, whose revenues range from $1.1 to $1.3 million. A coherent picture emerges nonetheless: the leader was Netscape, default home page of everybody who downloaded the browser. Then came the search engines and directories, more or less tied at $1.1 to $1.3 million, and then the top content sites, more or less tied at $.5 to $.8 million. Since discounts were common in the industry, all the Forrester estimates are probably somewhat high. HotWired, listed at $.7 million (the reality was $534,213), was booking a typical amount of ad revenue. Part of this, however, was due to the prestige of *Wired* magazine and the sales skills of Rick Boyce and his staff, who

The idea of a Wired search engine did not sit well with Beth Van-derslice, who used all of her levelheaded charm to dissuade Andrew and Louis. She repeated the famous axiom of Jack Welch, the head of General Electric, who said that companies should avoid wasting resources on endeavors unlikely to lead to a first- or second-place position in the market. HotWired, Beth thought, was too far behind.

Of course Andrew's aim had nothing to do with Jack Welch's philosophy of business. The split between perception and reality, so difficult to manage at Wired, touched every company in the Internet industry, even the best. For the week of February 15, 1996, Marc Andreessen was on the cover of *Time* magazine. The editors posed him barefoot on a throne, with the palm of his hand pressed against his cheek and the cuffs of his jeans turned up. The headline read:

THE GOLDEN GEEKS

THEY INVENT. THEY START COMPANIES.

AND THE STOCK MARKET HAS MADE THEM

INSTANTAIRES.

But Netscape's browsers were still available for free, and so were the new browsers from Microsoft, and that same week, at Richard Saul Wurman's TED conference in Monterey, California, an AOL executive named Ted Leonsis looked out over the packed hall and pointed out that web development was being conducted as a non-

---

were getting the highest CPM of all the sites listed. Even so, each new HotWired site lost money at this CPM, and the CPMs were falling.

profit enterprise. People were connecting for nothing from their schools and offices. The websites gave their content away for free. Netscape and Microsoft handed out browsers for free. For there to be a business there, somebody there had to be doing business!

Ed, who was in the audience, admired this speech. He loved a good, honest diatribe. A few days later, writing under the name Strep Throat, Ed gave Ted Leonsis a hearty welcome to the Suck universe:

> Content producers, in Leonsis's view, need to wake up, turn off the Java, and smell the coffee. Web publishing needs to be a vocation, not an avocation. . . . "These aren't websites, these are gravesites!" the big man tells us, offering an opinion we've been known to embrace ourselves.
>
> "Where's the money?" he rants on. People aren't paying to get on the net—most access is paid for by work or schools, and when users foot their own bills, it's usually some ridiculous flat fee. Where's the money?! People aren't paying hourly connect charges. Can't anyone see how wrong this is, Ted implores, and then begs us to help him put an end to this madness. Browsers given away free! Servers given away! No one's making any money here!

Ed wrote that he would like to make Leonsis an honorary Suckster for his dazzling insights, but the funny thing was—Suck praise aside—Leonsis's speech convinced nobody. Boosters pointed out that his company had an ulterior motive in his attack on webonomics. Though AOL benefited from a rising stock price, it was nonetheless attempting to make money in a traditional fashion.

AOL members, in early 1996, still paid for access by the minute. Using AOL was like making a long-distance telephone call. The more of their services you used, the more revenue the company banked. Somebody who spent two or three hours a night on AOL got a bill at the end of the month for more than two hundred dollars. This overly rational business style was allowing competitors to grab market share by aggressive giveaways. No wonder Leonsis hated the web.

In the spring of 1996, HotWired's burn rate was nearly five hundred thousand dollars per month. Andrew showed no signs of worry, but Beth was concerned; each new initiative launched by Louis and Andrew only increased the company's risk. Until now, it had always been possible to shift responsibility for business or operational failures at HotWired sideways or downward. Louis criticized Andrew for his loose style; Andrew pushed managerial responsibility onto Beth; Beth abhorred the business directors of the various websites, who were unable to keep costs down and develop new revenue sources; the business directors marveled at my reckless and disorganized hiring; while Chip reviled the engineering management, and the producers—the ones who were actually *planting flags*—were punished by everybody. The extreme-sports site, for instance, was by now a dismal and expensive failure, and during Louis's extended absence it was canceled and its young manager sacked. But mounting losses threatened to reverse the flow of blame, and Beth thought that senior executives would inevitably be called to account.

One day, when Beth was alone with Ed in the elevator, she begged him to give her the benefit of his wise counsel. Should Wired really be getting into this search-engine business? She worried that Ed might be blamed for a failure that was not his own. She told him he was one of the smartest people in the company. His intelligence was a key asset, and she did not want it to be wasted. Perhaps it would be better to resist Andrew's commands.

Beth's appeals were entirely lost on the young programmer. His extreme awkwardness neutralized her influence, and her flattery only startled him and made him suspicious. Also, he did not understand her business strategy. Beth seemed to assume that her job was to back up Wired's outrageous pronouncements with enormously profitable and popular products. Had she never read Suck? There were no profitable products on the web.

Ed much preferred being around Andrew, who, once he was sure of Ed's sympathy, allowed himself to be openly and honestly craven. Andrew was always talking about the tactics of deal making: who called whom, and how to get the other person to name the price. "Then, when they name the price," said Andrew, "always scoff."

Andrew treated business as a game. Ed's experiences had given him reason to believe this was how all real players looked at things, but nobody had ever invited him into the inner circle before. So what if HotWired was not likely to have the first-place or the second-place or even the third-place search engine? They were not going to build it themselves anyway. Ed and Andrew's idea was to find a partner, slap their name on somebody else's technology, grab as much ownership as their partner's ignorance permitted, and start posting some of that traffic.

Ed soon located a perfect victim. A Berkeley college professor named Eric Brewer, along with a graduate student named Paul Gauthier, had developed an ingenious method for indexing websites. Hoping to commercialize it, they formed a small company called Inktomi. Negotiations with Inktomi were easy. Ed loved being part of them. They hacked out the financial details via conference call. Andrew liked to press the mute button and look at Ed and say: "Just listen to this; they're going to say something completely stupid." Then he would take his finger off the button, listen for ten seconds, and reject the Inktomi proposal out of hand.

The structure of the deal was not a problem. Inktomi would build and operate the search engine; Wired would design the interface and sell the ads. Since Wired was merely handling marketing and sales, Inktomi proposed a seventy-thirty revenue split, in their favor. After several days of belittlement, Inktomi dropped the demand to sixty-forty. Andrew, in a half-weary, half-angry voice, said, "Fine, but then you pay sixty percent of the marketing costs."

According to the terms of the deal, Wired would gain two fifths of a search company as, more or less, an ad-sales commission. Moreover, Wired would own the web address, locking Inktomi into the partnership. Moreover, after giving up 40 percent of gross revenue, Inktomi would pay more than half of Wired's marketing costs. Ed felt a little bit sorry for the Inktomi guys, but not too sorry. It was all part of growing up. They would eventually learn how business worked, just as he had.

The technical labors were assigned to Inktomi, while Ed's attention was focused on publicity, design, choosing a name, and pressing HotWired's partner to make an early launch date that would justify the inclusion of the search engine in HotWired's pitch to investors. Inktomi, with its own sights set on instant riches, was also eager to show revenues as soon as possible. They believed that their search technology would allow them to offer the largest index of Internet documents yet created, and Paul Gauthier asked Ed to give them a sense of how much money they were going to make.

"Andrew, Paul wants financial projections," said Ed.

Andrew had already briefed Ed on this topic, and he felt it was time for his protégé to spread his wings and fly on his own.

"I believe in you," said Andrew to Ed. "You can handle this one."

The phone rang and Ed picked it up. It was Paul, asking again for the numbers. "Hmmm," Ed said. "I can see a number of scenarios. If you guys can deliver on the largest search engine, well, *you do the math*. Look at the other search engines. They are doing millions of pages a day. Look at our cost per thousand—we have the highest in the industry. We are talking about a lot of money here."

He held this line, encouraging but noncommittal, under increasing pressure for weeks. He was practicing his sleight of hand: HotWired's high ad rates were based on the fact that they were not a search engine but an elaborate editorial site with—presumably—loyal readers. They could hardly maintain these rates on their search engine. At this point, however, both parties were bluffing, for Inktomi was committed to delivering a search engine that did not yet exist. Andrew was warmly congratulatory and gave Ed a pat on the back.

The working name of the project was HotSearch, which Louis felt was unmemorable and lacked brio. The cover of the April issue of *Wired* proclaimed: BOTS ARE HOT! The story was about personal-information services that monitored the Internet and automatically retrieved just what you wanted. "Call it HotBot," suggested Susanna Camp, nicknamed Scamp, the manager of HotWired's chat space.

"That's just dumb," Ed answered.

But that afternoon there was the usual champagne toast to celebrate the Bots Are Hot! issue, and with the good cheer of the party pervasive, Ed felt free to joke around a little with his boss. "Scamp thinks we should call it HotBot," he murmured to Louis, with one of his soft, mock-hopeless laughs. He was surprised by the response he got. "HotBot is like Yahoo!" Louis said, repeating the name over and over. "Everybody will remember it. Nobody will misspell it."

The name HotBot struck the Inktomi engineers as childish and disrespectful. "They're threatening to quit if you call their search engine HotBot," Paul Gauthier told Ed.

Inktomi's pain decided the question. Andrew had been uncertain, but he now loved "HotBot" beyond measure. "I am not going to take marketing advice from engineers," he said, looking delighted. Even though Andrew made Ed's life difficult, Ed admired his jollity and competitive spark.

Ed was doing his best on HotBot, but his progress was halting. All spring, Inktomi's search engine had been either inoperable or very slow. Beth's warnings to Ed became severe. She was holding him responsible for success. "There is no need to push this forward if it's not ready," Beth said. She felt that if the HotBot launch went poorly, it would wreck everybody's reputation.

Ed resolutely ignored her. The stock market was in love with directories and search engines. In February and March three of them filed for IPOs: Lycos, Excite, and Yahoo. Ed mounted a prepublicity campaign that included interviews with every major computer magazine and many mainstream publications. The news he offered the press was: Wired's search engine indexes fifty million documents—the most on the web.

By mid-April, Ed found himself standing alone against a crowd of persecutors.

"How about if we launch with thirty million documents?" Eric Brewer suggested.

"That would not be the most documents, now, would it?" said Ed, displaying his frustration. "We cannot exactly launch under the slogan 'The Least Documents.' "

Boy, was Ed in trouble. The launch was scheduled for Monday, May 20. The day arrived, and there was still no HotBot. There were going to be stories the next morning in *The New York Times* and *The Wall Street Journal.* Andrew, out of town, called Ed to check in. Andrew was unconcerned. "Hey," he said, "we didn't say what time on Monday!"

Beth had a different take. "This does not have to launch, Ed," she said. She gave him a last chance to back out. "If you're worried, you can always stop it." She passed on the bad news to Louis and Andrew.

They ignored her. Louis frequently came by to see about Ed's progress, but every time Ed saw the company's founder he picked up the phone and pretended to be talking to somebody on the other end. Joey and Carl bothered him more.

"You are *saving the company,*" Carl said in his cruelest tone. Ed rested his face on his hands.

Very late that night, HotBot appeared. Ed went home. The next morning HotBot was still up, but it was painfully slow. Hundreds of thousands of users tried to access it. Most failed. It was the company's most public disgrace yet.

Andrew was calm. Beth was livid. She had been observing Andrew's pleasure in his own expert generalship with consternation. To her, HotBot was the natural consequence of a careless, overly rapid expansion. Louis believed himself to be building a real business, but his revolutionary style and insatiable ambition blinded him to the limits of the instruments—human and technical—he had at hand. Meanwhile, Andrew collaborated in the construction of these string-and-sealing-wax pseudoproducts that were good only for attracting publicity—and not always positive publicity, either. Beth's name for the search engine was HotBotch. According to what she had learned in business school, these sorts of mistakes were unforgivable.

During the next weeks Ed was the constant butt of jokes and criticism. More than a month went by before Wired and Inktomi's joint efforts uncovered the source of the problem with HotBot, which had been hard to unravel because it consisted of two unrelated bugs. When both were straightened out, everybody got a surprise. The traffic was unbelievable. It was huge. It dwarfed anything HotWired had ever done, and every day it increased. For the first time, Wired could compete with the major advertising-supported search engines that had passed it by.

Ed's idea was that the company had been saved. Beth's idea was that Ed should be fired. She stated her opinion selectively. Maneuvering among the conflicting requirements of Louis, Andrew, and an anarchic, dissatisfied staff, HotWired's president began to display a talent for leadership under the most difficult conditions. She had great poise, and she kept a wary eye on Louis, never acting on one of his demands until it was repeated often enough to convince her it would not dissipate naturally, without action. She never developed any hatred for him, because her natural reserve saved her from expressing assent she did not feel. Nor did she openly get in his way, because she could see there was no hope of internal reform. She simply waited for the next phase. After the company finally sold shares to the public, it would come under scrutiny from government regulators, financial analysts, and the press. There would be, at last, external parties who had an interest in their performance. Such scrutiny was likely to result in a change in management. For the first time, Beth began to look forward to the IPO.

On April 12 Yahoo had issued its first shares to the public. The starting price was $13, the opening trade was at $25.25, and the closing price was $33. More astounding was the implied valuation of the company. At the offering price, it had been $944 million. At the closing price, Yahoo had a valuation of nearly $2.4 billion. Andrew was not the only person to run his index finger over a calculator in the following weeks. The magic Netscape multiple had been sixty; the Yahoo multiple was eight hundred. With numbers this out of whack, no formula was trustworthy. Still, Wired's attempt to claim a value of $500 million on about $27 million in revenue looked positively sober by comparison.

The distance that had once existed between Louis and Andrew began to shrink. Louis wanted to grow the next century's most important media organization. Andrew aimed at realizing shareholder value through a terrific liquidity event. Each saw the other's desires as a subsidiary element in his own plans. Around the same time that Wired's IPO was announced, Jane let a few friends know she was pregnant. The timing seemed right. The company would go public in midsummer, providing an infusion of cash and giving her six months to hand off her front-line responsibilities to newly hired professionals before the baby came at the end of the year.

HotWired's harried employees soon noticed that all the executives were suddenly displaying a new unanimity and accord. Every element seemed to come together now, with surprising neatness. Louis in his madness or mad prescience had steered his companies into the most dangerous waters, far beyond any margin of self-rescue, and his timing was perfect, because a general madness, like the buildup of a Pacific swell, was lifting every vessel in the vicinity. He had only to get pointed right and head for shore. Once the IPO came in, everything would be sorted out: Louis rich and sovereign; *Wired* locked in its regular rhythms; HotWired reorganized and reformed by Beth; the Netizen carrying the message to the masses; and a host of European and South American editions chiming in with familiar yet exotic voices, like a chorus of foreign cousins. All spring the wave mounted, and Wired hung on its face.

—

CHAPTER 11

SINCERITY

Next came a number of small delays. The dizzying speed at which hundreds of Internet businesses had sprung up and thrived—assuming a ream of printed stationery as evidence of health—had given rise to a popular figure of speech that compared web years to dog years. Both web years and dog years were said to pass seven times more quickly than ordinary years, but what was true of speed was equally true of slowness, and the preparations for Wired's IPO, begun in February, were not completed until the end of May. Just a few months, in human time. Lengthy, interminable seasons, by the accelerated clocks of the boom.

All spring Rex Ishibashi and Jeff Simon worked to restructure the company in preparation for the liquidity event that would transform Wired's theoretical value into negotiable securities by means of the magic multiple. The roll-up had an interesting byproduct. When Wired and HotWired were combined, the executives had to specify in writing how much money each was worth.

Up until now, the value of the two companies had been settled by Louis and Jane in negotiation with their optimistic investors. Once a deal was concluded, the valuation was *fair* by virtue of the free participation of its partners. But a merger was different. The owners of each company were asked to turn in their old shares in exchange for shares in the new enterprise. The minority share-holders, while excluded from direct influence, had a right to re-view the logic that determined the relative value of their stake. Thus, a disinterested third party was hired to produce an opinion exposing the reasoning and testifying to its fairness. The third party was Robertson, Stephens & Company, a major West Coast investment bank.

Robertson, Stephens estimated that as a public company Wired Ventures ought to be worth between $620 and $939 million. As a private company whose shares could not be traded for cash, Wired's value, according to Robertson, Stephens, was subject to a discount of exactly 36.5 percent, leaving a range of $393 to $596 million.

In the wake of the fairness opinion, Rex Ishibashi raised $12.5 million from mezzanine shareholders, who received a little less than 4 percent of the company, implying a valuation of over $300 million. This answered Wired's immediate money needs and also supplied evidence that Wired's predictions were endorsed by pro-fessionals. In reality, however, the mezzanine investors were look-ing to the short-term future, where they saw IPO investors buying at an even higher price. These same IPO investors were meant to check their logic by looking at the past, where, in the eyes of mezzanine investors, they would behold a reflection of their own enthusiasm masquerading as objective support. Both parties thus enjoyed the prospect of an endless vista, like that produced by facing mirrors.*

Simultaneous with the mezzanine round, competing bankers eager to display their talents visited with the Bengal committee and offered to sell shares of Wired Ventures to the public. Louis and Jane chose Goldman Sachs, the most prestigious bank on Wall Street, to be their leading sales agent. But with the arrival of Goldman Sachs, the first tremors of disunity returned. The banker assigned to Louis and Jane was soon reduced to desperate measures.

"Tell him you won't sleep with him," she said to Jane, when she ran out of other approaches. Jane would have tried to help the banker understand the futility of this suggestion, but she hardly knew where to begin.

The problem was that Louis did not accept the Goldman Sachs policy of presenting every initial public offering in a softcover booklet measuring eight and a half by eleven inches, with black text on white paper, narrow margins, and small type. The booklet was technically known as a prospectus, but when Louis saw it he saw a magazine, and a very poorly designed magazine at that. He and John Plunkett had been studying the presentation of written material seriously for more than a decade, and they knew as well as they knew anything that long strips of type running margin to margin were difficult to comprehend. On a wide page, type should always be broken up into columns.

---

* The mezzanine investors included Nippon Telegraph and Telephone, CUC International, Tudor Investment Funds, and Advance Magazine Publishers.

Furthermore, Wired had gone to great lengths to select a typeface that, while perfectly legible, was suitable to the velocity of the
modern world. To use the same typeface that had clogged up every
Goldman prospectus since the time when these dubious documents were hammered into print by turn-of-the century Mergenthaler Linotypes was to betray the very essence of the digital
revolution. Louis insisted on changes, displaying that same soft-
voiced but implacable self-belief that had marked his character
since youth. Goldman would update the prospectus template for
Wired, or Wired would find a new banker that would. Kevin Kelly,
when notified of the crisis, advised Louis to stand firm. He loved it
when something unexpected and passionate occurred, and besides, looking purely at the facts, Louis was right.

The other party in this clash held that Louis had miscategorized
the object of controversy. Not every wafer made from flour and
water was a cracker, and not everything printed on paper and
bound between soft covers was a magazine. The goal was to un-
load shares, not engage readers in a fascinating dialogue about the
future of media.

Andrew agreed. "Feed the ducks while they're quacking," he
said. Internet stocks were popular now. Delay was inadvisable.

Louis insisted on publishing the prospectus with a cover and
overleaf in fluorescent *Wired* colors. Goldman Sachs informed
him that the prospectus was governed by strict rules promulgated
by the Securities and Exchange Commission. The founder of
Wired beat down this excuse with the results of some research he
had his lawyers perform: a letter from the Securities and Exchange
Commission to an inquisitive attorney, dated 1972, that stated:
"This Division will not raise objection if prospectuses which are

printed on colored and/or glazed paper are distributed." Louis, who had not failed in brinkmanship since his *Electric Word* days, was partially victorious. Goldman chose to keep its troublesome client at the expense of minor adjustments in the form of their prospectus. Louis could keep his overleaf and his font, but there would be no columns; instead the width of the prospectus was slightly narrowed.

Jeff Simon, the chief financial officer, negotiated back and forth with sober intensity and almost never made light of the stakes, though to a colleague he admitted, in a rare outburst of fancy: "I feel like a ball of string and Louis is a cat, and I keep hoping that I'll roll under the couch."

But there was a deeper problem: the Goldman Sachs bankers and the Wired executives had trouble specifying what linked all the company's projects together. Wired Ventures was not purely a search engine or web directory, like Excite or Yahoo. It was certainly not a technology company, like Netscape or Inktomi. But it was not a magazine company—or could not be, if the magic multiple were to remain plausible.

"Point of view," Jane insisted, echoing the principles Louis had outlined so many times. "Our business is point of view." The trick was to connect this philosophy to some familiar marketing language that investors would value. Finally, after much discussion, they settled on a trinity of attributes borrowed from firms long worshipped by Wall Street. These attributes were *branding, content,* and *attitude. Branding* was the most traditional word, associated both with Procter and Gamble's valuable household products and with Nike's remarkable marketing campaigns. *Content* was a term that had gained currency among companies operating in several media; it meant information in all its forms. *Attitude* referred to a self-confident and devil-may-care tone of voice: for instance, MTV. Wired, announced the prospectus, was a new type of global media company that sold *branded content with attitude.*

By the time the prospectus was written, Andrew was exhausted. He left for a vacation in Hawaii with his family. Like so many other Wired executives, he was bothered by nearly constant urges to quit his job. How could Louis persist in risking the safety of the company over minor issues, elevating even the most trivial challenges into heart-stopping last minute face-offs, games of chicken, Russian roulette? He just failed to see the humor in it. Nitpicking as a negotiating tactic was more than familiar to him, but Louis was embarrassingly sincere. The unanimity that greeted the announcement of the IPO had been superficial. And now it began to fray.

Andrew's wife asked him to sit tight for a while. His exit strategy was now in its final phase. After the IPO, there would be a six-month holding period when the employees were forbidden to sell their shares. Then it would be over. He just had to hold his breath. Though Andrew was immune to many of the stresses that tormented his subordinates, he shared with them this difficult period of waiting, as if they were underwater together, counting seconds until they could pop up.

The company had gone silent. There were no rousing press releases during the spring, because once a corporation files to issue shares to the public, extraneous publicity is forbidden by law. The prohibition on hype during the run-up to an IPO is known as a "quiet period," and it is enforced by the Securities and Exchange Commission as a way to protect investors from buying shares at a price inflated by the executives' big talk. All the justifications for purchase must be in the prospectus, where they can be examined calmly. Neither Louis nor Jane had realized that an IPO would necessitate public silence. And they chafed under these restrictions.

The only good news about the quiet period was that it would not last long. Jeff expected to receive comments on the draft prospectus from the SEC in about thirty days. There would be a week to make corrections, drop in the financial results from the second quarter, and get the final version printed at an overnight press. In mid-July Jeff, Louis, Jane, and Andrew would review their oral presentations with their banker, then begin a stretch of brutal travel. During the final five days, the Wired team was scheduled to run through their slides and answer questions in Minneapolis, Chicago, Kansas City, Denver, Philadelphia, Baltimore, Boston. The road show would end in New York, where, on Thursday, August 1, Wired's stock would appear on the Nasdaq exchange, represented by the symbol WWWW.

During this time their company proceeded to fall apart. The magazine held up the best, as it was staffed by now with editors and designers who had witnessed every sort of melodrama, and it had earned the respect of advertisers. The June issue, finished in April, had a photo illustration of a pudgy Bill Gates floating on a yellow inflatable raft in an brilliant blue pool beneath a fuschia-and-yellow *Wired* logo that looked like it was pulsing with reflections from the sun. Inside was a detailed report on Microsoft's massive new investments in media businesses. The issue was more than two hundred pages thick, with more than a million dollars in billable ads. But still no issue escaped without at least one blood-curdling conflict, no issue made it to the press on time, and no issue got in and out of Louis's office without last-minute, peremptory, and frequently contemptuous alterations. John Battelle, who had been an effective leader of the editorial staff, was preoccupied with creating new projects and no longer functioned as a shield.

The circulation department was an isolated kingdom of its own. Louis had remained true to his promise that every card filled out by a subscriber would come to the magazine's headquarters, in San Francisco. But the staff had long ago given up on processing these requests themselves. Instead, they packed up the cards and sent them in bulk to NeoData, in Colorado. Usually this delayed fulfillment by only a few days.

Wired sent out millions of solicitations. Many readers found the magazine daunting and did not renew. To its credit, *Wired* was never an easy read. The deficit was made up by new subscribers and, later, through the purchase of subscription lists from smaller magazines that went belly-up.

At the online division there appeared to be a number of cases of incipient insanity. Carl, on May 22, proposed to increase traffic by staging his suicide on the web. HotBot, while impressively popular, was frequently broken. Beth was promising to fire Ed; the engineering department was a free-for-all; and the programmer responsible for running traffic reports, Doug Kensey, was spending his time loading historical stock-price data into a database as an aid to his own speculations. This made it impossible to get good statistics on viewership.

Doug proudly showed Carl what he was doing.

"Why did Doug show me that?" Carl later asked Ed.

"It's a typical evil-genius thing to do," Ed explained. "What's the point of doing it if you don't tell anybody?"

HotWired's closest competitor that season was Halsey Minor and Shelby Bonnie's CNET, located on the other side of Market Street. CNET was modeled on a trade magazine, narrowly focused on serving computer professionals, and unburdened by association with a successful monthly magazine, or by much in the way of revenues. This was a distinct advantage in 1996, when it was unclear whether popular enthusiasm for net stocks would last another few months. CNET had filed for its IPO in late spring, using a streamlined process designed for smaller companies. Soon they would be ready for their road show. Wired was still not ready to go.

On June 11 Louis attempted to bring more mature leadership to HotWired by jumping David Weir, the Netizen editor, to the top editorial position. That day the Nasdaq index peaked, closing above 1,230. During the next week it lost fifty points and kept going.

Internet stocks led the retreat. On Tuesday, June 18, Yahoo was down more than 10 percent, closing at $20.50, but at least Yahoo remained above its offering price of $17. Excite fell to just over $10.50, meaning that investors who got in at the offering price of $17—or at its first-day close of $20—had watched as much as half their money disappear.

This was terrible news for Wired. For months investors had been eager for anything associated with the Internet. If not for the delay associated with the roll-up, Wired would already be a public company. Now the market's unanimous confidence seemed to be cracking.

"People sell the companies with no earnings and no fundamentals first. That's Yahoo," said Stefan Cobb to a reporter from *The Financial Post*. Cobb was a fund manager who had gotten in on the Yahoo IPO and quickly got out again with a profit.

On Friday, June 21, after most of the staff had gone home, Andrew sat with Louis, Beth, Chip, and me, and explained, in case we were worried, some of the reasons a return to rationality might actually benefit Wired. When markets grew weaker, Andrew explained, there was something called *a flight to quality*. The investors took their money out of the more speculative issues—the flight—and put it into companies whose strength was proven—the quality. "When it gets jittery," Andrew said, "the investors won't buy just anything. The sign of the top is when they will buy anything, like Excite."

Andrew asked us all what websites we would like to buy as part of a post-IPO expansion. I had already begun discussions with Feed, a small, well-edited, and popular New York site. Steven Johnson, one of the founders, wanted a million dollars, about five times their yearly revenue. When he heard Steven's price Andrew laughed with honest delight. "Let me give you some advice," he said. "Buy low and sell high."

His remark confused me. I had assumed Feed was cheap. Its multiple was only five. Wired's was twenty. If Wired was *quality*, then Feed was super quality! Andrew waved off my objections with his hands. Of all of us who worked with Louis, he was the closest and the most exposed. The more stressful things became, the more he found comfort in clowning around.

"Stop making that gesture, Andrew," I said. "You're worrying me."

Andrew smiled and waved his hands again. I went and got my camera. "Let's see all the executives shrug at the same time," I asked.

Louis did and Andrew did, while Beth, who was standing in the back, kept her face set in an expression of disdain.

Later, I found myself wondering why Louis had shrugged. Andrew was playing his favorite role, the grinning bandit. But Louis had no inherited wealth. Louis had no protective cynicism. Wired was his great accomplishment, whose influence he intended to grow and protect into the next century. Why mime a carelessness he could not feel?

As the flash went off, Ed Anuff entered the office, and when I brushed by him on my way out the door the much maligned Hot-Bot manager said, in his muttering voice, "That camera contains the most value you will ever realize from this endeavor."

CHAPTER 12

THE ROAD SHOW

Three months later, they were finally off. The jet was a Falcon 50, with room for nine passengers, a bar up front by the flight deck, and a cushiony three-seat divan. It came with a flight attendant and traveled five hundred miles per hour. Their first presentation was in Minneapolis, and they arrived on October 8. Their last presentation would be October 24, in New York City. Jane wrote back to her friends at the company that the road show had dazzled the bankers at Goldman Sachs, and that demand from eager investors in Los Angeles had been so great that the Falcon had to wing back to the city for an extra meeting.

Getting away had been very tough. About the same time Excite and Yahoo were tumbling in mid-June, a draft of Wired's unique prospectus had been released to the public. It was greeted by howls of ridicule. *Newsweek* honored the offering document with a two-page review by the magazine's Wall Street editor, Allan

Sloan. Sloan thought Wired was "an interesting company. You have to love people who have created a hot magazine and consider attitude a corporate asset. But if Wall Street can actually sell this stock at its top offering price of $12 a share, the company will be valued at half a billion dollars. That's beyond attitude, that's insanity."

Sloan was openly biased against both Wired and its story, and his review showed how much resistance was left in the market. In newsrooms all over the country, Wired's IPO offered a chance for journalists and analysts to show that their faculties of discrimination were sharp. In *The New York Times,* Lawrence M. Fisher reported that industry observers were looking at the Wired deal with "a mixture of fascination and concern." *The New York Observer*'s Christopher Byron read the prospectus and concluded that, without an IPO, Wired Ventures would soon be bankrupt. He blamed the bankers at Goldman Sachs.

> Hey, they're adults! This, I am sure, will be Goldman's defense when the alleged "class act" in investment banking circles finally has to explain the garbage it's been pushing through its IPO sausage grinder lately in the name of "hightech investment opportunities." The firm will no doubt piously hide behind the cautionary warnings and disclaimers in its offering statement—phrases like "highly speculative" and that sort of thing. But Goldman won't really be any different from the tobacco company that points to the Surgeon General's warning on the cigarette box and says, *Hey, we ain't hidin' nuttin'!*

In Goldman's case, first came Yahoo Inc., a so-called Internet search engine—a software program that helps you find valuable (a.k.a. "cool") stuff on the Internet, like downloadable graphics of Hillary Clinton's hairdos. This pipe dream investment went public in April at $13 per share and instantly soared to $43 on the first day of aftermarket trading as the fools rushed in. They were lured there, in no small part, by the name of the underwriter on the offering statement: Goldman, Sachs & Company, a moniker that is supposed to be synonymous (if the self-congratulatory crowd at the firm are to be believed) with the highest standards of investment professionalism currently available on Wall Street. So where's Yahoo's stock selling now? Try $28 and weakening.

Which surely foreshadows what lies in wait for Goldman's *next* foray into cyberspace, Wired Ventures. This deal turns out to be even worse than the one for Yahoo, if that's possible. Wired Ventures is simply the fancied-up corporate name for a three-year-old magazine, which is basically a wisecracking fanzine for the Internet. The magazine has never made a dime of profit, and is currently losing money at an accelerating rate.

So Goldman has been hired to raise some cash for the operation, with—what else—an IPO. Goldman has thus set out to dump a few million shares of this dog on the greater fools of Wall Street by hyping the company into the status of a multimedia cyberspace operation. According to the IPO's offering statement, Wired Ventures is not simply an old fuddy-duddy print operation but "a new kind of media company engaged in creating compelling, branded content with attitude for print, on-line, and television." In other words, "smart media for smart people around the world"—though let's hope that doesn't include the investors.

So what does this "content with attitude" multimedia operation really amount to? Apparently, quite a lot, according to the IPO. Goldman hopes to sell the public a total of roughly 6.3 million shares—about 13 percent of the company's fully diluted shares—at $12 per share. That translates into somewhere around $65 million for the company (net of Goldman's take), and results in a market capitalization for Wired Ventures of somewhere around $565 million. How big is that? Well, it's bigger than the Quaker State motor oil company; bigger than United States Trust; bigger than Tootsie Roll Industries. Bigger, in fact, than 75 percent of all publicly traded companies in America.

But there's nothing in the IPO itself to say that Wired Ventures is actually worth more than 10 cents.

The Wall Street Journal, the most influential financial publication, was less hysterical. Wired, to the *Journal,* seemed merely a bad idea, not a loathsome one. "The planned offering by Wired Ventures Inc. may be the latest sign that the hype about the future of Internet-related companies continues to far outrace reality," wrote G. Pascal Zachary.

In reading all these reviews, it is important to note three things. First, the date is June 1996, before the imaginations of fiscal analysts were forced to adjust to the great run-ups that followed. Second, by agreeing to merge Wired and HotWired, Louis and Jane seemed to have cast their great accomplishment into shadow. *Wired* was nearly breaking even, would soon be profitable, and was far more than a fanzine for the Internet. But in the excitement they had helped to create, this fact was lost. Third, and most important, the outrage that greeted their prospectus was not aimed at them alone. Wired had claimed leadership of a digital revolution and had encouraged the confusion of the revolution and the crazy rise in stock prices. To outsiders, the rout of the vanguard would herald the return of reason. Therefore, they piled on.

During the rise, web companies had gained momentum from *Wired*'s intimidating propaganda. Now this association became dangerous. CNET, initially priced at $16 per share, had sold its first shares to the public on July 9, 1996. The first trade was at $16.75, after which CNET dropped straight back down through its offering price. By July 16 it was at $12. The CNET road show had some difficult moments as the company tried to disentangle itself from any link to Louis and Jane. Yes, both companies were in San Francisco. Yes, they both ran popular websites. But CNET was an intensely focused business aimed at servicing computer users. There was no magazine with 300,000 subscribers, there were no plans to revolutionize popular culture, there was only a twentieth of the revenue, and, most important, the company awarded itself only a $212 million valuation.

During a presentation in Boston, Mary Meeker, the equities analyst for CNET's underwriter, Morgan Stanley, was questioned so aggressively about Wired's prospectus that she had to admonish the questioner that CNET, not its notorious neighbor, was the topic of the day. Meanwhile, the advertising-supported search engines that had already gone public were cratering. Excite had dropped by the second week of July to a bit over $6. Lycos, which had once been above $21, was $7.5.

A circumspect and self-interested man would have curtailed his activities and buttressed the magazine's survival by devoting to it the main supply of his remaining cash, but Louis held that providence favors action, and he advanced on every front. Andrew also pressed forward, since he was desperate for exit, and Jane was devoted, and Plunkett was demoralized, and Rex Ishibashi had given up resisting because Louis, he said, "was like a mountain that simply got bigger as you came to the crest." Among the rest of the staff it was common knowledge that promotion hinged mainly on bravery, and so they concealed their fears.

By now there was nobody in his vicinity to warn Louis to stop, and if there had been anybody, he would have ignored them.

By Sunday, July 14, both the Dow Jones Industrial Average and the Nasdaq index had dropped sharply from their spring peaks. After the market opened Monday there was panic selling of Internet stocks. Eighteen months into the Internet boom, the end had come. The Nasdaq dropped 43.30 to 1060.19, the second-biggest single-day fall in history. Soon it might be below a thousand again.

"Technology stocks are in a free fall," complained one money manager to *The Wall Street Journal*. "The way these stocks act, it's as if the United States of America was going out of business."

Jane called the company together that afternoon. At lunchtime the employees began showing up in the dank, unfinished ground-floor space that was held in reserve for Wired TV. Jeff Simon spoke first. "I called you here to talk about the IPO and disperse the rumors," he said. He was not a good public speaker and immediately turned the microphone over to Jane.

"As you know," said Jane, "there has been a stock-market correction."

Jane pointed to a chart behind her that showed a yellow graph of the Interactive Week Internet Index, a composite index that included 46 stocks. The graph showed a pink line in the shape of the Matterhorn, with its peak corresponding to the days in late spring when Wired's registration finally cleared the SEC. From there the line plummeted nearly straight down.

"We are going to wait until this storm has passed," Jane said. She searched for a metaphor that would help people understand that the IPO was postponed but not abandoned. "It's like the space shuttle," she said. "We're delaying launch but not taking it off the launch pad." Her figure of speech backfired, as all the workers in the room who considered themselves to be clever turned left and right with cruel remarks. The tenth anniversary of the *Challenger* disaster had just been celebrated, and the memorial images were still fresh.

During the next ten weeks the stock market slowly climbed back. On August 2 the Nasdaq index closed above 1,100. On September 16 it hit 1,200 again. It was a precarious moment of doubt. Lawton Fitt and Brad Koenig, the senior bankers at Goldman, searched for the point of intersection between the company's price and the hints of resurgent enthusiasm. Investors were buying Internet stocks again, but would they keep buying for long enough so that Wired could go public? The prospectus was redrafted and the valuation of Wired Ventures reduced to about $250 million. The bankers advised that if Wired was going to make another try, now was the time.

In early October the Nasdaq jumped again, erasing its summer losses and surpassing its June peak. But this didn't seem to make Wired's IPO more palatable. Released to the press once again, the revised prospectus attracted comment that was, if anything, even more vituperative than the first time around.

Business Week wrote that the prospectus "sounds like a cry for help." *U.S. News & World Report* quoted a Silicon Valley venture capitalist who said that the document "reads like a copy of Mad Magazine." The reduction in the valuation was taken as a sign of bad faith.

On Monday, October 14, the Nasdaq index set a new record, reaching 1,256.81. That night Louis, angered by press criticism to which he could not respond because of a quiet period that had now been in force for nearly four months, decided to send a private message of encouragement to his staff. Composed at 11:30 P.M. in his hotel room, his note evoked, for those who had worked closely with him, the unmistakable sound of his fingers pounding the keyboard:

Wired Ones,

Back in the fourth issue of Wired magazine, we ran a story by Michael Crichton called Mediasaurus, which took Big Media apart for being clueless, comparing their defective work product to the junk coming out of Detroit in the early 80s.

So it should come as no surprise to us to find the shoddy, if not malicious stories that have run recently about Wired and its IPO in Business Week, MSNBC, the LA Times, and US News. No surprise, but still not easy to swallow.

Once again, we are hampered in our ability to defend ourselves by the SEC's so-called "quiet period," which forces us to respond only by referring to the prospectus—which document the authors of these stories apparently don't know how to read.

What's particularly frustrating about these stories, of course, is that they are so at variance with the reality of the company we know. This is a company of great people who make great products—and who are building a great business.

At Wired magazine, we have just closed the two biggest issues in our history, with ad pages of 166 and 175 pages, bringing the total ad pages for the year to over 1,300.

At HotWired, monthly pageviews have skyrocketed from 1.8 million early this summer to over 18 million this September alone, and third-quarter revenue is up 100 percent over second quarter.

At HardWired, two of our first six titles have been selected as Book of the Month Club Alternates. And one, Mind Grenades, has made the Borders Top 50 bestselling books in America (less than a month after release) and is already back on press—an amazing start for a new company.

And Wired TV's first Netizen TV show will air on MSNBC on Saturday, 2 November, the weekend before the election—

again, another amazing achievement, especially for a team that didn't even exist six months ago.

It's facts like these which speak louder than clueless reporting. Jane, Jeff, Andrew and I have been on the road a week now, and we've made two dozen presentations in 11 different cities. One thing that we've discovered is that sophisticated investors are pretty immune to bad journalism—and they can read the prospectus. How's it going so far? Let's just say that in a crowded Fall market for IPOs, a lot of investors are making a point of coming out to hear our story.

So, as Jeff would say, what's the takeaway? The takeaway is that media envy and ignorance are rampant (no surprise). That Wired is on track to conclude its IPO and execute its business plan. And that in the end, as F. Scott Fitzgerald put it, success is the best revenge.

Louis

This e-mail was meant only for employees, but among the recipients was Mike Godwin, a loquacious, pugnacious, and somewhat paranoid attorney who served as the staff counsel for the Electronic Frontier Foundation. In the spring of 1996, very much in need of money to pay off his law-school debts, he had agreed to cohost Wired's first television program. He had received a freelance payment, along with a small grant of stock options.

Godwin's experience on *The Netizen* had been distressing. The first producer, a well-regarded veteran of CNN named Grant Perry, had been fired by Louis in short order, for Louis did not want business as usual, and Perry seemed intent on producing something that had a polished, professional look, like every other political show. After Perry was dismissed, Louis also fired Godwin's cohost, Lawrence O'Donnell, and replaced him with two young *Wired* editors who could be trusted to follow his directions. The fact that these new hosts had never worked in front of a camera before and had some of the inevitable tics and affectations of first-timers did not bother Louis at all: he hated TV and felt that an authentic amateur production was unquestionably superior to a slick professional one. He gave the hosts scripted questions to read, such as, "In the global village, isn't it time to separate the nation from the state?" Guests were to include the writers and futurists familiar to readers of the magazine, including Alvin Toffler, Paul Saffo, and John Heilemann.

When Andrew Lack, a top NBC executive, flew out to see how the show was coming along, Louis left him in a conference room and sent his subordinates to tell him that he would not be granted a meeting, nor would he be permitted to view the facilities. MSNBC had agreed to broadcast the first program, but its commitment did not extend beyond the payment of a $200,000 advance, and Godwin was certain the program would be terminated quickly. He himself had never been formally fired but had simply stopped receiving calls from the television division and eventually concluded that he was no longer an employee. He was very angry at being treated so casually.

When Godwin opened Louis's e-mail, his pulse quickened. Louis was forbidden from communicating any news outside the prospectus. Godwin pondered whether he was obligated, by virtue of his legal training and his professional license, and also by virtue of his commitment to good citizenship, to report the violation to the Securities and Exchange Commission.

Godwin was especially bothered by some of the statements Louis had made in the e-mail. Louis wrote that Wired's first TV show, *The Netizen,* would be broadcast on MSNBC on Saturday, November 2, the weekend before the presidential election. This fact was offered as evidence of Wired's amazing skill at building businesses. But Godwin knew that the TV division was a shambles.

Louis's optimism about the TV division was perhaps exaggerated. Could it really be a crime? As an attorney Godwin was used to examining things from all angles and facing up to the worst possible interpretation of evidence. In this case, he allowed himself to believe that Louis had not only violated securities regulations, but that he was also trying to fool investors with outright deceit in the service of a fraudulent stock operation. Godwin contacted a criminal lawyer. After some discussion, he decided not to report the e-mail directly to the authorities. He waited twenty-four hours. During this time, the Nasdaq set yet another record. On Tuesday, October 15, it hit 1,269. Wired was ready to go.

For people of conspiratorial temperaments, possession of a secret document offers temptations too difficult to resist. For reasons that were not clearly explicable even to himself, Godwin forwarded Louis's private note to his friend Gerard Van der Leun. He could not have chosen a more devious or effective way to deliver a blow. Van der Leun was Boswell, the WELL prankster who had not had any contact with Louis and Jane in more than three years, and who had been waiting all that time for an opportunity to injure them in exchange for having been omitted from the magazine's New York launch party in 1993. Boswell posted Louis's e-mail to the WELL under the ambiguous heading "This just in from Louis." He then strategically disappeared for three days, so that no further information about how he acquired the e-mail could be ascertained.

Once posted to the WELL, the mail was read by scores of journalists, who recognized that if it had been intentionally released, sanctions were likely. Sure enough, a letter soon arrived from Abigail Arms and William L. Tolbert, Jr., of the Securities and Exchange Commission, requesting copies of Louis's e-mail communications. *The Wall Street Journal* announced the snafu prominently.

Jane fumed. Her cheery e-mails notwithstanding, things had grown a bit dicey on the road show. The hurt feelings from the company's rough negotiations with Goldman Sachs had never entirely healed. The game of selling stock to the public involves, under the best of circumstances, so many discursive elisions and leaps of faith that the intrusion of purely personal elements is always dangerous, and if these elements are at all exotic, the danger is greater. In a world of even-voiced, gray-haired corporate presidents, an excitable thirty-five-year-old woman in her seventh month of pregnancy whose official communications back to the company included the news that her belly button was beginning to turn inside out was an exoticism in itself; combined with the revolutionary claims of a prospectus wrapped in a neon-yellow gatefold, the exotic threatened to become eccentric, or even, in the eyes of the old regime, absurd.

Though Louis had cut his hair and, the day before the road show, taken his personal assistant on a quick shopping trip to purchase the CEO's first pair of dress shoes in twenty years, such minor concessions hardly made up for the trouble he caused. These were among some of the guesses Jane made as to why Goldman Sachs seemed indifferent once the road show finally began. When Brad Koenig, the Goldman banker, had presented them to an audience in San Francisco, he could barely muster a word of praise. He gave the briefest of introductions and abandoned the stage. Now that Jane was facing investors, she felt more alone than ever.

In city after city, Louis attempted to correct a persistent confusion. The investment managers looked at the company's revenue statement and saw that a great majority of cash was coming from the magazine side of the business. Therefore, they mistook Wired for a magazine company. Even using a generous formula, a magazine company losing $15 million per year on $35 million in revenue could hardly be worth upward of $200 million on the public market.

Louis and Jane tried to make investors understand the elegance of their business plan. Wired's online division was within striking distance of the leaders, while spending only a fraction of the tens of millions that bigger companies, such as Time-Warner, were blowing on their net operations. Traffic on HotBot was growing, and advertising revenue along with it. HotWired's value compared favorably with other public online companies supported by advertising, such as Excite, and Excite had no magazine, no television, no books, and no brand.

They were met with coolness. On October 18 the road show arrived in Boston. Andrew was not feeling well, and the investor they were visiting with was unenthusiastic. They took a break, and when the investor left his office for a moment Jane stretched her legs, walked around his desk, and took a glance at his computer monitor. The screen was a matrix of names and numbers, most of them highlighted in red.

"What does the red mean?" she said to Jeff Simon.

On the road show, travel had been by private jet, ground transportation by limousine. Jeff's picture had recently been published in the company newsletter over the captions "Jeff gets to play in the cockpit! Jeff gets to ride in the town car!" He was the chief financial officer, and very much implicated in this adventure.

"Red is not a good thing," Jeff replied. After its peak on Tuesday, the market had stalled, and now it was tanking again.

Wired had never succeeded in a financing round that did not come to the edge of failure, and this one, Jane saw, would be no exception. They were scheduled to go public in a week, on Friday, October 25.

The following Thursday, all the executives went to a party to celebrate the success of *Mind Grenades,* which was a compilation of the multipage illustrations *Wired* published every month in front of its table of contents. The party was held at a small bookstore on the Upper East Side. John Plunkett, who came to New York for the celebration, was beset by congratulations, not only on the book but also on his soon-to-arrive millionairedom, which was a marvel to everybody who had known him during his time as a commercial designer.

John himself struggled to accept the reality of this pending fact, for he never really expected the magazine to be successful, and when it was, he thought Louis would ruin the business with his headlong forays into British publishing and web publishing and book publishing and television, and when these resulted in a huge mezzanine round of investment that implied his stake was worth millions, he still refused to think about it because, as he reminded himself, "There is still too much time for Louis to fuck it up."

Now, with less than twenty-four hours to go, he finally sat down in his hotel room on West Forty-fourth Street and asked Barbara to sit down with him.

"It looks like this is really going to happen," John said to his wife and partner. "Why don't you and I just talk about it for a minute. What are we going to do?"

John had been in the audience during the last road-show presentation, in a ballroom at the Waldorf-Astoria. There was seating for 150 people, but only 50 had shown up. Louis, that day, had not been his usual unyielding self. He seemed reflective and unhappy. But all the Wired executives had their material down pat, and John had allowed himself to feel impressed. Now, amazingly, the time for failure had run out, and this deeply resistant man was finally forced to confront his good fortune. He and Barbara talked for a few minutes, just touching on the most important issues. John wondered if there was a way to share some of his new wealth with his family without inciting resentment. For themselves, they knew what they wanted. After four incredible years, they would escape from San Francisco, escape from Wired, and, most of all, escape from Louis and Jane. Barbara had been raised in Montana; this was where they would look for a ranch.

While they were talking, the phone rang. It was Louis. "It's over," he said.

CHAPTER 13

SACRIFICE

O f course it was not over. Many of the greatest companies in history have touched on bankruptcy during their early years—some more than once. The night before Wired was scheduled to appear on the Nasdaq exchange, Louis got the bad news from his bankers. *The book,* as the list of orders was called, was only two-thirds subscribed. When an offering is undersubscribed, it's hard to carry off in fractional amounts, as the excess supply casts a pall over the market. Louis was angry.

"They could have cleared that inventory," he later complained. At the time of the Wired IPO Goldman was earning tens of millions in fees for comanaging an IPO for Deutsche Telecom, the recently privatized German phone company whose offering would eventually prove disastrous for investors.*

---

* The Deutsche Telecom IPO was notable because of its large size: it raised more

Louis knew that the Deutsche Telecom IPO was vastly oversub-
scribed. Everybody wanted in on it. It was an open secret that
stock salesmen who controlled access to coveted shares in a hot
IPO could easily pressure investment firms to choke down a few
million dollars of a less popular offering; this technique helped in-
sure a big brokerage's reputation for always getting the job done.
But Goldman declined to use any such tactics for Wired.

"At the end of the day, investors make up their own minds,"
said Lawton Fitt, the lead Internet banker at Goldman, when interviewed about Wired's spectacularly botched IPO by Jerry
Useem, a reporter for *Inc.* magazine. "Had the market not been so
volatile," she continued, "I believe the offering would have been
quite successful."

Volatility was just one of the problems. On the road show,
many attendees had been put off by Louis's vast ambitions. "Too
pie-in-the-sky," said Zach Guevara of the Capital Group. This
comment was typical. While many Internet companies had now
carried off successful IPOs, few of them required the savvy institu-
tional buyers to swallow an undiluted dose of world revolution.

---

than $13 billion in capital. It was oversubscribed by 5 to 1. It opened on No-
vember 18, 1996, at above $21; five and a half years later it was at $12, and
$7.5 billion in market value had vanished. Yahoo, Goldman's most famous
1996 IPO, makes an interesting contrast. Yahoo's market capitalization at the
time of its IPO was less than a billion dollars, and it raised about $34 million
from its offering. Six years later, even after its price had dropped 90 percent
from its peak, its market capitalization had reached $8 billion. Shareholders
who got in at the offering price of $13 saw their stock rise by more than 1,200
percent; those who braved ridicule and bought on the open market that day at
above $30 still saw their money grow 500 percent.

"Game over," said Andrew, when he found out that the stock would not open on Nasdaq the next morning. "Let's sell to Yahoo."

Yahoo looked like the survivor in the great web wipeout. Though it had closed below sixteen once or twice over the summer, it had never dropped below its offering price, and by October it was above twenty again.

His bosses ignored him. They returned to San Francisco and began to rally the staff for a lengthy, difficult, temporizing campaign. Mary Meeker, the Internet analyst at Morgan Stanley, predicted that web-based advertising revenue could hit eight billion dollars in four years. This would be more than the total for all outdoor advertising, and more than half the total for the entire magazine industry. Web revenues had tripled since the first quarter, and HotWired's sales had kept pace. Louis and Jane's idea was to wait out the down cycle in the market, but to do so they would need more cash.

It was good to be back in the office. The issue of *Wired* in production when Louis and Jane arrived was the best they had yet published. Conceived at the height of the company's confidence, it included a forty-thousand-word travelogue by Neal Stephenson that told the story of the wiring of the planet, starting with the completion of the first transatlantic cable in 1858 and ending with the paranoid adventures of fiber-optic installers running lines through the jungles of Thailand. In the same December 1996 edition, there was a beautifully photographed story about the logistics of Federal Express, a disturbing essay on the obsolescence of privacy, a detailed account of Steve Case and Ted Leonsis's attempt, at AOL, to grow into a major media corporation, and a touching profile of an engineering genius whose favorite form of social interaction was giving and getting piggyback rides. There were 175 pages of advertisements, bringing in more than three million dollars in revenue.

Amidst this plenty were two articles that insiders found very curious. Occasional readers of *Wired* sometimes saw in it a blind faith that reminded them of a cult, but in fact the magazine was shot through with contrarianism, and just at the moment Louis and Jane were desperate for money, their magazine slipped in two vicious exposés of the web. One of these was a little chart and a hundred-word story put together by John Browning, the executive editor of the U.K. edition, using data from Jupiter Communications. The data revealed that the top six web publishers—Netscape, Infoseek, Yahoo, Lycos, Excite, and CNET—accounted for six of the top nine web advertisers. In other words, the top suppliers of ad revenue to the web publishing industry were the publishers themselves. Advertising numbers were growing, to be sure, but the growth took the form of a loop, or at least a spiral. "Diversify or die," Browning wrote.*

The second story was a more detailed assessment of the current realities of web media by Hunter Madsen, the Harvard Ph.D. whom Louis had, after their interesting interview, hired as

---

* Each of these companies had sold shares for the public and was pouring a portion of its accumulated resources to fuel the banner market. Of the three top advertisers who were not on the list of the top six publishers, one, the McKinley Group, had already been purchased by Excite by the time the issue hit newsstands. The other two were Microsoft and AT&T, two huge publicly held firms that had large investments in the Internet.

HotWired's top marketing executive. Madsen pointed to falling banner prices, consumer indifference, and unsupportable costs, mounting an attack that gave the weight of objective research to the witticisms Ted Leonsis had made at TED nearly a year earlier. Even with banner prices falling, there were enormous amounts of unsold inventory, and hundreds of new publishers were being seduced into the field. Madsen reported that most content sites were covering no more than 20 percent of their costs with ad revenues.

Wired's numbers were not quite that bad, but they were bad enough, and at the beginning of December 1996 Louis looked at a calendar showing the words "no more cash" written across the squares marked January 13 and 14.

And still, all the while, the web grew and grew. The week the Wired road show failed, AOL hit seven million members. Two months later there were eight million. All of them could now browse the web as much as they liked, for on December 1 America Online finally began offering its members unlimited access for a flat price of $19.95 per month. More than 150,000 new web pages came online daily.

Among the many people tracking this growth was Paul Salem, a managing director at the private investment firm of Providence Equity Partners. Together, Salem and his partners controlled about five billion dollars, and their annualized rate of return over the past ten years had far exceeded their usual expectation of 30 percent. Salem had analyzed many companies, and with the calm of a person uninfected by futurism he sized up the situation at Wired and made a rescue offer full of hideous conditions and entanglements. "If you don't like it, don't do it," he said.

Salem was a fan of *Wired,* and he guessed that the magazine, with its steady revenue stream and predictable expenses, easily had a value of between thirty and sixty million dollars. But the magazine's parent company was a different story; it had more than 360 employees, half of whom worked on the website, and it was now burning through more than $1.5 million per month. Salem called Bob Forlenza, a banker at Tudor Investment Corporation, one of HotWired's original investors, and Forlenza confirmed that Wired was desperate.

Salem and Forlenza offered these terms to Louis and Jane: together, Providence Equity Partners and Tudor Investment Corporation would put about twenty million dollars into the company. But if this money proved insufficient to get them to profitability and Wired ran out of cash, the bankers would have the right to sell the assets and make off with a vastly disproportionate share of the proceeds. The terms were complicated, but even under the gloomiest of circumstances they were virtually guaranteed to double their money.

Louis and Jane knew they were in trouble. "I do not even know how to describe it," Jane later said, when asked about her state of mind. For the first time in their lives together, they were accepting terms dictated to them by others. Bankruptcy loomed, and at the end of the year the exactious agreements were signed. They had now pawned their achievements of a decade for twelve months of operating capital.

As expected, MSNBC canceled its contract with Wired in December, ending the company's foray into broadcast television. *Wired U.K.*, the British edition, was burning half a million dollars per month while serving fewer than ten thousand subscribers; in February the staff was fired and the office shuttered. At HotWired,

Beth Vanderslice, still obeying the dictates of ordinary business, demanded a plan of contraction, and her obedient managers prepared a list of people to dismiss. They would eliminate the entertainment channel, the health channel, the channel devoted to recipes for alcoholic beverages. But, surprisingly, these defensive maneuvers were rejected. Louis was determined to defend HotWired, for the online operation was to be the foundation of his future businesses, while Andrew, who was still HotWired's CEO, saw no point in giving up anything piecemeal because this would only forestall the moment of capitulation when his equity would be translatable into cash. Andrew owned hundreds of thousands of shares. A breakup of the company and a liquidation at current values would net him at least a million.

The most valuable digital asset, by far, was Ed Anuff's HotBot. But Ed had a problem: Inktomi had wised up. One day back in August, when Ed had gone over to Berkeley to berate his partners a little and emphasize their debt of gratitude to Wired for introducing them into the world of high-stakes business, he got an unpleasant welcome. He knew something was up because Eric Brewer looked extra chipper. He guessed at the cause. Inktomi had a new CEO. They had hired a man named David Peterschmidt.

Peterschmidt was a new type of individual, as far as both HotWired and Inktomi were concerned. He had been the chief operating officer at Sybase, a powerful database company, and he had been in the group that had taken Sybase public in 1991. Three other things impressed Ed when he looked Peterschmidt up on the web. First, he was nearly fifty years old. Second, he had been an Air Force pilot in Vietnam. And third, he had recently left his job at Sybase after the company took a brutal hit in the market for missing its revenue projections. Ed suspected that Peterschmidt's age and experience would make him a little less likely than Eric Brewer and Paul Gauthier to swallow Andrew's glib assertions trustingly.

Ed had arrived at Inktomi ready to demand some more concessions, and when he got there the Inktomi team just sat happily waiting, unwilling to start the meeting until their new boss walked in. Ed had brought his list of all the things Inktomi was going to have to do to justify its miserable existence, but he never got a chance to present them, because Peterschmidt, serious and relaxed in his business suit, simply delivered a little speech about how he was committed to running Inktomi in a way that acknowledged the interest of all the *stakeholders,* and that he would be doing a complete evaluation of all the *issues,* and that he would be sure to let them know when he had concluded his analysis. Then he smiled, rose from the table, and left.

Eric Brewer continued to grin.

"Uh, Andrew, they have a new CEO," said Ed later.

Andrew asked what he was like.

"Uh, he seems pretty serious," said Ed.

"Well, you told him that their mistakes had cost us all this money," began Beth.

"We really didn't get a chance to bring it up," interrupted Ed. "I think you guys are going to have to handle this."

A few weeks later, having repelled HotWired's team, Peterschmidt went on the offensive. He visited Third Street. Beth, who had very good manners, attempted to bond with him.

"It is *so* difficult to find database programmers," she said. "Do you know any? I have to pay them so much, I've been thinking about learning how to do it myself."

Peterschmidt fixed her with his polite stare. "That's a good idea," he said. "You *should* learn how to do that."

He was very pleasant but would not give them any information about Inktomi's plans. He was sizing them up. He did not seem intimidated. He gave his stakeholders speech again. Then, on his way out the door, he said that it looked like Inktomi might be owed a little bit of money. "I'm having the accountants come in and audit the books," he said. He promised to get back to Andrew before long.

Wired's control over its partner, built on a bluff, deteriorated, and although HotBot continued to add more and more users, Inktomi extracted itself from the disadvantageous contract, backing out of its marketing commitment and winning the right to provide its search engine to any number of competing companies.*

Beth pulled Ed off the project. *HotBotch,* she murmured, whenever the painful topic arose.

"The jig is up," Ed said soon afterward. We sat across from each other now. Ed expected to be fired at any moment. But neither Louis nor Andrew wanted contraction at HotWired. Ed sat at his desk and waited. Nothing happened.

Sometimes Carl came by. After selling Suck to HotWired, Carl and Joey had hired a staff, but Carl was not a talented manager, and he slowly backed away from the project. Suck was still widely

---

* In June 1998 Peterschmidt would take Inktomi public in a hugely successful IPO.

read, but as the universe of websites swelled, it lost its unique allure. Eventually, Carl moved his bed out of the office, and soon he stopped showing up altogether, except at odd hours. He didn't even keep his computer at Wired anymore, and he informed curious colleagues that he was "working from home."

His chair was quickly stolen. On his desk there remained only a symbolic representation of his employment in the form of a cheap coffee mug emblazoned with his name.

Morale was very bad. Some months earlier, while ringing in the new issue with a glass of champagne, Jane had looked over at the pastries Wired had supplied for the festivities and called out gaily to her staff: "Let them eat cake!" Her remark was still being repeated in the spring of 1997 by disappointed shareholders among the employees, who took it as evidence of ill will. Some of their negative comments reached Jane's ears, and she did her best to attribute them to lingering resentment over the failure of the IPO. But there was something older and more powerful at work. She and Louis had started their company as a rebel enterprise. They had never acquired any sort of executive dignity. In times of stress, Jane's youthful sociability grated, as did Louis's pride.

"The sarcasm was always there," Jane later said. She gave birth to a boy, named Orson, in January. While she retained her formal role at the company, she backed away from daily operations.

Wired missed its first-quarter financial goals. The Nasdaq index was even more anemic that spring than it had been during the fall. It struggled to stay above 1,200, and in the first days of April 1997 it dropped lower. Salem anticipated further declines. The faster Wired's assets could be liquidated, the better chance shareholders had of realizing value before a complete collapse.

"Why should the market collapse?" Louis asked. It seemed obvious to him that the opposite was about to happen. Nothing had ever slowed the influx of newcomers onto the Internet. After the nadir in early April, the stock market rallied, and a series of great days in late April and early May brought the Nasdaq above 1,300.

The cover of the July issue of *Wired* showed a happy face made from a photo illustration of the earth. The face floated against a bright yellow background, and a purple daisy emerged from its blissful grin. Underneath, in pink letters, it read:

THE LONG BOOM: WE'RE FACING
25 YEARS OF PROSPERITY, FREEDOM, AND A BETTER
ENVIRONMENT FOR THE WHOLE WORLD.
YOU GOT A PROBLEM WITH THAT?

If the December 1996 issue was the best *Wired* ever published, the July 1997 issue quickly became the most notorious. Initially, it was very popular; the office couldn't keep up with requests for reprints. But the ambiguity it toyed with was treacherous.

Ostensibly, the Long Boom had little to do with weekly or monthly fluctuations of the stock market. The lead author, Peter Schwartz, was a cofounder of the Global Business Network, and in his introduction to the story he insisted that the Long Boom was not a prediction but a *scenario,* which he defined as a plausible future meant to inspire hope. New technologies and the breakdown of national and cultural borders could make the world better. Why not look into the details of how this might work?

Schwartz and his coauthor, *Wired* editor Peter Leyden, reviewed a series of trends that seemed to bode well for humanity, including networked communications, Asian prosperity, European union, alternative energy. They also dutifully listed a set of *scenario spoilers,* including technological failures, global warming, and terrorism leading to renewed nationalism. The story ended with a peroration:

> A global transformation over the next quarter century will bring a tremendous amount of trauma. The world will run into a daunting number of problems as we transition to a networked economy and a global society. And all along the way the chorus of naysayers will insist it simply can't be done. We'll need an optimistic vision of what the future can be.

Fair enough, but as Louis had written in his first note to *Wired* readers, "In a world of information overload, the ultimate luxury is meaning and context." The context for the Long Boom cover was one of the most remarkable stock-market rallies ever seen.

The Nasdaq hit 1,600 in the first days of August, up more than 40 percent in less than a year, and *Wired*'s Long Boom cover cemented the magazine's reputation as an uncritical tout. It also sent a contradictory message, for if popular monthlies were proclaiming that the stock market was going to go up like this forever, it had to be nearing the top.

That fall Paul Salem came out to check on the company. When he arrived, Louis told him the good news. Wired had missed its financial targets during the first quarter, which gave them a slight cash-flow problem, but they had gotten on track in the summer and fall, and if Providence would put in another five million dollars, Wired would be making money by the end of next year. Then they would possess an asset of stupendous value in a buoyant market: the world's only profitable new media company. The rally had continued to set records in September, and on October 2 the Nasdaq closed above 1,700. Internet stocks were leading the way.

Salem saw things differently. Louis, with his obstreperous sincerity, was a burden to the company's other shareholders, who needed to be prepared to get out quickly when the market turned. Providence Equity Partners and Tudor Investment Corporation would not be putting more cash into Wired except to prepare it for a sale.

The new investors' rights were protected by a complicated double mechanism. If Louis needed more cash, Tudor and Providence would take over the board. Moreover, Louis and Jane had to sign away the rights they held as shareholders to vote on a sale. These mutually reinforcing arrangements—control of the board, plus control of the founders' shares—were meant to give potential buyers confidence that a sale would not be held up by shareholder conflict.

"It was a good deal for us," Salem later acknowledged. "People who saw our structure said, 'Can we copy that?' "

In November, Louis and Jane's last battle to salvage their company began in earnest. Their enemy had every formal advantage. Paul Salem had well-designed contractual assurances of control, and his aim was straightforward: to extract his guaranteed profit. But there were other, complicating factors. Every aspect of Wired's operations still revolved around the company's founder. Louis remained *Wired*'s publisher and editor and HotWired's director of programming, as well as the chief executive officer of Wired Ventures and the chairman of the board. Given that he also possessed unshakable confidence, vast reserves of belligerent energy, and more than 15 percent of the company's outstanding shares—Jane owned another 15 percent—the outcome of their struggle, contractual terms notwithstanding, was difficult to predict.

Unfortunately, Louis's first move was a mistake. He had been editing *Wired* every month for five years. As each issue closed, stories would pile up on his desk awaiting comment, while headlines would vaporize at the last minute when his disapproving eye finally fell on them. The strain of producing a glossy monthly is enormous even when the editor in chief is not launching an Internet company, a book-publishing company, a television show, and attempting to bring off a fifty-million-dollar stock offering. In the summer Louis had asked John Battelle, his longtime right-hand man in editorial affairs, to take on most of the chief's duties. Battelle was tempted but refused, and soon launched a competing magazine devoted to reporting on web business. Called *The Industry Standard,* it was an instant success. This left Louis without a replacement.

After months of futile interviews with outside editors, Louis turned to Katrina Heron, a former *Vanity Fair* and *New Yorker* editor who had been working for the magazine for several years. Louis wanted a trustworthy subordinate, but Heron was worldly enough to bid for explicit control. She insisted that her name be at the top of the masthead; otherwise she would not accept the job. Louis was stymied for days, and finally, in the utmost frustration, he asked his unyielding employee where on the magazine's masthead she thought his own name belonged. She reached her finger out decisively and pointed: at the bottom. Louis acquiesced. This was an irreversible error, for the magazine was the company's single unimpeachable asset, and its founder had been thought indispensable as a hands-on editor. Now he had done what any buyer who valued the magazine would hardly have dared to do: he had fired himself.

Paul Salem opened lines of communication with all the top executives, trying to understand the right way to liquidate the company and sell the assets, piecemeal if necessary. Beth Vanderslice was especially helpful. At long last, she had renounced her conventional ideas. Beth believed that *Wired* magazine was the obvious candidate for sale. As long as the bubble lasted, *Wired* magazine's worth would be limited by the fact that it was a regular, profit-seeking enterprise. HotWired could only ascend into the stratosphere when its ties with a regular business were loosed. A block away on Third Street, the magazine executives expressed equal eagerness to see the two companies split apart. From their vantage point the Internet business had never been anything but a drain on cash. They were working at America's best new magazine. HotWired was an embarrassment.

Beth's superb balance served her well, and as hostilities between Louis and his board of directors intensified, she maintained good relations with both sides. To Paul Salem, she provided regular reports designed to prove that the websites should not be discounted. Again and again she repeated the phrase *maximizing shareholder value*, and since she was an insider but also a realist, he relied on her analysis. To Louis, Beth offered practical advice on how to cut expenses while preserving the core of his Internet business. Since his survival depended upon forestalling bankruptcy, she was his ally, too.

This was not good news for Ed. As the winter of 1997 set in, Ed's voice seldom wavered from its tone of ironical woe. Sometimes I looked up from my desk to see Carl standing there talking to his old friend—they were trading office gossip and thinking up improvements for HotBot. "But Ed, Louis *can't* fire us," Carl liked to say, in his terrible flat voice.

Carl felt even closer to Louis that year. He had watched as the failure of the IPOs provoked yet another wave of criticism in the press. The widely read Silicon Valley monthly *Upside* published a cover illustration of Louis and Jane as a naked Adam and Eve. The story described Louis as a zealot who had lost all sense of reality. Bringing him down a peg would be a good step toward correcting all the exaggerations of the recent boom. The *Upside* article concluded with a direct admonition:

> The '60s are over, dude. Everybody's grown up now. No matter how much you detest authority, the world remains full of parents who know they're the ones who'll have to clean up the mess when the storm's over.

Amy Harmon, at the *Los Angeles Times,* also took aim at the magazine: "The rap on 3-year-old Wired," she wrote, "has always been that its unabashed boosterism for the high-tech future pandered to the industry at the expense of the truth."

Louis responded by keeping himself away from the press. Driving Wired to profitability was the only statement he felt like making. He refused requests for interviews. He seemed, to Carl, to think of everybody as his enemy, to be isolating himself, as if he alone could advance the revolution. His young employee sent him an emotional e-mail, encouraging Louis to be more open and more forgiving and, above all, not to lose faith in his story.

"You can create wonderful, brilliant things that others can't," Carl wrote.

Remember the way you felt when the first Wired magazine came off the press, and you held it in your hands? I felt some of that, some weeks later, in a snowy Minneapolis, 2000 miles away. But people react in different ways. Remember what the nuns used to say, Louis—you have a God-given talent, one that you should use to serve your fellow man.

He quoted Nietzsche to his boss, choosing a passage on the downfall of heroes:

Divine envy is inflamed when it beholds a human being without a rival, unopposed, on a solitary peak of fame. Only the gods are beside him now and therefore they are against him. They seduce him to a deed of hubris, and under it he collapses.

Louis e-mailed Carl back: "Is it hubris to have dreams? To try to make them real?"

"One of us was being an idiot here," Carl said later. "I suspect it was me."

By this time, Andrew was sick of arguing with his boss. He wanted the websites sold quickly, but Louis refused. Louis was clinging desperately to his brand. He could not admit that his big ideas had become dangerous, that the financial community had turned against him, that he was an object of ridicule.

"You know I love to fight," Andrew said to me one day. "I love politics, I enjoy playing the game. But now it just feels like being in a room with very, very stupid people." Andrew threw up his hands, but the gesture lacked its old jollity.

As Andrew retreated, Beth advanced. On November 13 David Weir, the managing director of the websites, was summoned to Louis's office, where, when he entered, he found Beth facing him with a piece of paper in her hand.

"David," she said, "we have recently reorganized Wired Digital, which includes some streamlining of the company and reallocation of people. As a result of the restructure as well as the need to contain costs, your position has been eliminated effective today." Her script had been prepared by a human-resources professional, and she did not fail to read it word for word. There were many more meetings still to go.

Counting on his brain to save him, Ed went to pitch Beth on a new product for HotWired. What he had in mind was an easy-to-use tool kit for corporations that wanted to build a central website for their employees. Beth fired him on the spot, and he left that day. Later in the afternoon I caught sight of Carl, who was walking quietly into the HotWired office. Carl surveyed the empty desk where he was supposed to have been working, sighed, and caught my eye. He had talked with Beth, and now he, too, was cleaning out his desk. Clutching the cup that said C A R L, he padded out. If HotWired was sold for a discount, the small number of shares he had received in exchange for Suck would be worth next to nothing.

On December 17 Louis, Jeff, Jane, and Andrew sat down with Walter Forbes. Forbes was an entrepreneur Louis respected. He had created a direct-marketing company called CUC, which had been one of the original HotWired investors. If Louis had to submit to being controlled by a higher commercial power, he preferred Forbes to whatever horrible fate was being prepared for him by Paul Salem. Louis explained to Forbes why it made sense to keep the magazine and the online divisions of Wired together. They were united by a brand, whose value was intimately associated with the most important business and cultural trends of the coming decade. At the end he paused, and Andrew quickly jumped in.

"But if you just want to peel off the digital part of the company, we would be open to that, too," Andrew said, as Louis stared.

Andrew's outburst was calculated. Immediately after the meeting, Louis took Jeff Simon aside. "I want him gone," Louis said.

The next day Jeff took Andrew over to Zeke's, the nearby sports bar where Hunter S. Thompson was said to have hid from Jann Wenner in the early days of *Rolling Stone*. They sat in a booth, and Jeff offered him six months' salary in exchange for his resignation. Andrew agreed to depart for double Jeff's offer, and promised not to appear in the office again so as to spare Louis the disgust of setting eyes on him. He retained his significant ownership stake. He expected a battle, and he settled back to observe it from a distance.

Most of the company's cash was gone. Salem was pressing them closely. Soon after the turn of the year the investor demanded acknowledgment that Wired had failed to meet its financial targets— this was a formal trigger for the board takeover. To keep the company from collapsing altogether, Salem offered a loan of up to ten million dollars. He demanded repayment within three months, and would charge a rate of 18 percent interest plus a $100,000 fee. If not repaid on time, the loan would convert into a new grant of stock, with preferences so onerous that they would consume all remaining value.

With these new conditions, the evisceration of Wired Ventures would be complete—a result rather easily foreseen. "It did not surprise us that they did not make their numbers," Paul Salem later said. "They *never* made a number."

The saddest thing was that Salem's statement was not true. *Wired* magazine had exceeded every expectation for years. In only one quarter since its creation had it failed to bring in more money than planned. Even the digital part of the company had better numbers than many of its peers. But there is no benefit, when fighting a creditor, in pointing out others more deserving of ill treatment. Salem was ready to take control of Wired and liquidate it. Louis stalled and raged. As the days to insolvency counted down, he refused to sign the agreements authorizing the loan and he refused to turn over control of his shares. He told Jeff Simon that he preferred to declare bankruptcy and suffer a court-supervised reorganization.

On Monday, March 9, 1998, Jeff packed up his office. The company had made its last paycheck. But at the last minute Louis, whose intention to wreck the company looked all too real, extracted an important concession. Paul Salem would make his loan, but the repayment period would be extended from an impossible three months to an improbable six months. This was their last window for rescue. Louis and Jane signed the loan agreement, and a new majority was constituted on the board.

As soon as Paul Salem gained control, he convened a board meeting by telephone. Jane, Louis, and Jeff Simon sat together in Jane's office, and Bill Jesse, their first banker and the person who had guaranteed payment for printing the inaugural issue, told Louis and Jane through the speakerphone that they were fired.

Jane stood up quickly and walked out of the building. For a moment Louis felt surprised. Jesse had not even bothered to show up in person. But Louis was the last person to be knocked off balance by merely personal considerations, and he spoke up for a full minute before following Jane out the door. He told the other board members that they were displaying their typical lack of intelligence. How were they going to replace him? Had they given any thought to the public repercussions of his dismissal? Did they at least have a press release prepared?

To be honest, the other board members had not yet completely developed their picture of what would happen after he was gone, beyond the general impression that management would instantly become more reasonable. They knew that with each increase in the price of Internet shares, Louis's faith in the Long Boom became more dangerous. The board knew that Dana Lyons, the advertising director of *Wired,* could take over as publisher, that Katrina Heron was now the editor in chief, and that Beth Vanderslice would gladly run HotWired. But as for what exactly was to be done to ensure that the founders gave up all influence and control over their staff, and what exactly would be said to the employees and to the outside world—this had not yet been discussed. It never occurred to them to secure the founders' offices or call a general meeting.

Later in the afternoon Jeff went to John Plunkett. "I want you to know that Jane and Louis were fired today," he said.

On the following Monday John observed that his ex-partners were very much in evidence. They walked confidently into their offices and began giving orders to their three assistants.

"What's going on here?" John asked Jeff, who was supposed to be the new president. Jeff just shook his head mournfully.

"It's more complicated than you think," he answered.

No further moves were made to evict them, and Louis and Jane simply continued to come in every morning, issue commands, and plot the downfall of the Salem group. To John Plunkett's amazement, they still appeared to be running the company.

Despite his weakness, Louis was a dominating presence. His lieutenants avoided him, and told one another he had gone crazy, and plotted humorously to save themselves from him, and in the overwrought atmosphere sometimes believed themselves to be at risk of bodily harm. He was their leader and at the same time their enemy. Louis's dismissal, they hoped, would be consummated any minute.

"Off with his head!" John Plunkett said later, recalling their fantasies at the time.

CHAPTER 14

THE END

In tragedy everything is lost, in comedy everything is gained, but romance is a mixed genre, whose happy outcome is never free of shadows. If Louis had seen the end of Wired back when he was bent over the broken printers at Ink, he might have accepted it gladly. His magazine was a success; the next stage was to become rich. Sometimes people tried to offer Louis this interpretation, but the transition from intoxication to sobriety is painful, and he would never accept that Wired was merely the product of an unusual interregnum, a period of lucrative optimism in a brief decade between wars.

All through 1998 the smartest insiders were thinking about transforming the idea of a digital revolution into assets that would hold their value through the next cycle. But Louis kept insisting that his main concern was not escaping in time. He believed that Wired's most impressive accomplishments were still in the future.

For his colleagues, this was evidence that he was either lying or out of his mind.

Meanwhile, Louis was being chased from the scene by a man who was not even a skeptic about the possibility of a global revolution in which all authorities would be overthrown. The topic merely failed to interest him. Paul Salem had acquired control of a very good magazine at a reasonable price, which he intended to re-sell at a profit. That was the essence of good business.

All spring and summer, Louis appeared to be routed. First he lost his magazine, and then he faced losing the rest of his company. On the last day of April 1998, the board of directors agreed to sell *Wired* to Robert Miller, the publisher of *Spin,* but before the deal was signed, Si Newhouse got wind of the secret negotiations and jumped in with a higher bid. After a quick, panicky auction, Paul Salem used the power granted to him by the voting trust to sell the magazine to Condé Nast for ninety million dollars.

Miller, who believed he was negotiating under an exclusive contract, threatened to sue. The last-minute confusion gave Louis the pleasure of sowing fear among the board, annoying his disobedient staff members who had already begun friendly discussions with Miller, and advocating on behalf of an investor who had supported Wired from the beginning. But in the end, Miller did not sue.

Announcing the sale in an e-mail to his staff, Louis pointed out that in April 1998 Wired Ventures had shown its first monthly profit; sadly, the company that reached that milestone was already gone.

Most of the money had come from the magazine. The breakup

put this revenue, and any reprise of Andrew's *scheme of the multiple,* out of the picture. The arrival of new executives also made the defense of Louis's office in the *Wired* magazine building moot. The scene of action shifted down the street, to where the web business was. On Sunday, May 3, the founders moved all of their computer equipment and files into their home.

The Condé Nast deal seemed to leave Louis a narrow chance for victory. He had feared that Salem would throw away his Internet company for next to nothing, and the banker surely would have, if either Newhouse or Miller had been willing to pay even a token amount. But they saw only losses and refused. Condé Nast left Wired Ventures all of the online assets.

Moreover, money from the sale of the magazine, which came in before the six-month deadline, paid back Paul Salem's loan. There would be no new set of devastating preferences layered on top of the old ones. When Louis examined the outcome, he saw a growing Internet company with—after debt repayments—more than forty-five million dollars in the bank. In revenue, Wired Digital ranked eleventh among major sites. In traffic, thanks to HotBot, it ranked fifteenth.

All month the market posted stunning gains. The day Louis left his office, the price of a single share of Amazon, a Seattle-based online bookseller that had gone public a year earlier at $18, reached $95—an advance of 500 percent. Amazon was not a media company, but through a marvelous chain of inductive reasoning in which every step is defensible, and the result absurd, the growth in the firm's value was transmitted through the entire market, producing a series of more or less synchronized ripples.

Commercial websites, to this point, had been stuck within the confines of the media industry. Amazon's demonstration of the possibilities of e-commerce expanded the game into retail, where mail-order sales alone were worth more than all the advertising, promotion, and marketing in America combined. The result was a recapitulation of the mania that had followed the Netscape IPO, only more quickly, more broadly, and with a corresponding decrease in intelligence. Rick Boyce, the chief of HotWired's advertising department, experienced the Amazon effect directly. His first call came from Barnes & Noble, a national bookseller that was racing to catch Amazon. Barnes & Noble wanted to be the exclusive bookseller on HotBot.

What did it mean to be the exclusive bookseller on a search engine? The origin of the idea came from Netscape's mistake. Back at the dawn of the boom, they gave Yahoo a free link on their home page. Their reasoning was that Yahoo, by compiling a directory, was giving customers a reason to purchase a browser. But Netscape was giving away browsers, not selling them, and meanwhile Yahoo's revenue from advertising was soaring. The practice of giving away free links soon ceased. After the success of the Amazon IPO, high-traffic sites started selling links to newly formed web retailers of books, cosmetics, music, pet supplies, and airline tickets. As Amazon shares rose, all of these businesses found an easy source of capital in the stock market.

"It was eye-opening to see what kind of deals were out there," Rick recalled. "The numbers were staggering." The greatest achievement of what came to be known as *business development* would come a year later, courtesy of drkoop.com, a site devoted to health products and medical information. In exchange for the right to appear prominently on AOL for four years, drkoop.com offered $89 million. The day the deal was announced, drkoop.com's stock price shot up more than 50 percent.

With its obstreperous magazine out of the way and a pile of money in the bank, Wired was finally ready to benefit from the delirium. The deals were getting richer by the minute. On July 17, 1998, the Nasdaq index reached a remarkable milestone, closing slightly above 2,000 for the first time.

"Bob Davis was calling me at six this morning," Beth Vanderslice said to Jane one day, when they encountered each other at the office. Though Louis and Jane did not have jobs at Wired Digital, they remained board members and the largest shareholders and felt free to stop by and check on things. Jane took Beth's announcement as a rebuke. Bob Davis was the chairman and CEO of Lycos, a HotBot competitor and one of the company's suitors. That he was calling Beth showed how little the founders' opinion mattered. Though Jane was busy raising Orson, and she and Louis hoped to have another child soon, she had no intention of abandoning her interest in the company she had helped to build. She was hard at work looking for an investor who would help them win back control.

Absurd and offensive—this was Louis's opinion of the offer Lycos made. The world was finally acknowledging the truth of what Wired had been saying for years. This was no time to sell out.

"It's like taking a Ferrari and selling it for scrap!" Louis said. His point, in talking to Salem, was always that Wired would be worth more later. He was not opposed to the investors taking profits; but today's profits were insufficient. Wired, he argued, would soon be worth billions.

Paul Salem disagreed. On July 28, 1998, Lycos offered more than $140 million for HotBot and the rest of Wired Digital. Any day now, when America came to its senses, they might be worth nothing.

Salem's urgency was real. No sooner had the Nasdaq index peaked in July at a little over 2,000 than it began to drop again, crossing back through 1,900 at the end of month, breaking 1,800 a week later, and giving up on 1,700 on August 27. Then, on August 31, in the largest single-day decline in its history, the Nasdaq index fell 140 points. "You could see the whites of people's eyes," said one trader to *The Wall Street Journal.* "There was relentless and indiscriminate selling."

September 1 saw the index below 1,500. There had been drops before, including the ones that killed Wired's IPO in 1996, and they had proven to be false alarms. But the party had to end sometime, and the latest plunge seemed decisive. After some painful negotiations, during which the price dropped to $84 million to reflect the market crash, Paul Salem and the rest of the Wired board accepted an offer from Lycos, over the usual tiresome objections from the largest, but neatly handcuffed, shareholders. The founders would earn a modest fortune from the proceeds of the sale and—their ex-partners prayed—would never be heard from again.

The contract took a few weeks to complete, and the deal was announced on October 7, 1998. Louis was crushed.

Then, at long last, the unlikeliest heroes arrived. They came out of the margins of capitalism, the dregs of the revolution whom Louis had scorned six years earlier, when the company was launched. Two weeks before the announcement of the Wired sale, a Silicon Valley enterprise specializing in the auction of collectibles—including rare and popular editions of little stuffed animals called Beanie Babies—bucked the market's downward trend and managed to sell shares to the public. The company was eBay, and its shares—priced by the bankers at $18 each—made their first trade on opening day at $53.

There were two reasons for eBay's success. The first was exogenous, or, as HotWired's engineers would have put it, *random.* In late summer 1998 the economies of Southeast Asia were melting down. There was a risk of a global recession. The normal medicine would be a cut in interest rates, but this risked sparking another bull run in the American markets.

Should Alan Greenspan and his colleagues at the Federal Reserve Bank sit on the sidelines and trust the international situation to take care of itself? Or should they abandon Wall Street's less careful speculators to the inevitable consequences of another market orgy? The speculators, making advance bets, drove prices up. They were not disappointed. At the end of September Greenspan cut rates. After a brief dip as sellers took their profits, the markets took off again. From below 1,400 on October 8, the Nasdaq index rallied to 1,500 on the twelfth, closed above 1,600 on the fifteenth, and reached 2,000 again six weeks later.

The second reason was endogenous. The debate, so long ago, between Louis and the young idealists in his company about the meaning and purpose of the World Wide Web was resolved at long last. Louis had once laughed at the idea that when people got used to browsing the web, they would spend their time searching the small nooks and crannies and relaxing, as he put it, with "Uncle Moe on his digital front porch." But he did not anticipate that Uncle Moe might be having a garage sale.

By the date of its public offering, there were nearly a million items for sale on eBay. The auction site took a fraction of every sale, plus a cash fee for each listing. eBay was profitable, its investors were rich, and proof had arrived at last that a web business could make money. Within months, a share of eBay purchased at the offering price of $18 was worth more than $700.

The rally was general. On November 12, 1998, AOL exceeded fourteen million members, and on November 17 its stock split two-for-one. On December 22 AOL was added to the S&P 500, and a week later it surpassed fifteen million members.

Wired's failure to go public with a valuation of $500 million and only $30 million in revenue was long forgotten. A company called Earthweb went public in November with just $1.5 million in revenue, and two days later theglobe.com went public with $1.7 million in revenue. They were soon trading at prices that suggested a capitalization of $315 million and $500 million, respectively.

Success gave rise to peculiar difficulties for the greatest speculative winners. The exit strategy for a small-time player was simple: sell your few thousand shares of eBay at three hundred dollars to any available eager beaver who shows up late in the game and hopes he can still get rich. But what if you control a whole company? The situation of Bob Davis, Wired's buyer, turned paradoxically grave just at the moment of widespread celebration.

Davis, whose company was based in Waltham, Massachusetts, far from the center of the boom, had proved himself an excellent strategist. Eighteen months earlier, the price of his company's shares was below twelve dollars, and his search engine reached less than 15 percent of web users. His technology was not good, and his traffic was languishing. He had only one thing going for him—Lycos was already a public company.

Davis went on a buying rampage, using his stock to purchase every company with good traffic that was not yet public. Rick Boyce watched his moves with admiration. "They bought everybody in the top twenty who was out of money, desperate and fucked," Rick recalled. "The next thing you know, they were saying, We're as big as Yahoo!"

His biggest purchases were WhoWhere, an online directory; Tripod and Angelfire, two sites offering free home pages; and, if the deal went through, HotWired, whose HotBot traffic made it one of the market leaders. With the announcement of the Wired deal, Lycos could claim to reach 40 percent of web users. His stock price soared. It doubled, then doubled again, then tripled. By the beginning of the new year it topped $145. Later, in a memoir called *Speed Is Life,* Davis explained that after purchasing other web companies "our cash position would often improve due to the cash on hand of the company we acquired, and our market capitalization would typically jump by a good deal more than we'd paid for the business. In essence, the acquisition was free."*

Davis's success caused two simultaneous crises. First, it threw a

* The acquisitions by Lycos were not really free; they were paid for by the buyers of Lycos's stock whose eagerness drove up the price of shares and whose cash compensated any insiders who took advantage of their new liquidity to sell out.

wrench into the Wired deal. The deal had Lycos buying Wired for $84 million worth of stock; but this was before Lycos shares skyrocketed. When Lycos went into orbit, Wired shareholders stood to gain more than $200 million over the original price.

Given the feelings of the board members toward one another, a dispute naturally arose about who would carry off the greatest portion of this unexpected bonus. Louis felt that this money should be shared by everybody in proportion to their ownership in the company. Salem argued that the rise in value of the Lycos shares should benefit the last round of investors in accordance with their preferences. A great deal of money was at stake. Everybody conferred with their lawyers. The sale to Lycos was delayed. Without the traffic from Wired, Lycos could not say they were challenging Yahoo.

Bob Davis's second problem was worse. eBay's profits, while wonderfully encouraging, had not been transferable to run-of-the-mill websites and search engines. These were not viable businesses. Davis now controlled a five-billion-dollar company at what might be the peak of the market. How could he lock in his gains? He had cannily acquired huge capital value in the bubble economy, but keeping it was another matter.

The greatest exit strategy at this grand scale was the one that would eventually be executed by AOL's Steve Case, who managed to purchase Time-Warner just months before the crash, using his vastly inflated stock for currency. But Bob Davis was no Steve Case. He occupied a second tier, and required a second-tier partner, and he found one in USA Networks, owned by Barry Diller.

The deal would be a merger. Davis would supply his search company, with its enormous valuation, its forty million dollars in annual revenue, and its regular losses. Diller would put in the Home Shopping Network, Ticketmaster, and some other businesses that together earned $300 million in profits on more than a billion dollars in revenue. The merger would marry the story of the Internet to the cash flows of mainstream media.

What it was was the *scheme of the multiple,* and the market violently hated it. The day after the merger was announced, Lycos stock dropped like a stone. By weighing down his search engine with a conventional business, Davis was renouncing the magic that was making everybody's shares float so buoyantly. Once he merged with USA Networks, investors would evaluate his company like a regular media enterprise, just as they had evaluated Wired Ventures like a regular magazine. In March a major Lycos shareholder was campaigning against the deal, and by April it was in deep trouble.

There are few financial positions more nerve-wracking than sitting on a pile of stock you cannot sell at a moment of wild inflation. Each jump in the price only adds to the stress, as it increases the money you stand to lose if you fail to get to the exit in time. Ed Anuff had been through this once before, and by the time he escaped he was just about broke. However, in May 1999 his mind was at rest, because he owned zero shares of Wired. At the time he was fired, in late 1997, he had owned a small number of options to buy Wired stock, but the company was in bad shape, and he was unhappy at being forced to abandon the search engine he had helped build, and he could not see adding to his humiliation by writing the company a check to pay for his options, whose value would then be controlled by Beth and other people he intensely disliked.

Ed had enough distance to watch the endgame with bitter glee. He was happy he no longer worked at HotWired. He was rooting for Louis to trash the deal and ruin the company, and leave everybody with nothing. Louis was angry, and appeared to be extremely reckless.

Wired's founder mobilized for a war over distribution of the proceeds of the sale to Lycos, deploying, first, all the resources of his rhetoric, and second, the threat of a value-destroying lawsuit he described as *Armageddon*. He rallied the other shareholders to come to his aid. He pointed out that the Lycos sale was negotiated by Paul Salem and other late-arriving investors, who controlled the board and hired the attorneys. Now, Louis claimed, they were making a grab for the proceeds. He accused them of cronyism, of fiduciary irresponsibility, of theft.

"Wired was ahead of the curve here," Louis would later say, referring to the failures of corporate governance that would gain so much attention in the Enron scandal. "This is the point where greed slips over into malfeasance and crime: the manipulation of a company for the benefit of those who control it to the disadvantage of the rest of the shareholders."

To Paul Salem, however, protecting the rights of the rest of the shareholders meant completing a sale of Wired while their ownership stake still had value. He saw that Louis was angry about losing control of the company, and he interpreted his attack as a transparent scheme to undermine the sale. Salem was under no obligation to share Louis's faith in the boundless future of Internet media. Besides, he also had a fiduciary duty to the shareholders in his investment fund. They expected him to be rational. He would concede none of his preferences, which he believed gave him a clear right to a disproportionate share of the extra $200 million.

Louis hoped that if he could get enough of the original owners to oppose the terms of the sale, he would be able to block it. Many refused. Andrew took a leading role in organizing the defectors, always emphasizing Louis's ability to produce a defeat out of the most promising material. John Battelle, who had his hands full at *The Industry Standard,* sent a message that he would accept any compromise that left him with enough money to build himself a carport for his new home. Sadly, what the idealists of the Grotto had once been to Louis, Louis had now become to the board members in charge, and even to some of his old companions and friends. He seemed interested only in exercising his talents, in inventing a new medium, in changing the destiny of humankind. His claims about Wired as a billion-dollar company failed to disguise motivations that had nothing to do with money. He wanted to complete his mission. *He was not maximizing shareholder value.* At a time when smart people were cashing out, this was the worst thing you could say.

John Plunkett got opposing calls from Louis and Andrew. John no longer worked for *Wired.* His mania for control and his unusual talent, which were held in check and given direction by Louis's domineering manner, had been impossible to integrate into the more workaday processes of Condé Nast. He had resigned under pressure. But John's unhappiness at being ejected from *Wired* did not make him nostalgic for Louis's leadership, and he thought he would probably take sides against his ex-friend. After all, Louis had never done anything to protect his feelings. Louis's

disregard had extended even to the last day of his editorship, when
Steve Florio, of Condé Nast, along with a couple of other Man-
hattanites in admirable business suits, came out for a ceremony of
transition. The staff gathered in the lunchroom, and Kevin Kelly
made a short speech. Louis was touched, and his emotions affected his staff, who understood the magnitude of the change.
When his turn to respond came, Louis said that in all the praise
and admiration for the magazine, there had been perhaps less than
just attention to another person whose hard work and total dedi-
cation had been absolutely crucial—even as crucial as his own
labors—to its success. John agreed with these words and stood
modestly in the back ranks savoring them; then there was a polite
burst of applause when Louis named Jane.

Now Louis was asking for John's help. He talked to John about
the importance of sticking together, and John silently remembered
the great employee rebellion of 1993, when Louis and Jane and the
other board members sneakily tried to create a superior class of
stock for themselves. John's opinion was that he was destined to
get a better deal from Paul Salem and Louis's other enemies than
he ever would if Louis had any control over the situation. So he
was open to any good compromise, but when he received a document to sign there was no spreadsheet attached showing how
the money would be parceled out. He later described calling Bob
Smelick, the Sterling Payot partner who had been an original
Wired investor and who was now crunching the numbers, and
asking for the details.

"I can't show you the spreadsheet," John remembered the
board member saying. "It's confidential." He asked John to sign a

letter of agreement whose terms would be revealed to him later, after the deal was completed.

John was surprised by this protocol. "How can I sign this sheet saying I've read the proposal if you can't show me the proposal?" he asked. He got angry and decided to stick with Louis. Kevin Kelly never wavered in his loyalty to Louis; Nicholas Negroponte and Charlie Jackson, Wired's original angels, stuck by him as well.

The forces were therefore closely balanced. The terms of the Lycos offer forbade Wired from negotiating with other potential buyers until June 15. Louis managed to hold things up as the deadline approached. After this date, all bets would be off, and everybody knew that confusion would ignite Louis's dream of retaking control. Of course, it might also result in everybody's shares becoming worthless.

Louis was unfazed. "We are being shortchanged in this transaction!" he told Jane.

Jane and Louis were out of money again. They were supposed to be receiving severance checks from Wired, but because they had refused to sign a statement renouncing the right to sue the company, their severance checks had been stopped. They had no funds in the bank, for at no point had they been able to exchange any of their Wired shares for cash.

Jane and Louis were now expecting another child, due in early summer. Jane had witnessed numerous instances of Louis's dangerous behavior, and she could not say that his bold decisions had always turned out for the best. She had no doubt Louis was willing to wreck everything for the sake of his principles. It was not hard for her to imagine a setback so damaging that they might never recover from it. But they were no longer completely free to uproot themselves and start again from scratch. They had new responsibilities.

Jane controlled her own shares with complete independence. She owned nearly as many as Louis did, and they were worth millions even if Salem's group took a large portion they did not deserve. By fighting with the board, Louis risked driving Lycos away. What if the market tanked before they figured out their next move? Salem and his partners were appealing to her to save the deal and rescue her own future.

Negotiations stretched into May. Jane was not shy about fighting with Louis, and the verbal fireworks that had frightened employees in the first days of the magazine recurred frequently during that difficult spring. By May 5 the Salem group finally offered to split the difference. Jane told Louis that they should accept this compromise. Louis refused.

He was happy to watch the deal fall apart. If it did, Wired could try to go public again, this time as a profitable Internet company. "How great would that be?" he asked.

"The whole idea that we would try to go public again was terrifying," Jane later said. She did not think she had it in her.

For weeks Jane had suffered as the intermediary between increasingly furious combatants, and whenever she got off the phone, after an hour or two or more of listening and responding and taking notes, and reviewed the latest compromise with Louis, his answer was invariably no, often expressed less pleasantly. Jane reflected on the fact that she had now been answering the phone for Louis for ten years. She could handle small talk and the human interest very well; he could not do it at all.

By May 7 the merger between Bob Davis and Barry Diller was widely known to be on the verge of collapse. This helped Lycos's share price, as buyers got used to the idea that it would stay a pure Internet company. But another broken deal would be dangerous for Lycos.

Bankers know nothing if not how to exploit desperation, and Bob Davis soon learned that if the Wired deal was to be rescued, he was going to have to pay more. A clever expedient was found: since Wired had tens of millions of dollars leftover from the sale of the magazine, and since Lycos would be acquiring this cash along with the company's other assets, Davis would agree to pay for Wired's cash in Lycos stock, and he would value the stock at the price agreed upon at the time of the deal, last October, rather than the current, much inflated price. This would put about thirty million dollars more into the kitty, which the warring shareholders could split. Louis, as always, was inclined to refuse.

In all these proposals, a pool of money was set aside for the common shareholders among the employees. Originally, it was 10 percent of the total proceeds. This amount was whittled down during negotiations between Louis and the board, with portions of it being handed out to classes of shareholders who, unlike the employees, were directly represented. There was some concern that there might be an exodus of employees as the sale was going through, and the board counted upon Beth Vanderslice to hold things together. In accordance with the prevailing theories about executive compensation, the board diluted the common stock and issued Beth four million dollars' worth of new shares. Rick Boyce, who was managing the advertising staff, got three million dollars' worth. This emptied more than half of the employee pool.

These facts drove Ed crazy. Though he no longer had any stake in the settlement, he wore himself out criticizing it as unjust. Most of the value at HotWired was due to HotBot, and Wired's original participation in HotBot was mostly due to him—and he was to get nothing. Beth had not even supported HotBot!

Over drinks one night, Andrew outlined the process bankers use to determine the distribution of proceeds from a sale. "The people at the table," he said, "grab as much as they can." That was the whole of his lesson.

Andrew was holding forth at the end of two small tables pushed together in a North Beach bar. Carl and Ed flanked him on either side, and at the far end sat Chip and me. It was a reunion of sorts. Carl had become the back-page columnist for John Battelle's *Industry Standard,* and he called himself a microstar, devoting himself to fulfilling the obligations of celebrity—or microcelebrity—with all the same deadpan earnestness he had formerly given to Suck. He stayed out very late, and wore expensive shiny shirts, and grew his hair long; it fell straight down from his forehead and then curved lightly to the side, almost covering one eye.

Andrew had lost weight and regained his relaxed and self-pleased expression. "I came out of it best," he said. "Just add up the numbers and you'll see." Andrew's shares would be worth several million under the latest plan.

Such a statement was sure to gall Ed, but Carl piped up first; surely Louis and Jane, he said, had outdone Andrew! If Louis went along with the latest settlement, he would get more than fifteen million.

"Louis worked for five years for no salary," Andrew said. He argued that these uncompensated years should be taken into account, reducing their average annual pay and putting him on top. It was a silly argument, but it had its intended effect. Ed could barely talk.

Finally, Ed got his words of protest flowing. Why had Andrew not looked out for him? He had followed Andrew's every command. "It would have been more fair to let us know at the beginning it was every man for himself," he said.

Andrew laughed. "What is this, *Sesame Street*?" he said. "Every man for himself means every man for himself!" Andrew explained that the very *point* of being a banker was to have an unfair advantage, and the best way to get an unfair advantage is for the other person not to suspect that you have one.

"That is why Andrew is my hero," said Carl. Carl admired how well Andrew had positioned himself in relation to Louis's story— not as a believer but as a fake believer, a double agent. This allowed him to retain his pride while jumping over to the winning side.

"It's all a rationalization for how badly he fucked up," Chip countered. Andrew's scheme of the multiple had directly led to the company's breakup and sale. His dumb idea ruined everything. That Andrew would get rich off the proceeds was a mere accident.

"No," said Andrew. He was afraid he had been misunderstood. He was not presenting himself as a genius. "It's not that I sat down in 1994 and said to myself, Here's how I'm going to screw everybody. It's just how I am."

"Beth did well," I pointed out.

Andrew felt that he deserved some of the credit for the vast dilution of the common shares. "She asked me how much money to give herself," he said. "I told her, 'Rip as much as you can out of this pig, because that's what I would do.' "

"Andrew did not have a plan," murmured Carl softly.

"There was no grand plan," said Andrew. "We were just looking out for ourselves."

"But Andrew," Carl said, and he suddenly sounded plaintive. "*You were in charge.* Did you ever look at your business card and notice those letters after your name, CEO?"

"I didn't start out as the CEO," said Andrew, with a grin for the ages. "I worked my way up to it."

But Andrew was counting his money prematurely, for the deal was not complete. Louis invited various subordinates to discuss his plans, should a last-minute savior be located. Carl, for instance, believed that he would become the ruler of Wired Digital in place of Beth, who would be dismissed. But Carl was in no shape to give orders, whatever happened, as he had found some new drugs to experiment with, and some new late-night companions who valued his microcelebrity and loved to lead him astray.

Bob Forlenza, representing Tudor Investment Corporation, called frequently to discuss a compromise and to explore the chance that a separate peace could be negotiated with Jane.

Louis was doing little to strengthen their love. On May 9 the sun was coming in through the west-facing windows of the Berkeley house, the living room was like an oven, and Jane felt as heavy and immobile as only a woman in the last weeks of pregnancy can feel on a sticky afternoon. A new proposal had been faxed that morning. The phone rang, and Louis looked at her from across the room. He did not move.

She could pick the phone up, but when she did, she would be in control of what came out of her mouth—not Louis. The phone stopped ringing, then started again.

He was not pregnant, and he was as close to it as she, but he did not move—and neither did she. The phone stopped ringing, then started again.

Louis and Jane looked at the phone.

Orson, their firstborn, had been suffering from a lack of attention for weeks. His parents were spending all their time behind closed doors, arguing and talking on the phone. He toddled across the floor and looked at Jane unhappily.

"Mommy, answer the phone," Orson said.

She ignored him.

Orson weaved across the floor, pulled the phone off the hook, and left it dangling. Jane looked at Louis for the last time. It was his turn to carry the burden. He did not get up.

"Hello," said a small voice coming out of the swinging handset. "Hello! Hello!"

Louis just laughed. Then Jane laughed too, though perhaps her tone was different, and she heaved herself from her chair.

"You have to give me an answer now," said Bob.

This was her moment to save herself, but it was too late. She was giddy and exhausted, and honestly beyond caring. Louis had worn her out.

"No," Jane said, "we do not accept this deal."

Louis looked at her proudly. "Perfect!" he crowed.

The next week Paul Salem took the only action left that would stymie Louis's campaign to wreck the sale: he agreed to most of their financial demands. This rational maneuver made further protests impossible. The sale was ratified. The total price for all of

Wired—more than $90 million from Condé Nast for the magazine and nearly $300 million from Lycos for the rest, was higher than the value Louis and Jane had claimed for their company during the road show. For Louis, this was defeat masquerading as victory. He would lose his company, and he would become very rich.

On June 29 the Wired board of directors had a meeting open to all shareholders to vote for the final terms of the sale. Since the biggest shareholders, including Louis and Jane, had signed statements pledging their affirmation, the meeting was a formality, but the prospect had a gloomy appeal, so a few of the employees went.

The setting was a conference room on the twenty-fifth floor of Maritime Plaza, an enormous building with a reception area on the second floor and a desolate, street-level lobby. There was a paid security guard outside at the door, and a long table manned by attorneys where the stockholders were asked to show their driver's licenses. The Wired executives were prepared for a crowd. The Securities and Exchange Commission had insisted on an explicit accounting of the executive's profits, and there was no telling how the common shareholders would react.

The windows of the conference room opened onto a view of the Golden Gate Bridge enshrouded in fog. As it turned out, one security guard was plenty. The meeting was attended only by Beth Vanderslice, two attorneys, a company accountant, Barbara Kuhr, John Plunkett, two young designers, an ex-Wired publicist who had recently become successful selling temporary tattoos, and me.

One of the attorneys, preparing to open the meeting, said: "I'm afraid your investment in getting here will exceed the return." He meant that the meeting would be brief.

Another attorney was appointed *director of elections,* and the company's accountant was appointed secretary, and the time was read—9:02 A.M.—and pledged votes were declared by the accountant, and the time was read again, and the meeting was adjourned. Officially, it had taken two minutes. Wired Ventures was erased.

During the next four weeks, as the documents and contracts were hurried to completion, the price for Internet securities rose and fell. On the date of closing, a share of Lycos was worth ninety-five dollars. Louis enjoyed noting that every investor who had ever touched Wired made money, but for the most part he was depressed. When he spoke, his tone was recriminatory.

The value of Louis and Jane's portion, together, was more than thirty million dollars. Some fraction of this money would go toward the purchase of an ancient apartment on the Herengracht in Amsterdam. There was a flower-filled garden, and a delicately tinted ceiling whose cherubs had been painted in the eighteenth century. Jane gave birth to a daughter named Zoe in June, just before Louis's fiftieth birthday, and their first summer after *Wired* would be spent in an old château in the South of France, with dinners prepared by the staff and served on china on the lawn. The little bungalow in Berkeley grew into a full-size home that cut into the rocky hill, and the shaggy tree over Strawberry Canyon was taken out, yielding a classic view. The sharp and—to some— odious identity of his unusual magazine and even more unusual organization dissipated under the influence of Condé Nast and Lycos, and the splash Louis had once made in South Park settled down, for a time, into smooth prosperity. Louis was an angel now, and he listened to pitches from other dreamers, and tried to help them see the future more clearly. He diversified his investments, gaining security for his family that, properly managed, could last through generations.

Jane diversified her investments, too.

On the question of financial value, the final resistance was overcome. The Nasdaq index broke through 3,000 in November 1999. It hit 4,000 a month later. And on March 9 of the following year, not long after Steve Case announced his purchase of Time-Warner for $106 billion in AOL stock, the index closed above 5,000 for the first time. The very next day *The Wall Street Journal* ran a front-page story whose headline read: "The New Chips: Conservative Investors Are Finally Saying: Maybe Tech Isn't a Fad."

The last skeptics were now in the market, and two weeks later the collapse began.

ACKNOWLEDGMENTS

Louis Rossetto gave me access to his files and censored nothing. I respect his courage enormously. Andrew Anker, Ed Anuff, Joey Anuff, Martha Baer, Chip Bayers, Bill Jesse, Jane Metcalfe, John Plunkett, Peter Rutten, Paul Salem, Kristen Spence, Carl Steadman, Randy Stickrod, and dozens of other people associated with Wired shared their stories with me. I owe them many thanks. John Brockman, my formidable agent, launched the project. Scott Moyers, my editor at Random House, supplied unflagging support. In early 2003, Jonathan Karp at Random House took over and graciously saw the book through.

Special thanks to Susan Lehman, at Riverhead Press, for her valuable editorial help. Kevin Kelly pushed hard to have the story told and opened the most important doors. Thanks also to Lesley Bonnet, an indispensable copy editor, to Andrea McCloud for assistance with research in the early phases, to Melanie Cornwell for advocacy and encouragement, to Erik Adigard and M.A.D. (madxs.com) and Carl Steadman (members .plastic.com/carl) for much and varied aid, and to my generous first readers: Martha Baer, Cate Corcoran, Carol Lloyd, Sarah Miles, Davitt Sigerson, and Joan S. Wolf.

For documents, discussion, and alternate histories: www.aether.com.

INDEX

ABC-TV, 80, 97

Abolitionist, The, 6

Adigard, Erik, 70–71

Advance Magazine Publishers, 191*n*

advertising:

  for Apple/Macintosh, 20–21

  blink tag for, 120

  cost-per-thousand pricing of, 134,
    167, 176, 183, 221

  HotWired, 107, 109, 112, 113,
    133–34, 136, 166–67, 176, 183

  icons in, 71

  income from, 31, 84, 106,
    176–77, 214, 220–21, 242

  loop of, 220

  and mass marketing, 107

  membership-and-password system
    for, 107–8, 120–21, 137, 142,
    150

  online, 62, 106–7, 109, 113,
    133–34, 166

  sales of, 70, 84, 106–7, 133,
    176–77, 209, 220

  shrinkage of, 94

  targeted, 107, 134

telemarketing, 21–23

user-tracking of, 134, 137, 143,
  150

web, 62, 107, 109, 120–21,
  133–34, 136, 156, 166–67,
  176, 183, 219, 243

Afghanistan, mujahedeen in, 9

African National Congress, 13

Alameda Newspaper Group, 93,
  94

alternative health, 54

Amazon, 241–42

America, 32

American Society of Magazine
  Editors, 88

anarchists, 52, 98–99

Andreessen, Marc, 101–4, 120, 142,
  178

Angelfire, 247

angel investors, 29, 62, 70, 253,
  261–62

Anker, Andrew:

  and bankruptcy, 235

  on deal making, 181, 182, 183,
    186, 224, 241, 256–58

Anker, Andrew (*cont.*)
  early years of, 57
  and endgame, 256–58
  exit strategy sought by, 167, 176,
    206, 223, 235, 251
  and First Boston, 57–58
  and HotBot, 184–87, 224, 225
  and HotWired, 107–8, 112, 113,
    125, 133, 134, 137–38, 140,
    142, 150, 180
  and IPO, 173–76, 192, 194, 195,
    198–99, 210, 214, 219
  liquidity event sought by, 157,
    166, 187, 223, 233–34, 235
  and the multiple, 172–73, 187
  and Netizen, 158–59, 164, 166
  and Sterling Payot, 64–65
  and Suck, 169, 170
  and web business, 106, 157, 166,
    171
Anuff, Ed, 75–76, 152–54, 176,
    180–81, 197
  and bankruptcy, 232, 234
  and endgame, 249–50, 256–57
  and HotBot, 184–86, 199, 223–25
  and Inktomi, 182–84, 186,
    223–24
  and Suck, 154, 167, 179
Anuff, Joseph (Joey), 152–56,
    168–70, 185, 225
AOL (America Online), 111, 178–80
  and access to the web, 132, 138,
    165, 168, 180, 221
  and acquisitions, 167–68, 248,
    262

  advertising on, 243
  as commercial system, 102, 132,
    138, 168, 179–80, 219, 243
  growth of, 138, 165, 221, 246
  stock price of, 168, 179, 246
apocalypse, 53–54
Apple computers, 20–21, 33, 42, 46,
    70, 139
Apple Multimedia Lab, 51
Architectural Digest, 87
Architecture Machine, The
    (Negroponte), 50
Arms, Abigail, 213
Asimov, Isaac, 147
AT&T, 112, 220*n*
Awaken, 140

Baer, Martha, 93–95, 100–101
Baffler, The, 147, 148
banking:
  and junk bonds, 57–58
  and *Wired,* 58–59, 60, 64–65, 70,
    81, 82, 85–87
Barlow, John Perry, 36–38, 98–99
Barnes & Noble, 242
Battelle, John, 64, 65, 95, 101, 112,
    157, 164, 171, 196, 230, 251,
    256
Bay Area Computer Currents, 47
Bayers, Chip, 109–10, 112, 135,
    138, 151, 157, 163, 180, 198
BBC, 97
Beanie Babies, 245
Behlendorf, Brian, 104
Bengal (IPO project), 175

Berners-Lee, Tim, 102

Bianca's Smut Shack, 126

Bonnie, Shelby, 197

Book of the Month Club, 209

Borders Books and Music, 156, 209

Boswell (Gerard Van der Leun), 81,
    212–13

Boyce, Rick, 112-13, 133-34, 150,
    167, 177n, 242, 247, 255

Brand, Stewart, 41, 44, 53–54, 64,
    68

Brass, Tinto, 8

Brewer, Eric, 181–83, 185, 223, 224

broadband networks, 97

Brooks, David, 130

Brown, Tina, 60

Browning, John, 220

browser wars, 103–4

Burda Digital, Inc., 137, 162n

Burn Rate (Wolff), 27

Business Week, 47, 208, 209

Byron, Christopher, 202

Caligula (film), 8

Camp, Susanna, 184

Campeau Corporation, 57

Canon copier, 46, 69

Cape Town, South Africa, 12

Capital Group, 218

Case, Steve, 219, 248, 262

Castillo, Nori, 84

CBS, 80, 97

Chapman, Gary, 129–30

Chung, Connie, 80

Cisco Systems, 139

Clark, Jim, 101

Clinton, Bill, 88, 128

Club Med, 112

CNET, 156, 176, 197, 205, 220

CNN, 65, 80, 210

Cobb, Stefan, 198

CoEvolution Quarterly, 41, 53–54,
    61, 66

Columbia Young Republicans, 6

Communism, collapse of, 72

CompuServe, 102, 168

Computer Graphics World, 29

Computer Lib (Nelson), 20–21

Computer Professionals for Social
    Responsibility, 129

Computers and Translation, 18

computer technology:
    buyouts and mergers in, 168–70
    color production in, 74
    design possibilities with, 34
    dynamics of complexity in, 55
    e-mail replacing postal mail, 138
    investors in, 141–42, 202–6,
        245–46; see also stock market
    as liberating social force, 16–17,
        20–21, 22, 26, 34, 43, 47, 52,
        55, 59, 71, 97, 128–29
    and the Long Boom, 227–28,
        237
    networks in, 42–55, 61–62, 81,
        97, 119; see also online
        networks
    object-oriented programming
        (OOP), 73
    profits taken from, 239–62

Condé Nast, 86–87, 106, 156, 240–41, 251, 252, 260, 261
copyright law, 73, 98–99, 105
Craig, Peter, 74
Crichton, Michael, 98, 208
Critchett, Amy, 76–79, 88
Critical Theory, 119
cryptography, 73, 83, 84
CUC International, 191*n,* 235
cultural resistance, 54
cybernetics, 53–54, 55, 129; *see also* computer technology
cypherpunks, 83, 122

Danbury Printing and Litho, 69–70, 82, 83, 84, 87
Darwin, Charles, 55
Davis, Bob, 243, 246–49, 255
Davis, Fred, 45–46
Delphi, 102
Details, 47
Deutsche Telecom, 217–18
DigIt, 30
Diller, Barry, 248–49, 255
disintermediation, 61, 83, 107, 119, 129
do-it-yourself media, 54
Drexel Burnham Lambert, 58
Drexler, Eric, 42
drkoop.com, 242–43
Drucker, Peter, 147
Dungeons and Dragons, 121

Earthweb, 246
eBay, 245–46, 248

Economist, The, 158
Egg, 31
Electric Word, 18–23, 28, 29, 30, 31, 36, 38, 43, 44
electronic bulletin boards, 61–62, 102, 111
Electronic Frontier Foundation, 36, 48, 78, 81, 147, 210
Elmer-DeWitt, Philip, 97
Enron Corporation, 250
entrepreneurship, 54, 75, 107, 121, 123, 151, 181
ESPN, 156
E.T., 55
Excite, 184, 193, 197, 198, 201, 206, 214, 220

Fame, 31
Federal Communications Commission, 47, 97
Federal Express, 219
Federal Reserve Bank, 245
Feed, 198–99
feedback, 53, 54, 55
Felici, Jim, 29, 34
Felsenstein, Lee, 45, 47
Fido (FidoNet), 62
Filo, David, 139–40
Financial Post, The, 198
First Boston Bank, 57–58
Fisher, Lawrence M., 202
Fitt, Lawton, 207, 218
Fitzgerald, F. Scott, 210
Florio, Steve, 252
Folio, 74

Forbes, 100

Forbes, Walter, 235

Forbes ASAP, 100

Ford, Henry, 158

Foresight Institute, 42

Forlenza, Bob, 222, 258, 259

Forrester, Jay, 53

Free Software Foundation, 45

Ganesh, 110

Garcia, Jerry, 142, 143

Gates, Bill, 103, 195

Gauthier, Paul, 181–84, 224

Gibson, William, 44, 67, 99

Gilder, George, 100

Gilmore, John, 73

Gingrich, Newt, 128–29, 146–47,
    149

Global Business Network, 227

Global Network Navigator (GNN),
    167, 168, 171

Globescan, 5, 12

Godwin, Mike, 210–13

Goldman Sachs, 191–94, 201–4,
    207, 213, 214, 217–18

Good Morning America (TV), 80

Gopher, 119

Gore, Al, 128, 147

government-research networks, 62

Grateful Dead, 36, 111, 140

Greenspan, Alan, 245

Guardian, The (London), 96, 130,
    164, 175

Guccione, Bob, 8

Guernsey, Kenn, 171

Guevara, Zach, 218

Gulf War, 31, 32

Hale, Constance, 100

Hall, Justin, 110–11, 112, 124,
    126–27, 128, 136, 138–39, 140

Hambrecht & Quist, 141

HardWired, 164, 209

Harmon, Amy, 232

Hawken, Paul, 61

Haymarket Square Riots, Chicago,
    52

Hearst Building, 94

Hearst Corporation, 93–94

Heidelberg six-color press, 69

Heilemann, John, 97, 157–58, 211

Hennessy, John M., 58

Heron, Katrina, 230, 237

Hertzberg, Hendrik, 147–48

Hewlett-Packard, 42

Home Shopping Network, 249

HotBot, 184–88, 196, 199, 214,
    223–25, 232, 241, 242,
    243–44, 247, 256

HotMOO, 121, 122

HotSearch, 183

HotWired, 107–10, 119–20

  and Amazon, 242

  audiences of, 165, 183

  competition for, 139–40, 154–55,
    156, 166, 176, 197

  features in, 112–13, 140

  free content on, 142

  funding of, 125, 162, 235

  growth of, 125, 131–32, 135,

HotWired (*cont.*)
 152, 153, 163–65, 171, 175,
  186, 209
 icons for, 109
 launch of, 112–14, 120, 139, 182
 leadership of, 164, 197, 221, 229
 membership-and-password system
  of, 107, 108, 120–22, 127–28,
  136–37, 142
 merged back into Wired, 173–75,
  189–91, 204–5
 new ideas in, 162–63, 171
 office space of, 125–26, 138
 planting flags in, 132, 134, 150,
  164, 180
 profitability of, 133, 135, 162–63,
  172–73, 174, 180, 214, 219,
  222–23
 reasons for not using, 164
 repeat audience of, 136, 137, 164
 sale of, 247
 shareholders of, 125
 spinoff of, 125
 staff protests about, 121–24, 137
 and Suck, 169–70, 225
 value of, 189–91, 214, 223, 256
 web advertising in, 107, 109, 112,
  113, 133–34, 136, 166–67,
  176, 183
HotWired LLC, 125, 170
Hoyam, Andrew, 35
Hundt, Reed, 97

IBM, 139
image tags, 103, 119

Inc., 218
India, feature stories in, 67
Industry Standard, The, 230, 251,
 256
Infiniti, 46
Infoseek, 133–34, 139, 166, 220
Ink Taalservice, 12, 15–18, 21, 26,
 239
Inktomi, 182–84, 186, 193, 223–25
Internet:
 anonymity on, 127
 browser wars, 103–4
 business development on, 242–43
 connectivity in, 102, 105–6
 early years of, 99, 102
 growth of, 103, 106, 138, 189,
  227
 hobby sites on, 111
 investors in, 141-43, 145, 174,
  197-98, 206-8, 217-18, 220*n*,
  237
 links on, 134, 242
 as metaphor, 147
 as noncommercial, 102, 108, 109,
  113, 127, 138, 140–41, 142,
  145, 179
 perception vs. reality in, 178
 pirating on, 73, 99, 104, 110
 stock market losses, 197–98
 technical sites for, 139
 and the Web, *see* World Wide Web
 Wired link of, 105–6
Ishibashi, Rex, 171–72, 174, 189,
 190, 206
Italy, Red Brigades in, 9

Jackson, Charlie, 51, 70, 82, 253
Jennings, Tom, 62
Jesse, Bill, 64–65, 70, 72, 79, 81,
    82, 135, 171, 174, 237
Jobs, Steve, 33
Johnson, Steven, 198
Jones, Paul Tudor, 162*n*
junk bonds, 57–58
Jupiter Communications, 220
Justice Department, U.S., vs.
    Microsoft, 96

Kao, John, 171
Kapor, Mitch, 36, 48
Keizer, Maurice, 21–23
Kelly, Kevin, 39–43, 45, 52–53, 55,
    63, 171
  book by, 95, 100
  conversion to Christianity of,
    40–41
  and endgame, 252, 253
  as executive editor, 64, 66
  and IPO, 174, 175
  personality of, 52–53, 55, 63
  and *Wired,* 52, 54–55, 63, 64, 66,
    174, 175
Kennedy, Alison, 44, 48
Kensey, Doug, 196–97
Kesey, Ken, 44
Kid A in Alphabet Land (Steadman),
    119
Kisman, Max, 18–19, 109
Knowledge Bowl, 116–17
Koenig, Brad, 207, 214
Kreth, Will, 51, 62, 64, 72

Kuhr, Barbara:
  and endgame, 260
  and John Plunkett, 28, 29, 30, 33,
    34, 49, 63, 95, 216
  and *Wired,* 62–64, 66, 109, 171

Lacan, Jacques, 119
Lack, Andrew, 211
Language Technology, 18–21, 26,
    109, 151
Lanier, Jaron, 48
Law, John, xii-xiii
Leary, Timothy, 45
Leonsis, Ted, 178–79, 219, 221
Letters of Marshall McLuhan, The
    (McKenna), 45
Levy, Steven, 83
Leyden, Peter, 227–28
libertarianism, xi-xii, 6–7, 20, 52,
    129
Life, 74
Limits to Growth, The (Forrester),
    53–54
Links to the Underground, 110–11,
    124, 126, 128
Linotron, 6
Linotype, 5–6, 17
liquidity event, 157, 166, 168, 187
Los Angeles Times, 209, 232
LSD, 44
Lycos, 139, 184, 206, 220, 243–44,
    247–50, 253–55, 260, 261
Lyle Stuart, publishers, 8
Lyman, Kathleen, 70, 84
Lyons, Dana, 237

McDonald's, 98, 153
mcdonalds.com, 98
McFarland, Ian, 121–24
Macintosh, 21
McKenna, Terrance, 45
McKinley Group, 220*n*
McLuhan, Marshall, 71, 149
MacWEEK, 46, 47, 64
Macworld, 28, 30, 32, 62, 63, 72, 77
Mad Magazine, 96–97, 208
Madsen, Hunter, 165–66, 220–21
M.A.D. studio, 70
Magazine Consulting Group, 74
magazine industry:
  competition in, 48
  distribution in, 60
  economics of, 60–61, 74, 81–82
  and Gulf War, 31, 32
  manifesto in, 33–34
  National Magazine Award, 88
  new launches in, 31–32, 60, 127
  as out of touch, 45, 74
  pushing the limits in, 69, 84
  return on investment in, 60, 74
  trade journal of, 74
  traditional, *see* mainstream media
mainstream media:
  ambush of, 96
  attention paid to *Wired* by, 65, 80, 99, 113, 201–5, 208–10, 232
  bankers and, 58–59, 60
  computer culture to supplant, 100
  conservative and servile, 61

  defective output of, 16
  election coverage by, 157–58
  electronic routing around, 97, 127
  future of, 94
  Louis's hatred of, 16, 59
  magazines in, *see* magazine industry
  online versions of, 119, 154, 156–57, 242
  as out of touch, 71, 97–98, 100, 107
  traditional production of, 93–94
Malone, John, 97
Manhattan, Inc., 31
Markoff, John, 99
Marxism, 147–48
MCI, 112
Meadows, Dennis and Donella, 53–54
Media Lab, 88
Medium is the Massage, The (McLuhan), 71
Meeker, Mary, 205, 219
Mergenthaler, Ottmar, 5
Mergenthaler Linotype Company, 5–6, 17, 192
mergers and acquisitions, 58
Merry Pranksters, 44, 45
Metcalfe, Jane:
  as advertising director, 64
  and bankruptcy, 222, 226, 229–30, 235, 237–38
  and Barbara and John, 28, 30
  and Barlow, 36–38

and cash flow, 82–83, 84

children of, 226, 243, 259, 261

complaints handled by, 78–79

and endgame, 253–54, 256, 258, 260, 261–62

firing of, 237–38

first meetings of Louis and, 10–12

and HotWired, 163–64

houses purchased by, 170–71, 261

and incoming mail, 75–77

and IPO, 195, 198, 204–7, 210, 212–16, 226

move to France, 261

move to New York, 25–34

move to Oakland, 85

move to San Francisco, 34–38, 43

in Paris, 17–18

personality of, 226

phone solicitations by, 21–23, 43, 47, 62

as president, 64

and Real Invest, 11

and *Wired* beginnings, 30–38, 146

and *Wired* future, 174

and *Wired* ownership, 82

and *Wired* U.K., 175–76

Microsoft, 67, 73, 96, 141, 178, 179, 195, 220*n*

Microtimes, 47

middlemen, economic role of, 61

Miller, Robert, 240–41

Mind Blowing and Its Methods (Rheingold), 108

Mind Grenades (book), 209, 215

Minneapolis Star-Tribune, 119

Minor, Halsey, 197

Miramax, 60

Mississippi Company, xiii

MIT Media Lab, 50

Mondo 2000, 44–45, 47, 48

Morgan Stanley, 141, 164, 205, 219

Mosaic, 101, 102, 110, 119, 136, 141

Mosier, Eugene, 46, 64

Mother Earth News, 32

Mother Jones, 147

Mozilla, 101, 103, 120

MSNBC, 209–12, 222

Murdoch, Rupert, 25

Myhrvold, Nathan, 73

Nasdaq:

peaks and valleys of, 157, 197, 206, 207–8, 212, 226, 227, 228–29, 243, 244, 262

and Wired IPO, 195, 217, 219

National Center for Supercomputing Applications, University of Illinois, 101, 102

National Lampoon, 26

National Magazine Award, 88

National Security Agency, 97

Nature, 47

NBC, 97

NCSA Mosaic, 141

Negroponte, Nicholas, 50, 58, 59, 70, 82, 88, 253

Nelson, Ted, 20–21, 102
NeoData Services, 77, 196
Netizen, 158–59, 163, 164, 166, 171, 188, 197, 209–10
Netizen, The (TV), 210–12
Netly News, 156, 168
Netscape, 133, 136, 193
  free browsers of, 141, 178, 179, 242
  impact of, 147, 154, 162, 173, 220, 242
  IPO of, 141–43, 145, 146, 147, 162, 165, 242
  Mozilla browser as, 120
  multiple of, 172, 173, 187
  stock price of, 141, 142
  in top ten, 139, 220
Network Solutions, 155
New Age, 41
Newhouse, Si, 86–87, 240–41
New Republic, The, 130–31
News That Stayed News, 66
Newsweek, 80, 113, 201–2
New Yorker, The, 60, 87, 147, 230
New York Observer, The, 202
New York Times, The, 47, 99, 113, 166, 185, 202
New York Times Magazine, The, 6
Nietzsche, 233
Nike, 193
Nippon Telegraph and Telephone, 191n
Nixon, Richard M., 6, 7, 8
NTT, 162n

Odgers, Jamie, 51
O'Donnell, Lawrence, 211
Olsen, Jimmy (comics), 64
One to One Future, The (Rogers and Pepper), 107
online networks, 44–55
  advertising via, 62
  commercial, 102, 106
  competition in, 44–45, 99
  conferencing via, 62
  disintermediation in, 61, 107, 119
  electronic bulletin boards, 61–62, 102, 111
  government-supported research, 62
  pirating on, 73, 99, 104, 110
  pornography on, 73
  and privacy issue, 83, 97, 99, 123, 127
  spontaneous successes of, 131
  subscribers to, 123
Oracle, 139
Orca Bay Capital Corporation, 137, 162n
Origin, 70
Orlow, Dan, 74
Out of Control: The Rise of NeoBiological Civilization (Kelly), 53, 95
Outside, 47
Overman, Steven, 146
Ovitz, Michael, 88

Pacific Telesis Group, 162n
Paglia, Camille, 68

Paine, Thomas, 130

Pathfinder, 99, 120

Peck, Bill, 133–34

Pepper, Don, 107

Periodical Studies Service, 74

Perry, Grant, 210–11

Peru, Shining Path in, 9

Peterschmidt, David, 223–25

Petersen, Jim, 140

Petersen, Julie, 111, 140, 142

Petrow, Steven, 163

Pillsbury Dough Boy, 97

Playboy, 73

Plunkett, John, 3–5, 58

   and Barbara, 28, 29, 30, 33, 34,
     49, 63, 95, 216

   design by, 29, 34, 36–37, 50, 64,
     68–70, 72, 83–84, 112, 191

   and endgame, 251–53, 260

   and IPO, 206, 215–16

   and ownership, 82–83, 238

   and Real Invest, 4–5, 9, 12

   as resistant to Louis's ideas, 27,
     29–30, 32–34, 49, 63, 82, 96,
     171, 215–16, 251

   at TED conference, 49

   and *Wired,* 50–51, 62–64, 65–66,
     70, 72, 95–96, 100

Point Foundation, 44

pornography, accessible, 73, 97,
   110, 154

privacy, 83, 97, 121–24, 127, 219

Procter and Gamble, 193

Prodigy, 102, 168

Providence Equity Partners, 221–22,
   228, 229

psychedelic art, 50–51

Psychology Today, 32

Publish!, 29

Quaker State, 204

Queen Mu, 44, 48

Quittner, Josh, 98, 146, 147,
   168

Reagan, Ronald, 12, 128

Real Invest, 4–5, 9–10, 11–12

reality distortion field, 33

Reality Hackers, 44

recession, 245

Red Brigades, Italy, 9

Rheingold, Howard, 108–9, 111,
   113, 132, 140

Richardson, Eliot, 47

Road Warrior, 97

Robertson, Stephens & Company,
   190

Rogers, Martha, 107

Rolling Stone, 32, 89, 131, 235

Roosevelt, F. D., 7

Rossetto, Louis, 5–14

   ambitions of, 171, 186, 187, 218,
     223, 239

   in Amsterdam, 15–23

   audience understood by, 59, 72

   and bankruptcy, 222, 227,
     229–38

   control exercised by, 100, 136–37,

Rossetto, Louis (*cont.*)
  192–93, 196, 206, 211,
    230–31, 236, 238, 250–51
  editorial skills of, 19–20, 22, 29,
    73
  as editor in chief and publisher,
    64, 66, 83, 113, 229–31
  and *Electric Word,* 18–23, 28, 29,
    36, 43, 44
  e-mail address of, 73
  and endgame, 239–62
  family background of, 5–6
  firing of, 237–38
  and *Globescan,* 5, 12
  and Goldman Sachs, 191–94
  at Ink Taalservice, 12, 15–18, 21
  investors sought by, 29, 30–31,
    34, 36, 48, 62, 190, 217, 219,
    228–29
  and IPO, 191–96, 198–99,
    204–16, 217–18, 226
  and Jane, *see* Metcalfe, Jane
  leadership ability of, 51, 164, 166,
    188, 251, 297
  and libertarianism, 6–7, 52, 129
  management techniques of,
    122–24, 125, 126–27, 131–32,
    136, 137, 145, 150, 157, 158,
    166, 185, 186, 206, 215
  move to New York, 25–34
  move to San Francisco, 34–38, 43
  novel written by, 7–8
  personality of, 3, 6, 17, 26, 27,
    33, 50, 52, 55, 121, 146, 206,
    216, 226, 229–30, 238, 251

  on pirating, 99
  profit as focus of, 105–6, 108,
    121, 122, 123–25, 159, 166,
    232–33, 239
  and quiet period, 194–95, 208–13
  and Real Invest, 9–10, 12
  social change as mission of,
    16–17, 22, 23, 26, 34, 47, 52,
    59, 77, 97, 105, 111, 131,
    149–50, 157–58, 186, 251
  in South Africa, 12–14, 16
  staying on board, 243
  and tech network, 42–55, 120
  and television show, 210–11
  visions of, 29–36, 51–52, 67,
    70–71, 73, 74, 77–78, 105,
    111, 122, 130–31, 192, 218,
    228, 233–34, 237, 239–40,
    243–44, 245–46, 251, 253
  and *Wired, see Wired*
Rucker, Rudy, 45
Rutten, Peter, 15–17, 21, 80, 164

Saffo, Paul, 48, 211
Salem, Paul:
  and bankruptcy, 226, 235–36
  and control of the board, 229,
    235–38, 240–41
  and endgame, 240–41, 243–44,
    248, 250–52, 254, 259
  and liquidation, 231, 236, 240,
    241, 243–44
  and Providence Equity, 221–22,
    228, 229
Salon, 156, 163

San Francisco:
  counterculture in, 43
  daily papers in, 94, 156
  Gate Five Road in, 41–42
  as gateway to the Pacific Rim, 42
  and Gold Rush, 38
  literary magazines in, 133
  new forty-niners in, 38
  South Park area of, 38, 125, 162
  tourism in, 42
San Francisco Chronicle, 99
San Francisco Examiner, 93–94
San Jose Mercury News, 65
savings-and-loan debacle, 58
Schwartz, John, 80
Schwartz, Peter, 227
Scientific American, 47
Seagate, 70
Securities and Exchange
  Commission (SEC), 192–93,
  195, 207, 209, 212, 213, 260
Sequoia Capital, 139
7 Days, 31
SF Weekly, 47
Sherman, Bill, 69, 82, 84
Shining Path, 9
Sigal, Bill, 4–5, 9–10, 11, 12
Signal, 43–44
Simon, Jeff, 171, 189, 193, 195,
  206–7, 210, 215, 235–38
Singapore:
  as "Disneyland with the death
  penalty," 99
  feature stories in, 67
Sloan, Allan, 201–2

Small, Michael, 163
Smart, 32
Smelick, Bob, 58, 79, 81, 252
"S.M.I2.L.E.," 45
Smith & Hawken, 61*n*
Solinas, Piernico, 8
Sony, 46
South Africa, Louis in, 12–14, 16
Speed Is Life (Davis), 247
Spence, Kristen, 51, 52, 64, 72
Spin, 240
Sports Illustrated, 47
SportsZone, 156
Spy, 31–32
Spyglass, 141
Sri Lanka, Tamil rebellion in, 9
Stallman, Richard, 44–45
Stanford Research Institute, 48
Steadman, Carl, 115–22, 135–37,
  145–46, 150–56, 176, 185,
  196–97
  and bankruptcy, 232–33, 234
  and creation myth, 146, 150–51
  and endgame, 256, 257, 258
  and Suck, 154–56, 167, 168–70,
  225–26, 234, 256
  and user registration, 120–22,
  136–37, 143, 150
Steadman, Luke, 115, 116,
  117–18
Steinberg, Steve, 73
Stephenson, Neal, 219
Sterling, Bruce, 45
Sterling Payot, 58, 64–65, 81, 82,
  106, 135, 252

Steuer, Jonathan, 104, 105–6, 109, 110, 112, 113
Stickrod, Randy, 28–29, 32, 34, 35–36, 38, 43, 45, 51, 76, 80
stock market:
  AOL IPO, 168
  Deutsche Telecom IPO, 217–18
  diversification in, 262
  and fair valuation, 190, 205, 208
  flight to quality in, 198
  and global recession, 245
  and liquidity, 157
  Long Boom of, 227–28, 237
  mirror effect in, 191
  and the multiple, 172–73, 187, 189–90, 198, 241, 249, 257
  Netscape IPO, 142–43, 145, 146, 147, 162, 165, 242
  peaks and valleys, 157, 158, 174, 197–98, 203, 205–7, 215, 218, 228–29, 241, 243–44, 262
  and P/E ratio, 172
  and prospectus, 191–95, 201–5
  public sales on, 213
  quiet period for, 194–95, 208–13
  random success in, 245
  and search engines, 184–85, 242
  speculation in, 245
  Wired IPO, 173–76, 187–88, 189–99, 202–16, 217–19, 226, 232, 246
  WWWW symbol on, 195
  Yahoo IPO, 184, 187, 198, 218*n*
story stocks, 142

Strep Throat, 179
Students for a Democratic Society, 6
Suck, 154–56, 157, 167, 168–70, 176, 179, 181, 225–26, 234, 256
Suhler, John, 58–59, 85
Super Bowl (1984), 21
Sybase, 223–24

Takeover (Rossetto), 7–8
Talk, 60
Tamil rebellion, Sri Lanka, 9
TED conferences, 49, 74, 178, 221
Thau, Dave, 163
Thompson, Hunter S., 235
Ticketmaster, 249
Time, 97, 156, 178
Time-Warner, 99, 120, 156, 214, 248, 262
Toffler, Alvin, 83, 129, 146–47, 211
Toffler, Heidi, 129, 146–47
Tolbert, William L., Jr., 213
Tootsie Roll Industries, 204
To Renew America (Gingrich), 146
Tripod, 247
Tudor Investment Corporation, 162*n*, 191*n*, 222, 229, 258
"Tune In, Turn On, Drop Out," 45
typesetting:
  digital prepress systems, 68
  Heidelberg press, 69
  Linotype, 5–6, 17

Ultimate Porno (Salinas), 8–9

United States Trust, 204
universities, networks in, 62
Upside, 232
Uptime, 117
USA Networks, 248–49
Useem, Jerry, 218
U.S. News & World Report, 208, 209
Utne Reader, 148

Vancouver Stock Exchange, 76, 152
Van der Leun, Gerard, 81, 212
van der Meer, Jaap, 18, 21, 151
Vanderslice, Beth:
  arrival of, 135
  and bankruptcy, 231, 234, 237
  criticism offered by, 178, 186, 196, 224
  and endgame, 243, 249, 255–58, 260
  leadership of, 186–87, 231, 237
  and Peterschmidt, 224–25
  and search engine, 180–81, 184–86
Vanity Fair, 60, 87, 230
Veronis, John, 85–87
Veronis, Suhler & Associates, 58–59
Vidal, Gore, 8
virtual reality, 48
Vogue, 87
Volvo Corporation, 112

WAIS (Wide-Area Information Search), 167–68

Wall Street Journal, The, 47, 58, 185, 204, 206, 213, 244, 262
Walsh, Mike, 141, 142
Watergate, 7
Weinstein, Harvey, 60
Weir, David, 163, 197, 234
Welch, Jack, 178
WELL (Whole Earth 'Lectronic Link), 44, 61–62, 73, 81, 97, 108, 123, 130, 212–13
Wenner, Jann, 88–89, 235
White, Keith, 148–49
White House, 139
Whitman, Walt, 111
Whole Earth Catalog, The, 44, 61
Whole Earth Review, 41–42, 43, 53, 54, 66, 108
WhoWhere, 247
Wiener, Norbert, 53
Wigwag, 31
Wilkinson, Lawrence, 171
Wintzen, Eckart, 30–31, 38, 48, 70
Wired:
  ads for, 70, 84, 106–7, 123–24, 195, 209, 214, 220, 221
  allusive style used in, 73, 128
  "attitude," "branding," and "content" for, 193–94, 202–4
  audience for, 72, 77, 79, 85, 88, 106, 108, 131, 138, 165, 196, 220
  awards to, 88
  and bankers, 58–59, 60, 64–65, 70, 81, 82, 85–87

Wired (*cont.*)

and bankruptcy, 222–38

business model for, 106, 121, 123, 128, 137, 141–42, 143, 166, 214

cash flow in, 62, 63, 69–70, 78–83, 84, 85, 121, 138, 180, 203, 205, 206, 214, 221–22, 228–29, 235–36

competition of, 96, 99, 106, 111, 156–57, 158, 186, 205, 225, 230, 243

constant evolution of, 161–62

contrarianism in, 220, 227–28

control of, 66, 81–83, 100, 106, 172–73, 229–38, 240

creation myth of, 146, 150–51

critics of, 72, 74, 80–81, 84, 129–31, 148–49

and design, 50–51, 63, 68–70, 72, 83–84, 123, 195

disagreements within, 80–82, 105–6, 109–12, 121–24, 166

disintermediation in, 61, 83, 107, 129

early days of, 30–38, 77

electronic copies of, 104

employee e-mails in, 122–24, 127

endgame of, 239–62

exit strategy for, 229

facilities borrowed for, 36, 46, 47, 59

feature stories for, 67–68, 73, 83–84, 96–98, 100, 107, 128, 129, 147, 165, 195–96, 219–21, 227–28

first issue of, 67–74

Flux feature of, 73

foreign editions of, 96, 130, 155, 164, 175–76, 215, 220, 222

as forerunner, 59, 69, 131

founders of, 51–52, 95–96, 172–73, 237–38, 241, 243–44

friends and neighbors round, 65, 81

the Grotto in, 104–5, 108–12, 121, 125

growth of, 128, 131–32, 164, 171–72, 174–75, 186, 236

high price for, 61

and HotWired, *see* HotWired

Hype List feature of, 73

impact of, 165–66

improvisation in, 100

and Inktomi, 182–84, 186, 223–25

Internet link of, 105–6

investors sought for, 30–31, 34, 36, 48, 50–51, 59–60, 62, 65, 70, 79–80, 81, 85, 138, 171, 174–75, 190–91, 204, 217, 228–29

IPO for, 173–76, 187–88, 189–99, 202–16, 217–19, 226, 232, 246

job applicants in, 94–95

as lifestyle magazine, 130

liquidity event for, 189–90, 236

main recipe for, 66, 67, 128, 146

manifesto, 33–34, 36–37, 70–73, 130–31
media attention to, 65, 80, 99, 113, 201–5, 208–10, 232
as mouthpiece of digital revolution, 52, 55, 59, 67, 71–72, 77, 96–100, 105, 111, 127, 128–29, 130–31, 147–50, 165, 205, 218
name of, 30
online operation of, 106, 196, 214, 223, 241; *see also* HotWired
ownership of, 50–51, 52, 63, 70, 81–83, 85, 125, 135, 190, 224, 226, 229–36, 250, 255
perception vs. reality in, 65, 178, 236, 239
as pirate ship, 96
pirating content from, 98–99, 104–5
political hostility toward, 128–31, 148–49
preparation for sale of, 229–38
profitability of, 172–73, 232, 236, 240–41
prospectus for, 191–95, 201–5, 207–9, 213
prototype, 55, 62, 69, 70
public disgrace, 186
public reaction to, 73–74, 148–49
quiet period for, 194–95, 208–13
recruitment in, 51, 55, 62–64, 112, 132–33, 134, 138

reputation of, 62, 129
rescue offers for, 221–22, 245, 255, 258
restructuring of, 81–82, 189–91, 204–5, 234, 236
roll-up of, 173–74, 189–91, 198
search engine for, 176, 178, 180–88
second issue of, 83–84, 129
shareholder meeting of, 260–61
split of, 81–82
spontaneous order advocated in, 52, 129
staff of, 64, 65, 100
subscriptions to, 75–79, 84–85, 87–88, 98, 128, 131, 196
success of, 77, 79–80, 85, 95–96, 99–100, 106, 128, 236, 239
survival as goal of, 82–83
technical assistance to, 104
television series for, 158, 171, 209–12, 215, 222
as test victim, 98–99
trademark rights of, 82
value of, 189–91, 222–23, 226, 241, 244, 260
web archive of, 104–5, 106, 120
youth of employees, 95, 108, 121, 124, 126, 132, 155, 157, 186
"zero" issue of, 46–47
Wired Digital, 234, 241, 244, 258
Wired Holdings, Inc., 82
Wired U.K., 96, 130, 155, 175–76, 220, 222

Wired USA, Ltd., 81
Wired Ventures, 146, 171, 175,
    190–91, 193, 202–4, 207, 229,
    236, 240–41, 249, 261
Wolf, Gary, in *Wired* office, 101, 132
Wolff, Michael, 25–27, 29, 32, 43,
    70
world, computer simulation of, 53
World Wide Web:
    access to, 132, 138, 165, 168,
        180, 221, 246
    advertising on, 62, 107, 109,
        120–21, 133–34, 136, 156,
        166–67, 176, 183, 219, 243
    browsers for, 102–4, 120, 137,
        139–40, 147, 178, 179, 242
    commercial nature of, 156–59,
        167–68, 169, 242–43
    cost of publishing on, 138
    directories for, 167–68, 176,
        181–83, 242
    domain names on, 98, 153–54
    excitement of, 105, 139
    exhibitionists on, 138, 140
    free connections on, 178–79,
        181
    growth of, 103, 154, 221–22,
        245–46
    importance of, 104, 105, 245–46
    new forms of culture in, 132, 137,
        140, 242, 245–46
    ranking on, 177–78*n*
    tracking movement through,
        136–37
    user authentication on, 121
    Wired and, 106–8, 220–21
    see also Internet
Wozniak, Steve, 20–21
WPP Group, 162*n*
Wurman, Richard Saul, 49, 73–74,
    178

Xanadu Project, 102

Yahoo, 139–40, 176, 193, 197–98,
    202–3, 220, 248
    IPO of, 184, 187, 198, 218*n*
    and Netscape, 162, 242
    stock price of, 187, 197, 201,
        203, 218*n*, 219
Yang, Jerry, 139–40

Zachary, G. Pascal, 204
Ziff Davis publishing, 26, 70
Zima, 112
Zimmermann, Phil, 83

GARY WOLF (gw@aether.com) is a contributing editor at *Wired* and is currently at work on a novel. He lives in San Francisco.

For more on *Wired—A Romance,* please visit www.aether.com.

ABOUT THE TYPE

This book was set in Sabon, a typeface designed by the well-known German typographer Jan Tschichold (1902–74). Sabon's design is based upon the original letter forms of Claude Garamond and was created specifically to be used for three sources: foundry type for hand composition, Linotype, and Mono-type. Tschichold named his typeface for the famous Frankfurt typefounder Jacques Sabon, who died in 1580.